T0246576

Ian Kemish AM served as Australian High Commissioner to Papua New Guinea, Ambassador to Germany, Head of the Prime Minister's international division, and Head of the consular service in a diplomatic career that spanned twenty-five years. He was awarded membership of the Order of Australia for his leadership of Australia's response to the 2002 Bali bombings. He is an adjunct Professor in history at the University of Queensland, a non-resident fellow with the Lowy Institute, a director of the Australia–Indonesia Centre and an Honorary Fellow of Deakin University. Ian is also actively engaged in the international development and not-for-profit sectors, and writes regularly on Indo-Pacific strategic issues.

THE
CONSUL

IAN KEMISH

UQP

First published 2022 by University of Queensland Press
PO Box 6042, St Lucia, Queensland 4067 Australia
Reprinted 2022

University of Queensland Press (UQP) acknowledges the Traditional Owners and their
custodianship of the lands on which UQP operates. We pay our respects to their Ancestors
and their descendants, who continue cultural and spiritual connections to Country. We
recognise their valuable contributions to Australian and global society.

uqp.com.au
reception@uqp.com.au

Cover design by Luke Causby
Typeset in 12/16 pt Bembo Std by Post Pre-press Group, Brisbane
Printed in Australia by McPherson's Printing Group

 University of Queensland Press is supported by the Queensland
Government through Arts Queensland.

  University of Queensland Press is assisted by
the Australian Government through the
Australia Council, its arts funding and advisory
body.

A catalogue record for this book is available from the National Library of Australia.

ISBN 978 0 7022 6349 1 (pbk)
ISBN 978 0 7022 6646 1 (epdf)
ISBN 978 0 7022 6647 8 (epub)
ISBN 978 0 7022 6648 5 (kindle)

University of Queensland Press uses papers that are natural, renewable and recyclable products
made from wood grown in well-managed forests and other controlled sources. The logging
and manufacturing processes conform to the environmental regulations of the country of
origin.

For Roger

'Isn't it a great feeling, knowing we're doing this for Australia?'

Contents

Foreword

AUSTRALIA'S CONSULAR SERVICE IS AMONG the best in the world, and Ian Kemish has undertaken the important task of documenting its work over the past twenty years.

It is vital that Australians know more about the work of the specialists within the Department of Foreign Affairs and Trade (DFAT) who help Australians when things go wrong for them while overseas. Ian is the right person to tell the story as he managed DFAT's consular service in the early 2000s, during a time when the international environment was redefined by terrorism. He led the men and women of the service in responding to the September 11 attacks in 2001, the Bali bombings in 2002 and numerous other challenges. This book is also Ian's own story.

I came to know Ian well when he was serving as Australia's High Commissioner in Papua New Guinea from 2010 to 2013 – a pivotal strategic role that also involves its fair share of consular crises. He supported my determination – first as the opposition's spokesperson on foreign affairs, and from 2013 as Australia's Minister for Foreign Affairs – to engage closely with PNG as our nearest neighbour.

Foreign ministers and their officials must work closely together in responding to global challenges, while pursuing trade and investment opportunities, protecting the rules-based international order, working to keep our region stable and helping Australians in trouble overseas.

Each year, DFAT's consular officers assist thousands of Australians, people injured, assaulted, robbed, hospitalised, kidnapped, arrested, detained or facing other challenges overseas. Involvement in this area of work can be a life-changing experience, particularly when responding to a major crisis. I know this from my experience leading the Australian response to the downing of Malaysia Airlines Flight 17 over eastern Ukraine – an atrocity that took the lives of 298 people, including thirty-eight who called Australia home. Supporting the families of the MH17 victims was one of the most challenging, and emotional, experiences of my career.

The last twenty years have seen the progressive modernisation of the Australian consular service in response to the technology revolution, as well as changing public expectations and travel patterns. As foreign minister, I launched a comprehensive strategy in 2017 to ensure the service maintained world's best practice, expanding victim support services, while promoting a culture of more responsible travel and utilising digital technologies to promote better public engagement with the Smartraveller advisory service. These reforms were building on the work of past ministers and consular staff, including Ian and his colleagues.

It will be important for the consular service to remain responsive to changing trends as Australians emerge from pandemic restrictions and once again venture out into the world. The conflict that erupted in Eastern Europe in the first half of

2022 reminds us all of the ever-changing risks in the international environment. I am confident that our consuls will continue their commitment in the service of their fellow Australians, as Ian has eloquently articulated in this timely account of their work.

The Hon Julie Bishop

A Call in the Night

IT WAS ABOUT THREE IN the morning on 13 October 2002 when the home phone shattered the silence of our bedroom in the quiet Canberra suburb of Pearce. My wife, Roxanne, who has always been quicker to surface from sleep, picked up the receiver. She listened for a moment, then said, 'That's okay, Ric ... Yes, of course, he's just here.' She passed me the phone. 'It's Ric Smith calling from Jakarta.'

Ric Smith was in the process of winding up his posting as Australia's ambassador to Indonesia. It was about midnight in Jakarta, where he was attending a farewell dinner in his own honour, hosted by the Canadian ambassador. Gruff and battle-scarred, Ric was a true servant of the national interest, having also been ambassador to China, and with previous postings in New Delhi, Tel Aviv, Manila and Honolulu. We all liked him despite his hard-bitten style, because he took people on their merits, meant what he said and followed principle rather than fashion. He was a generation older than me, and a legend of the Australian diplomatic service.

Ric was grave, courteous and to the point. 'Sorry to wake

1

you, mate,' he said, 'but I've just been speaking to Ross Tysoe, and you've got some work ahead of you.'

Ross Tysoe was the Australian consul-general in Bali. He had rung in to report that there had been at least one, and probably two major explosions in the Kuta nightclub strip in Denpasar – a popular hangout for young Australians and other Western tourists. Ross had immediately gone to the scene. It was clear that there had been a significant number of casualties, including some Australians, but the situation was chaotic and the scale of the emergency unclear.

Ric said he understood from Ross that he had already been in touch with the standing twenty-four-hour Consular Emergency Centre in Canberra, which reported to me. 'I think this one is going to be a bit beyond them,' he said. 'My guess is we're looking at multiple medical evacuations, and you're probably going to need to get Defence involved. Sorry to start with you, but there it is.' The call probably lasted less than two minutes. Ric had given me an efficient heads-up and left me to get on with it. He had other calls to make.

Confusion and scant information were nothing new. It always started like this. I'd taken a few similar calls in the two and a half years since I'd been appointed as the assistant secretary, or head, of the consular branch at the Department of Foreign Affairs and Trade in Canberra. In this role, at the hub of Australia's global diplomatic network, I was responsible for leading and coordinating DFAT's consular function – its support for Australians travelling and living overseas. This support is provided by the men and women of DFAT's consular service, who, like other departmental staff, rotate through their careers between headquarters and Australia's overseas missions. The consular service also steps forward to coordinate the federal government's response when Australians are affected by a major crisis overseas.

This is a field of the public service that passes largely unnoticed by the 99 per cent of Australian travellers who have no need of it. Most Australians can confidently expect not to be assaulted, hospitalised or arrested – or even die – while travelling abroad. Statistically, Australians are no more likely to encounter accident, injury or other trouble overseas than they are in Australia. But it does happen, every day. It also seems that when a major transportation accident, militant attack or natural disaster unfolds – no matter where it is – there will inevitably be some Australians mixed up in it. We used to say that if a plane went down between Tashkent and Vladivostok, there would almost certainly be an Australian on board. Australian consuls respond when misfortune or tragedy strikes. Their work often involves supporting people at the most difficult moment of their lives.

I had no real idea of what lay ahead of me when I put down the phone that night, but I had every reason to be confident. My team and I had responded to thousands of difficult individual welfare, arrest, hospitalisation and death cases. It was our job to support the families of Australians killed in air crashes and natural disasters, and to coordinate evacuations from countries beset by conflict. Global jihadism had burst into the open on 11 September 2001, just over one year before, ending an age of innocence for Australian travellers and requiring a substantial upgrade of our capacities and procedures. Through all of this, I had seen my colleagues show extraordinary purpose and creativity in supporting their fellow Australians, often displaying a level of personal commitment that most members of the public would never expect.

They were about to do it all again.

CHAPTER ONE

New Frontiers

I BOARDED THE OVERNIGHT FLIGHT from Singapore to Copenhagen and eased into my aisle seat. It was 15 June 1991, and I was on my way to my best friend's wedding in southern Sweden. The man sitting next to me was in his mid-fifties. He was bulky and looked uncomfortable in the middle economy seat. His grey hair was close-cropped, and his jaw was covered in coarse grey stubble. He acknowledged my arrival with a gruff nod and resumed his conversation with the man sitting by the window. I could see they were both carrying Australian passports, but the language they were speaking sounded Eastern European. It soon became clear that the two men were connected with several other men scattered around the cabin. There was an air of grim excitement about them: they were restless, calling out to each other across the aisles.

A little after take-off, as drinks were being served, I caught my neighbour's eye and asked him where he was headed. He replied in a matter-of-fact tone that he was travelling on from Copenhagen to Zagreb. I was keen to display my knowledge of the world, and asked him how long he was planning to stay in Yugoslavia. His response was swift and dismissive. 'There is no Yugoslavia. That's all finished. We are Croatians and we are going home to fight for Croatia.' I did my best to cover my confusion with another question, but he soon turned back to his friend for better-informed conversation.

A keen student of global politics, I was embarrassed to think that I had missed some important international development. At that time, I was on my first diplomatic posting in the Sultanate of Brunei, on the north coast of Borneo, and had been absorbed with developments in South-East Asia. Even if I set that excuse aside, I feel I can plead some forgiveness for my late-twenties self. Yugoslavia was actually still intact when this awkward in-flight conversation took place. Granted, a majority of Croatians had voted the previous month to leave the Federal Republic of Yugoslavia, but Croatia's declaration of independence was still ten days away – an event that would precipitate the collapse of Yugoslavia into a series of violent conflicts.

As we flew on through the night, I had no idea what the fate of these men would be – or that in coming years I would become a close observer of the new war on Europe's doorstep myself.

Within a couple of weeks I was back on the job in Brunei. I was a third secretary – the most junior diplomatic rank – at the Australian High Commission in Bandar Seri Begawan, the sleepy riverine capital of Brunei. There's no practical difference between a 'high commission' and an 'embassy', by the way – they are both the formal representative office of one nation to another, located in the capital city of the 'host country'. It's just that if both countries are members of the Commonwealth of Nations, the political association which brings together former members of the British Empire, the office is called a high commission. Neither should be confused with 'consulates' or 'consulates-general', which are subsidiary offices of differing size located outside a national capital. The generic terms 'mission' or 'post' can be used to refer to any of them.

My role in Brunei involved engaging with the local authorities about issues like regional economic cooperation and territorial disputes in the South China Sea, and promoting Australia as an education destination for the wealthy Brunei elites. As the local liaison officer for our armed forces, I also spent some of my time supporting joint military exercises. Australian patrol boats visited regularly to conduct manoeuvres with the Brunei fleet, and Australian army units sometimes trained in the country's jungle interior. This occasionally gave me the chance to go to sea with the navy, and to fly in and out of remote army camps by helicopter. I was also responsible for preparing cables to Canberra on local developments of interest – of which, it has to be said, there were very few. The mission was so small that when the high commissioner was absent, I was left in charge, despite being very junior. It was a two-year rotation, and the breadth of work involved gave my diplomatic career a solid foundation.

The last decade of the twentieth century was underway. This was when I grew to maturity as an Australian diplomat – during a period of great change for the world, and for the Australian foreign service. The communications revolution was beginning to gather pace, but the global order was changing fast and the world seemed full of possibilities. Nothing but hope had been in the air in 1989, when the Berlin Wall was breached by excited East Germans, rushing into the open arms of their jubilant friends in the West. I had only just completed my initial training with DFAT at the time. Within two years, the Soviet Union had itself dissolved. In Washington and elsewhere, it was proclaimed that the West had won – that democracy had emerged as the final form of human government, and that the United States was the uncontested leader of the new international order. No one had any inkling that, more than twenty years later, bitterness about the Soviet empire's collapse would lead a future Russian leader to threaten global security by invading neighbouring Ukraine. What was clear, was that the communist regime in China was not looking to change – it responded brutally to pro-democracy protests in Beijing's Tiananmen Square in April 1989 – although most western policy makers found it inconvenient to think about that. I recall a lunchtime conversation during this time with a pompous American diplomat who repeatedly referred to his country as 'the world's only remaining superpower'.

As often in Greek mythology, Nemesis was to pursue hubris. The conflict in Yugoslavia that had called my fellow passengers 'home' in 1991 would become a series of ethnic-related insurgencies that would span the next decade, and quickly expose the impotence of the new international order. It would provide a developing jihadist movement with a key training ground, while also giving it the opportunity to hone its message and sense of purpose.

As the 1990s unfolded, this organisation would emerge from its origins in the resistance against the Soviet occupation of Afghanistan to become progressively better resourced, more flexible and more dangerous. Its founder and leader, Osama bin Laden, was already a hero in parts of the Arab world, but it would be ten years before his name, and that of his organisation, al-Qaeda, would become widely known in the West.

This movement would certainly recast our understanding of global power dynamics, but it would also change the way we thought about travel. It would force governments to strengthen and refocus their intelligence and security resources on the threat of terrorism. It would also lead governments to overhaul their consular and crisis management functions – to try to manage the new, serious risks to their citizens, and to ensure an effective response when intelligence inevitably failed and disaster struck.

The movement was already active when the Gulf War unfolded at the beginning of the 1990s. The United States and its allies felt they had strong justification for their firm military response to Saddam Hussein's August 1990 invasion of Kuwait. The coalition's repulsion of Iraqi forces in January the following year was backed by a UN Security Council resolution and had support from several other Arab states and many others in the international community – including from Bob Hawke's Australian government. But every action has a consequence, and the war to repel Saddam also drove the jihadist movement forward. By permitting the United States to base troops in the holy land of Mecca and Medina in 1990, the Saudi regime prompted Osama bin Laden's moral outrage, providing him and his followers with what they saw as justification to launch a truly global struggle. Bin Laden and his organisation were expelled from Saudi Arabia in 1991 for repeatedly criticising the country's alliance with the United States. They moved first back to Afghanistan, and then made their way, about twelve months later, to a new safe haven in Sudan, where they could continue their planning and activities with minimal interference or interruption.

The Gulf War also had unforeseen consequences in Australia's neighbourhood. South-East Asian governments generally went along with the international coalition's response, but a serious gap emerged between their official stance and a populist pro-Saddam view among their Muslim populations. It was clear to us that Saddam had strong popular appeal in Brunei. My wife, Roxanne, recalls being shadowed by young boys in the supermarket around this time. They were boasting to each other loudly in English, for the benefit of the Western woman, about their support for the Iraqi leader. 'I hope a thousand bombs drop on George Bush,' one said.

The guarding arrangements at the Australian High Commission were surprisingly low-profile and relaxed, particularly given that we shared a building with the US embassy. As I left the office one evening in February 1991, rushing home to catch the latest news about events in the Persian Gulf, I was astonished to see that the elderly private security guard at the front of the combined embassy building was wearing a baseball cap displaying the slogan 'I love Saddam'. I asked him to remove it, which he eventually did with great reluctance. I have no doubt that he put it on again as soon as I left.

In Indonesia especially, the gap between this kind of populist view and the official stance of the government led to demonstrations in Jakarta and elsewhere. As a firm anti-communist, President Suharto was still regarded by the United States as a staunch ally in the early 1990s but, aware of mounting feeling in the country, his government tried to walk a fine line – keeping away from the fray but condemning the invasion of Kuwait and calling for Iraq's withdrawal. This was not good enough for some Indonesians, who believed their country should be showing clear support for Saddam. Protesters criticised US interference and called for the removal of the UN representative office from Indonesian soil. Such divisions were to grow over the following years, and seriously challenge the country's internal cohesion. Resentment about what some perceived to be an unjustified attack against an Arab hero would provide fertile recruitment ground for the nascent South-East Asian subsidiary of the global jihadist movement.

The Australian consular function of the 1990s was ill-equipped for the challenges that this movement would throw at it in the early years of the following century. Looking back at that time, one former colleague has described DFAT's arrangements for supporting Australians in difficulty as 'little more than a cottage industry'. The department's consular arm had certainly evolved since the mid-1970s, when the advent of the jet airliner and more affordable travel had led to a surge in the number of

Australians travelling abroad. Since then, increased prosperity at home, combined with greater competition between airlines, had made international travel ever cheaper and more accessible – a trend that prompted what was then the Department of Foreign Affairs to complain, in its 1981 annual report, that 'problems associated with age, illness, immaturity, lack of experience and crime placed increased demands on the Department's consular staff'. The department cited 'cheap fares, the changing age [of] groups travelling and the growing attraction of more out of the way destinations' as contributing to the department's heavier workload.

The number of overseas trips made by Australians continued to climb steadily through the 1990s, from 2.1 million in 1990 to 3.5 million in 2000. The Australian figures reflected a clear global trend: the volume of international tourist arrivals recorded across the world grew from 435 million in 1990 to 674 million in 2000. The number of people travelling to developing countries was growing faster than for 'traditional' destinations in Europe and North America. The Indo-Pacific was seeing especially strong growth, particularly from Australians keen to become better acquainted with their own region.

The culture of the Australian foreign ministry took some time to catch up with these realities. Assisting Australian travellers and overseas residents was not regarded as core business for DFAT when I joined the organisation in the late 1980s, and this was reflected in relatively low funding and staffing levels for this field of work. Ambassadors and other senior diplomats often thought of consular support as a necessary but regrettable area of responsibility, and took little interest in this aspect of their posts' operations. This was not universally true, of course: some always understood its importance at a fundamental human level, and appreciated the impact that this work could have on DFAT's reputation among the general public – the people whose taxes paid their wages. But, overall, the organisation was only slowly beginning to understand that the global travel revolution required rethinking its priorities and responsibilities.

Assisting Australians in difficulty was the domain of the department's consular and administrative 'stream'. If the foreign ministry had been a military organisation, these people would have been its non-commissioned officers. They could not aspire to the department's most senior levels, but they provided its backbone. The more senior representatives of this stream at an Australian overseas mission carried two titles. They were known both as senior administrative officers – or, in everyday DFAT parlance, 'SAOs' – and as consuls. This latter title was elevated to 'consul-general' for the most senior. They balanced the books and supervised the locally engaged staff – accounts clerks, receptionists, drivers, cleaners and consular assistants – and stepped in when a case became particularly difficult. They saw their primary role as 'managing' their ambassadors – that is, ensuring that their ideas were consistent with the department's financial and administrative rules. They took a firm, rules-based approach to their areas of responsibility, including consular support, and their decisions were not to be gainsaid.

These titles and broad areas of responsibility remain much the same today, but the range of people who fill these roles is different. To begin with, that earlier generation of SAOs and consuls were almost exclusively middle-aged men. Change was coming to DFAT – there was an equal number of men and women in my 1988 graduate intake, and recent years have seen the organisation prosecute a serious and comprehensive diversity agenda. But this area of the organisation was one of the last bastions to fall.

I don't think I'd even heard of consular work when, as a young graduate from the University of Queensland, I was fighting my way through the series of exams and interviews that constituted the DFAT selection process. Uppermost in my mind was the prospect of living in exotic locations abroad and connecting with other cultures. Before moving to Brisbane in my high school years, I'd spent a very happy childhood in Papua New Guinea. A thirst for adventure had taken my parents there. They'd met in Nigeria in the 1950s – my father was serving in the northern city of Kaduna with the British Army, and my mother was posted there from Scotland to work as a secretary with the regional administration. They married and tried to settle back in the British Midlands, where my elder sister and I were born. But the world beckoned, and they migrated to Australia when I was an infant. But Brisbane of the early 1960s didn't quite satisfy their itch, and after three years we moved to PNG, where my father first worked as a stores and transport manager with the territory's electricity authority. They both later worked as administrative staff at PNG's fledgling national university. Holidays always trumped material possessions when it came to the family budget; my parents didn't buy their first home until they were in their late forties. It was from them that my siblings and I inherited a fascination with the wider world.

My interest in joining DFAT was also based on a passion I had developed as a university student for international politics. My vision of diplomatic life involved representing my country in international negotiations in the great capitals of the world, or advising the Australian government on the big foreign-policy issues of the day. But a more prosaic imperative – to find stable employment – was also looming as I approached the end of my honours year. Our first child, Annabelle, was born while Roxanne and I were still waiting to hear from DFAT whether I'd been accepted.

My first year in the department, as a graduate trainee,

encouraged my loftier expectations: we were busy debating themes such as international disarmament, human rights and peace-building, treaty making and trade negotiations. A briefing on consular operations must have been included in the course, but it left little impression on me. So while I embarked on my first overseas assignment with no real consular training, an encounter at a relatively early stage of that posting in Brunei taught me something about the human dimensions of consular work.

The SAO at our high commission, a consular veteran, was on leave back in Australia. It was late on a Friday night, and Roxanne and I were at our home in a quiet suburban district of Bandar Seri Begawan. Our infant children were asleep: Annabelle had just turned four, and Eloise was a baby. We exchanged perturbed glances and looked out the window. A man and a woman were standing out there in the dark. I opened the door and walked uncertainly to the gate.

'We're very sorry to disturb you,' the woman called out as I approached. 'We were told this was the house of an Australian diplomat, and we need help.'

I confirmed that I worked for the High Commission and introduced myself, wondering what this could be about. The man stood still and silent as the woman explained, in a torrent of words, that her boyfriend, the young man beside her, had been notified earlier that evening that his parents in Australia had been murdered, and that his brother had been charged with the crime. They were desperate to get home as quickly as possible but were short of money and didn't want to wait until the regular commercial service flew out via Singapore late the following day. They had heard that there were special direct night-time mail flights between Brunei and Darwin that might help them get home quickly at minimal cost.

I invited the distressed couple inside, and we made them a

cup of tea. I began by asking what they were doing in Brunei. They had taken a short-term work contract through a chance connection, and it was their first time outside Australia. Roxanne and I never fully understood what they were doing there, but the conversation left us in little doubt that their story was genuine. It was all very sad. I told them that there were no 'special flights' that could help them return home that night, and we began discussing their options.

I must have somehow imbibed the consular service basics by then, because I knew that the approved approach was to help them contact relatives or friends who might be able to wire them enough money for a flight. I explained this, but it made them very anxious. In those pre-internet days it would mean waiting until at least the following Monday to receive funds via the banking system, and they couldn't think of anyone who might be able to help anyway. The young woman then tentatively produced a folded piece of paper from her purse. It was a signed but otherwise blank cheque that her uncle had given her, 'just in case', before she left Australia. After further discussion, I offered to take them to the airport the following morning and try to help convince Royal Brunei Airlines to accept the cheque in exchange for two one-way tickets on the first flight to Australia via Singapore.

For better or worse, I was clear about what I was going to do. Knowing that this cheque would not be accepted without at least some evidence of official support, I drove into town in the middle of the night, opened up the office and sat down to type a letter of guarantee on my computer. It was completely against the rules, and I knew it. If the cheque bounced, the Australian government would not pay the couple's airfare and I would be personally liable. It was a substantial amount of money for our family at that stage of our lives, but Roxanne and I trusted our judgement about these people. We had been affected by their story, and both felt it was the right, human thing to do. We didn't think of them as a 'case'; they were people we had met who were in distress.

The following morning the airline accepted the cheque, backed by my letter of guarantee. The couple flew out of our lives and we never heard from them again. I don't claim that I showed much common sense on that occasion, but as it turned out my instincts were okay. I did receive a phone call from Royal Brunei Airlines about six weeks later, and my heart sank when the caller said that it was about the payment for those airfares. This was quickly followed by a wave of relief when they explained that the couple had been overcharged and were due a small refund. The cheque had been good.

I certainly never mentioned any of this to the High Commissioner, and the SAO was shocked when I later told him what I had done. Perhaps because of his reaction, I never shared this story with experienced members of the department's consular service when I was appointed as their leader several years later. But perhaps I should have. Over time, I came to understand that our empathetic response to our fellow Australians was actually a common phenomenon, and that even veteran consular officials sometimes stepped outside the guidelines if their instincts or common sense told them to.

My family and I had another, more profound encounter with the consular service during our Brunei posting. It would contribute even more significantly to the experience and thinking I brought with me when I was appointed, years later, to the lead consular role.

It began with a friendship I'd made a few years previously, during the DFAT training course. Roger Strickland was the best, brightest and simply nicest member of our 1988 graduate intake. A farm boy from Western Australia, he'd started his working life as a rural reporter for the ABC. He almost blew his chances in the DFAT selection process when he failed to turn up to his final interview – he'd got the date wrong – but he somehow managed to blag his way into the next round of interviews. Tall, handsome and endearingly daggy, he instantly became everyone's mate. I considered him my best friend in the group, and I know I was not alone.

Halfway through our training course, Roger and I were on a work trip to Melbourne, where I'd arranged to catch up with Roxanne's sister, Chrissy. When Roger walked into the bar with me, it was love at first sight. Chrissy and Roger were married two years later, around the same time Roger began his first diplomatic posting at the high commission in Port Vila, the capital of Vanuatu, and we were posted to Brunei. We were happy to think that our families would always be closely connected, and it seemed Roger and I would travel on similar career paths.

Then a phone call came that changed everything. It was very late at night in July 1991 when Roxanne's brother rang us in Brunei to tell us that Roger was missing. He'd been on a light plane that had gone down in dense jungle on the Vanuatu island of Espiritu Santo. Search and rescue teams were doing everything in their power to locate the plane. Roger's family and friends flew to Port Vila, the locals rallied, and everyone hoped and prayed for a miracle that would become another of Roger's hilarious adventure stories.

There was no miracle. Roger, the pilot and eight other passengers on the plane had died on impact. It took a week to find the crash site, and getting them all out of the jungle was both a logistical nightmare and a test of endurance. Chrissy, along with Roger's parents, Mary and Lester Strickland, were confronted with all the necessary but awful elements of the consular process – from identifying the body to the requirement, after so many days exposed to the elements, for a lead-lined coffin to pass through Australian quarantine. The consul in Port Vila, along with colleagues in Canberra and Perth, guided the family through the practicalities with kindness and sensitivity. Despite our grief, we were all impressed by the level of care shown by my fellow DFAT officers.

It was at Roger's memorial service in Perth that I first met Ric Smith, who was then deputy secretary of the department in Canberra. He'd flown across to Perth to represent the organisation. Ric spent some time speaking with Chrissy, Lester and Mary, before turning to me. He frowned and said, with some intensity, 'Listen, if this family needs anything from the department, you need to tell me. Don't worry about the bloody hierarchy – speak to me direct. Are you clear about that?' It was a fierce kindness that left an abiding impression on me.

When I look back now, I see that the experience of being on the receiving end of consular assistance was an important part of my personal preparation for the roles I would later take on. It reinforced the importance of human empathy in consular work, and also encouraged in me an abiding respect for the work of Australia's consuls, most of whom try to support their clients in exactly the way they hope their own families would be supported.

There was one other, perhaps less tangible but equally important legacy that Roger left me with. One wet Canberra morning, not long after we met, Roger and I were hurriedly dodging puddles on our way towards the DFAT building. He turned to me and, without a hint of irony, said, 'Isn't it a great feeling, knowing we're doing this for Australia?'

I looked over at him with surprise, and then realised that he was completely serious. Our own self-consciousness and the ironic, detached style affected by so many of our seniors generally discouraged us from speaking in such terms with each other, even in private. I smiled and shoved him in front of me through the doors.

In his own guileless way, Roger had dared to speak aloud the motivation that inspires many members of the foreign service. He understood the importance of our collective role as servants of the Australian public. They were words that would stay with me.

CHAPTER TWO

Muffled Drumbeat

'THERE IS A WAR BETWEEN the West and Islam,' a Saudi Arabian who'd fought in Bosnia during the 1990s told the BBC in 2015. 'Bosnia gave the modern jihadist movement that narrative. It is the cradle.'

I first flew into Sarajevo, the capital of war-torn Bosnia, in the back of a Ukrainian Air Force Antonov aircraft in mid-1995. I'd been unsettled by what passed as a safety briefing back in Zagreb: an unshaven and bleary-eyed pilot had pushed his face through the cockpit door to say, in his best English, 'Sara-hyavo … one hour … seat belt,' before flashing a tired thumbs-up at us. As the plane began its steep descent between the mountain peaks, I'd been disconcerted further by the knowing smiles that passed between two of the 'old hands' as I began to don the flak jacket I'd been given. A beefy American of military bearing leaned over and shouted above the din, 'No, sit on it – the snipers are below,' and he proceeded to show me by example.

I was by then on my second overseas posting with DFAT. I had been promoted a couple of times, and was a first secretary attached to the Australian embassy in Vienna, where Roxanne and I were living with our children. My role was to focus on Australian interests in three nearby countries of former Yugoslavia where Australia had no resident representation: Slovenia, Croatia and Bosnia. Over the three-year posting I probably spent about two weeks of every month in these countries of South-Eastern Europe, liaising with the different governments and factions of the region, as well as other international representatives, managing a modest aid program in Bosnia and generally reporting on developments.

This time, my reporting had a reasonably substantial audience among the officials back in Canberra. Our government required informed analysis about what was happening in that part of the world, as the conflict in former Yugoslavia was the subject of considerable debate and discussion at the United Nations and in major capitals, and international agencies were working to support traumatised people across the region. Australia was a conscientious contributor to these deliberations, and a significant financial supporter of the humanitarian effort. In addition, Australia was also host to large communities from former Yugoslavia – Serbs, Croats, Bosniaks and what we now call 'North Macedonians' – and a second major influx of refugees from the region was underway. In the ten-year period from 1992, about 100,000 people would be admitted to Australia as refugees or humanitarian migrants, and almost half of them were from former Yugoslavia. My work helped inform decisions on the shape of the annual intake, and I was sometimes asked to give my opinion on the merits of individual asylum applications.

A lot had happened in the Balkans since my awkward conversation on that flight to Copenhagen back in 1991. Croatia and Slovenia had declared independence on 25 June that year. The Yugoslav National Army retaliated first against tiny Slovenia, which quickly mobilised its territorial forces to inflict an embarrassing defeat on the federal forces. The conflict then shifted to Croatia, where Serb militia forces, backed by the rump regime in Belgrade, seized large swathes of Croatian territory – sometimes with unspeakable violence. When the Muslim-led presidency of Bosnia declared its independence in March 1992, the whole thing exploded into a terrifying and confusing triangular war: the Muslim, mainly urban-dwelling majority found itself under attack from Serbs and Croats alike. More than two million people were displaced. We had not seen population movements on this scale since World War II.

The war in former Yugoslavia took place on Europe's doorstep, and it laid bare the weakness of the new international order. The major powers traded recriminations as war criminals operated with impunity in the Balkan region. The United Nations Protection Force was deployed in an attempt to impose stability, but had limited powers and was regarded with contempt by the various ethnic factions. The image of Dutch UN troops standing by helplessly in Srebrenica in 1995 as more than 8000 Muslim men and boys were rounded up by Serb soldiers for mass execution will stand forever as a symbol of this impotence.

First-, second- and even third-generation Australians participated on all sides of the conflict. Regrettably, there were even Australian links to some of the war crimes committed during the war. Dragan Vasiljković, who migrated to Australia at the age of thirteen, was extradited from Australia in 2015 and found guilty by a court in Croatia of war crimes committed there in the 1990s. Zoran Tadic, another accused war criminal, spent fifteen years hiding in plain sight in Sydney and escaped extradition by fleeing to Serbia in 2019.

My work drew me into contact with many Australians who had been drawn by bonds of family and heritage back to the region as it underwent extraordinary political change. Only a small proportion had returned to take up arms. Others were interested in revisiting their ancestral homes, meeting long-lost relatives, or perhaps reclaiming property that had been confiscated decades earlier by the state. But most of the Australians I met of Croatian, Bosnian or Slovene heritage were unified in their desire to help rebuild their homelands free of what they saw as the shackles of the autocratic, Serbian-dominated federal regime. Some of them held a staunch ethno-nationalist view of the world; others were more moderate.

These people might have felt passionately about their familial homelands, but they also identified strongly as Australians. They were proud to carry Australian passports and prized the benefits that went with it. They were entitled to Australian consular support when overseas, just like any other Australian, although they were generally confident and connected enough in their other country of nationality to not require Australian help if they fell into trouble. Our honorary consuls in Croatia and Slovenia – prominent local figures with Australian connections who acted as agents for the Vienna embassy in return for a modest honorarium – were kept busy enough with routine consular work, including passport renewals and pension-related inquiries, and were supported by the professional consular staff back in Vienna. We had no representation at all in Bosnia; our engagement there relied solely on my periodic visits.

My frequent encounters with these Australians of Balkan heritage highlighted for me that those who draw on the government's consular support overseas come from many different cultural backgrounds. Consular support is not limited to those of Anglo-Celtic heritage. There have been moments in recent history when some Australian media commentators, politicians and members of the public have seemed to struggle with this point – such as when the consular service moved to evacuate thousands of Lebanese Australians from war-torn Beirut in 2005, or when Australians of

Indian origin were seeking in mid-2021 to return to the safety of their adopted country amid the Covid-19 pandemic.

As is always the case in regions of conflict, there were also Australians working with international agencies in former Yugoslavia to promote stability and alleviate suffering. I learned a great deal about what was actually going on in Bosnia from Lisa Jones, a fellow Queenslander in her twenties who was working as a United Nations High Commissioner for Refugees protection officer and spokesperson in Sarajevo. Over half of Bosnia's population of 4.4 million people were displaced by the conflict, and Lisa and her colleagues at UNHCR were working alongside the International Committee of the Red Cross to provide them with emergency relief and whatever protection they could. Another great source of insight was Ken Lindsay from Perth, a Royal Military College Duntroon graduate who was working on secondment with European Union institutions dedicated to monitoring and supporting the peace-building process. They had a much tougher, leaner life than I did – they lived in a city under siege, where every spare patch of land was either devoted to growing cabbages or was a makeshift gravesite. They were also sources of enormous practical assistance, information, analysis, friendship and humour. We had many intense conversations over dinner about the state of the conflict, and what seemed the region's very dim prospects for the future. One of my contributions was to bring good Australian wine with me from the UN commissariat in Vienna. These were welcome moments at the end of the day, after hours spent in depressing engagements with harassed local officials.

A common theme of these dinnertime discussions in Sarajevo was the problem of the 'foreign fighters' who had begun flowing into Bosnia from Iran, Arab countries and Afghanistan in late 1992. The narrative that rallied them to join the conflict was that their fellow Muslims were under fire from orthodox Christian Serbs and Catholic Croats, and that the Western powers were allowing it all to happen. As far as they were concerned, a struggle for survival was underway between Islam and the West. About 1500 of these volunteers had come together in a 'mujahedin battalion' under Bosnian Muslim leadership in 1993. Among these 'holy warriors' were Afghan-trained Islamic militants loyal to Osama bin Laden who had a longer-term strategy in mind. They inflicted bloody reprisals, hunted down non-believers, abused prisoners of war and desecrated Christian religious sites. They targeted UN peacekeepers and even fought with Bosnian Muslims. Using the conflict as cover, they began to establish a European domestic terrorist infrastructure, which would later be used to plot violent strikes against the United States.

By the end of my first year in the role, in November 1995, the warring parties concluded a peace agreement at US-sponsored talks in Dayton, Ohio. I was in Sarajevo as the negotiations were being completed, and remember clearly how the city's inhabitants were glued to the CNN coverage on television screens in every cafe and restaurant. They greeted the news, when it came through, with a mixture of relief and scepticism.

The Dayton Accord ruled that the foreign mujahedin should leave the country within a month. While some married locally, took out Bosnian citizenship and stayed, most of the voluntary fighters left. Bosnia had been a useful training ground for them, and they considered that it was time to move on. Within a few months of the war's end, terrorist sleeper cells began to appear in the cities of Western Europe. Among the 'graduates' of the Bosnian conflict were at least two of the September 11 hijackers, the British-Pakistani national who would be convicted for murdering US journalist Daniel Pearl in Karachi in 2002, and several other al-Qaeda operatives.

In retrospect, the scale of terrorist planning and activity that we saw in the 1990s should have left little room for doubt about the extent of the movement's ambition. Energised by a greater sense of purpose, the Bin Laden group had begun to flex their operational muscle as early as 1990, when the FBI unearthed evidence of a plot to blow up New York skyscrapers. In 1992 the group launched attacks on hotels in Yemen where US troops were known to be staying, and showed the first signs of what was to be a decade-long preoccupation with the Manhattan skyline. Then, in 1993, a group affiliated with al-Qaeda detonated a bomb under the World Trade Center, killing six people and injuring hundreds. The mastermind, Ramzi Yousef, joined his uncle, Pakistani Islamist militant Khalid Sheikh Mohammed, in a plan to bring down eleven Asian airliners, assassinate the Pope and fly · an aircraft into CIA headquarters. The plot was foiled, but a bomb was detonated on Philippine Airlines Flight 434 as part of a 'test run', killing one Japanese passenger. In a fatwa published in 1996, Osama bin Laden declared war on the United States and Israel, claiming they had turned Saudi Arabia into an American 'vassal state'. More than eighty foreign tourists were murdered while visiting an archaeological site on the banks of the Nile in 1997.

However, the growing drumbeat of international terrorism was muffled by the many distractions of the era – including, in the first half of the 1990s, the release of Nelson Mandela, the election of the young American president Bill Clinton, genocide in Rwanda, a ceasefire in Northern Ireland, and a peace accord between the Palestinians and the Israelis.

In those first few years after the fall of the Berlin Wall, Australians still carried abroad that secure, slightly smug view that everyone loved us, and that we were welcome pretty much anywhere. And we were, increasingly, everywhere. Tourists flocked to destinations which recent, dramatic geopolitical change had made newly accessible. Reconciliation and reform in South Africa had begun to restore the country's reputation, and Kruger National Park became a must-see location. Australians and others flocked to places that had until recently been locked away behind the Iron Curtain, from Buda Castle in Hungary to Bran Castle in Romania. They marvelled at the extraordinary architecture of Prague and drank the excellent Czech beer. In Moscow, Australians queued up with everyone else to visit Saint Basil's Cathedral, Lenin's mausoleum and the new McDonald's on Pushkin Square.

International travel was different then. We carried cameras and guide books with us, and paid with traveller's cheques. International phone calls were very expensive, and if we really needed to call home we kept it short. Mobile phones were uncommon. We still sent postcards. We generally travelled for longer than in more recent times, to be sure that the trip was worth the cost. There was some security screening at airports, but it was nothing compared to the hassle and indignity of subsequent years. We did not really understand the growing threat.

It took the devastating bombing attacks against the American embassies in Kenya and Tanzania in August 1998 to bring al-Qaeda to widespread public attention, and for Bin Laden to be added to the FBI's 'ten most wanted' list. The embassy attacks actually had little dampening effect on Westerners' enthusiasm for travel, but they were a very clear statement that al-Qaeda had the 'world's only superpower' firmly in its sights.

The Australian High Commissioner in Nairobi at the time, Philip Green, was in his office speaking to an Australian business visitor when the bomb went off at the US embassy. They heard and felt the blast. The explosion destroyed the US embassy building, along with most of the mission's vehicles and equipment. It killed 213 people, including eleven Americans, and injured about 4000. The Australian team lost no time in providing staff to support the US embassy's recovery efforts, along with vehicles and communications equipment. Under Philip's direction the Australian team asked the nearest hospital what they needed, contacted a medical warehouse and went around to load up a truck with urgently needed supplies. Delivery was completed within twenty-four hours of the bombing.

There was something particularly Australian about that self-initiated emergency response by the High Commission in Nairobi. It contrasted with the inaction of many other diplomatic missions, which even days later were still awaiting instructions from their governments. It reflected an important cultural strength of the Australian service – one which would work to our benefit when we had to deal with disasters that directly impacted Australian citizens. The team on the ground felt confident enough to do what was plainly needed, without feeling they had to seek permission first.

It was also something their American colleagues didn't forget. Years later, Green encountered a high-ranking US diplomatic official who'd been based in Nairobi at the time. A day or so after the attack, he told Philip, he'd finished work late at his temporary office and jumped into the back seat of the car allocated to him by the security guards. It was a Land Rover, but he knew the US embassy didn't have any of those. When he asked about it, the Kenyan driver told him that he worked for the Australians. 'My High Commissioner told me I should work for you for as long as you need me,' the driver added.

My posting in South-Eastern Europe came to its end in mid-1998. I had criss-crossed the region for more than three years, watching, engaging and reporting as NATO military forces worked to promote stability in Bosnia, and as the conflicting sides slowly moved towards a political accommodation. By the end of my posting the security situation had improved to the point that I felt comfortable driving all the way to Sarajevo from Vienna. It was a ten-hour drive via Zagreb, and often during the last several hours I chugged slowly through mountain passes behind either a British tank or a horse-drawn cart.

Consistent with normal practice, my next rotation was back at headquarters in Canberra. I was appointed to the department's South-East Division, where I helped formulate Australian regional policies and guided the political and economic work of some of Australia's missions there. My work had a particular focus on Myanmar, then known as Burma, where the military regime was refusing to join the rest of the region in embracing democratic reform. I visited the country regularly, calling twice on Aung San Suu Kyi, the pro-democracy leader and Nobel laureate who was then under house arrest by the military authorities. Regrettably, things don't look much different today – a decade of hope came to a crushing end with another military coup in early 2021. Aung San Suu Kyi, who was released in 2010 and went on to become the country's State Counsellor and foreign minister, is again under house arrest.

By contrast, things were happening fast in Indonesia, Australia's largest neighbour. Indeed, upheaval in Indonesia was a major Australian foreign policy preoccupation in the last years of the 1990s. Economic problems, including food shortages and mass unemployment, had triggered widespread riots across the country in May 1998. These problems ultimately led to the resignation of President Suharto after three decades of military rule, and marked the beginning of a new democratic era for South-East Asia's most populous nation.

We know now that the end of military rule in Indonesia also emboldened the leaders of Jemaah Islamiyah, an extremist group dedicated to the establishment of a pan–South-East Asian Islamic state, to return from hiding in Malaysia. They subsequently established contact with Bin Laden's al-Qaeda network, leading to a boost both in JI's operational capacity and in their own prestige within the movement. One of the men who slipped back into Indonesia as the 1990s drew to a close was Abu Bakar Ba'asyir, who would become infamous in Australia as the key figure behind the 2002 Bali bombings.

Australia attracted the attention of the jihadist movement in 1999, when the Howard government abandoned Australia's long-held position of de facto support for Indonesia's annexation of East Timor. It all came as a bit of a surprise. The new and unpredictable president of Indonesia, B.J. Habibie, acted much sooner than expected on a suggestion made in late 1998 by Prime Minister Howard that a referendum on East Timor's self-determination be held 'at some stage in the future'. The resulting UN-sponsored referendum in August 1999 showed overwhelming support among East Timorese for independence, but this sparked a violent anti-independence campaign by local Muslim militia groups.

Ironically, after years of quiet but steadfast support for Jakarta's de facto rule in East Timor, Australia now found itself leading an international peacekeeping effort to quell those fighting to preserve that status quo. In the eyes of the radical Islamists, Australia was now the leader of an anti-Muslim conspiracy. Osama bin Laden would state, in November 2001, that the 'crusader Australian forces were on Indonesian shores, and in fact they landed to separate East Timor, which is part of the Islamic world'. Australia was an enemy in what Bin Laden saw as a 'war of annihilation in the true sense of the word'.

It seems so clear, looking back, that serious trouble was brewing at the close of the 1990s. The decade had seen the build-up of a global terrorist movement that would shock the Western world to its core on 11 September 2001, while its South-East

Asian subsidiary, Jemaah Islamiyah, was preparing to unleash Australia's worst consular disaster a little over a year later. Western intelligence agencies were conscious of the growing threat, and governments were beginning to reflect their concerns in public advice to their citizens. But no one at the time, in Australia or elsewhere, understood the true scale of the threat.

CHAPTER THREE

The Inheritance

DR ASHTON CALVERT HAD BEEN appointed Secretary of the Department of Foreign Affairs and Trade in May 1998, only months before I'd returned to Canberra at the conclusion of my posting in Vienna. The holder of this position may not have much profile outside Canberra, but is Australia's top professional diplomat – and so, as far as departmental officials are concerned, the real boss. Prime ministers and foreign ministers might determine government policy, but they came and went. Importantly for the organisation's ambitious diplomats, the secretary was the key decision-maker on postings and promotions.

Ashton was an intellectual heavyweight. He'd been a Rhodes Scholar and had a doctorate in mathematics from Oxford, where he'd also been the president-cox of the rowing team. In the decades leading to his appointment to the top role at DFAT, he had been assigned four times to the embassy in Japan, the last time as Australia's ambassador. He'd also been posted to Washington and had served as international adviser to Prime Minister Paul Keating. He had a reputation for being very details-oriented, and very exacting. He was to leave a strong imprint on the organisation, upgrading its administrative efficiency and insisting on consistently high-quality output. He was also a cerebral and committed adviser to the government of the day.

Someone once turned up a couple of minutes late to Ashton's first meeting with the DFAT's division heads – a leadership group of about twenty senior officers. Many had already served as ambassadors, and some took themselves quite seriously. Ashton looked up as the latecomer entered, commented crisply that he expected people to be on time and ordered the humiliated offender to leave. The message ricocheted across the organisation: punctuality was no longer negotiable. If you were running late for a meeting with the secretary, it was best not to come at all. His reputation was unnerving, but as I was to discover over the years to come, there was another side to him. Not everyone remembers him this way, but he could be thoughtful, generous and very funny. He was also the leader from whom I learned most.

I took a welcome call from him in the lead-up to Christmas 1999, when I was on holiday with my family in Queensland. He told me that he had decided to promote me to the first rung of the department's senior executive service, as an assistant secretary. At this level, one might head a branch of thirty or so people in Canberra. It also meant that my next overseas posting might be as ambassador to a small or medium-sized mission, or perhaps as deputy ambassador to a larger one. I was also very happy to be told, when I returned to work a few weeks later, that I was to be the head of the consular branch. This placement had appealed to me from the start: I was attracted to what I saw as the 'human dimension' of supporting Australians in difficulty overseas. I also knew that the consular branch was increasingly being recognised within the department as an important one.

DFAT had only just begun assigning people like me, who had joined as policy specialists through the graduate trainee scheme, to these kinds of roles. Things had moved on a little since I'd joined back in 1988, and the categorisation of consular and administrative officers as a separate – and lesser – 'stream' within the organisation had been recognised as elitist and inappropriate for Australia's foreign service. Ashton was keen to send a message to the organisation that things were changing – that strong achievement in the consular field, as well as in areas of corporate management such as finance and personnel, could be a platform for those aspiring to the organisation's upper levels. Foreign and trade policy credentials were still important to the department's overall function, but they were no longer the only things that mattered.

Most members of the consular branch in Canberra, and the Australians who worked as consuls overseas, nonetheless tended to be people who had grown up in the system doing only consular and administrative work. It was what they knew best, and they rightly prided themselves on the specialist knowledge they had attained over their careers. These 'real' consular officials were too polite to say anything, but they were probably surprised at my appointment. I was still – just – in my thirties, and had no obvious formal consular background. Some were probably asking themselves what personal experience and attitudes I was bringing to the job.

I enjoyed getting to know my new consular colleagues. In addition to the experienced consuls on home rotation working at more senior levels within the branch, there were retired military personnel embarking on a second career, part-timers with young children at home, and people just starting their careers. Most of those who were attracted to the field brought an impressive strength of mind to the work, along with a solid dose of compassion. They dealt with extremely difficult cases with patience – and sometimes, a bit like nurses, with black humour. I am reminded of some of these consular types when I meet Australians who do voluntary work at drop-in centres for the homeless, or who work with the victims of domestic violence. When I took up the role, there were very few officers in the branch who had joined through the annual graduate trainee scheme, but that was soon to change: others would be attracted by the growing profile of the work, and the realisation that it could be good for your career. Those who did join us invariably found, as I did, that it could be very fulfilling.

The branch in Canberra was the hub for the global consular service, and at the end of the 'spokes' were the consular officers assigned to Australia's missions overseas. At the heart of the branch was the consular operations (or 'con ops') team, whose roles involved working with our missions overseas to support consular clients and their families. The normal division of labour saw the con ops team liaising primarily with the next of kin when an Australian abroad encountered some serious difficulty. This team made up about half of the roughly thirty-five men and women who reported to me in Canberra; the others worked on things like consular policy, contingency planning, crisis management support and travel advisories.

These were the people under my direct, everyday supervision. But I was also accountable for the work of the global consular service. Australia had just under 100 overseas missions at that point – it's a little more than that now – and the network of consular officers assigned to these missions reported back to my branch. We provided our colleagues overseas with guidance and instructions on complex cases, we liaised with concerned family members and we stepped in to provide direct assistance when a mission encountered a particularly demanding situation.

It's not always understood that the majority of staff engaged at Australian overseas missions are actually local people – generally citizens of the host country. They watch their Australia-based (or 'A-based') supervisors come and go on their three-year or four-year postings; some raise an eyebrow when a new SAO arrives from Canberra full of enthusiasm and a desire to implement change. Local staff provide the network with long-term local knowledge, contacts, and an ability to navigate administrative hurdles and often complex political currents. The system could not function without them. Many of them have shown extraordinary loyalty and commitment to Australia. Some of them, but not enough, have been recognised through awards in the Order of Australia.

Much of the everyday support to Australians overseas is provided by locally engaged consular staff, working under the supervision of an A-based consular officer. I sometimes cringe a little when I ponder what these people must think of Australian travellers. Many sensible Australians encounter difficulty overseas through no fault of their own. But sometimes the people who turn to our overseas missions for assistance – because they run out of money, lose their passports, are unable to cover their medical costs, have been arrested or just want the embassy to help them hire a car – are not the best representatives for our country. Many years later, when I was serving as Australia's ambassador to Germany, our highly professional consular assistant, a typically plain-speaking East Berliner, would look at me severely and say, 'Australians are so helpless!' I would plead that she wasn't seeing the 99.5 per cent of Australian travellers who were managing their lives perfectly well without any help from the consular network, but it never seemed to wash.

When I arrived in the consular branch, the service was managing about 21,000 cases every year. Our consuls had been managing a steadily increasing workload for years, consistent with the growth in the number of Australians travelling overseas. That growth seemed daunting at the time, and it was to grow much further in the years that followed. The casework extended well beyond the thousands of lost passports and encounters with petty thefts that were recorded each year. The single largest category was 'welfare and whereabouts' cases. This was a broad descriptor which covered a myriad of situations – from anxious inquiries lodged by families that had lost contact with a loved one for too long, to people who just showed up at embassy reception desks unable to look after themselves. Australians were dying overseas at a rate of almost two each day, and a similar number were being arrested. The number of hospitalisations requiring official Australian intervention was a little higher. These numbers would more than double over the following twenty years.

To put it all in perspective, only six out of every thousand Australians travellers were turning to the official network for help; the others were either encountering no serious difficulties or sorting their problems out on their own. But the consular department's staffing resources had not kept up with the growth in the caseload, and the workers were feeling the strain.

The service had also been grappling for some time with a clearly discernible increase in traveller expectations. Sometimes these expectations were completely ridiculous. Australians would occasionally show up in embassy foyers seeking help buying tickets for the opera or the metro, or asking if the consul could feed their cat while they went away for the weekend. Ridiculous requests like these were made by only a tiny minority of travellers, but they were the thin end of the wedge. Too many people seemed to have a wrongheaded understanding of where personal responsibility should begin and end after they left Australia's shores.

The frustratingly low proportion of travellers who took out travel insurance was one manifestation of this trend. Many people think about travel insurance as a way of covering the loss or theft of their personal effects, or the cost of flight cancellations.

But this is actually the least important reason to take out cover. Injury, sickness or death overseas can be a very expensive business, and when people neglect to buy insurance it can lead to a double dose of tragedy. Each year Australians are shocked to learn that their government cannot just step in and cover the costs of their hospitalisation and repatriation when they or their loved ones meet with serious misfortune. While DFAT will not let anyone die for lack of medical support, any official financial intervention takes the form of a short-term loan, and even this is only approved as a last resort. Australians are regularly forced by circumstance to sell or remortgage their homes to cover the costs of medical evacuation or treatment abroad for themselves or someone they love. Young people and budget travellers are more inclined to skip insurance, and also the most likely to call on consular assistance.

In my first months on the job, a young man suffered serious burns in a fire on a resort island in South-East Asia. He had no travel insurance, so we stepped in urgently to arrange his evacuation to the national capital, on the basis of an understanding reached with the man's family that they would have to cover the costs later. Family members flew from Australia to be at his bedside, and they supported him for several months until he was ready to return to Australia on a medical evacuation flight. The whole thing cost the family scores of thousands of dollars. Later that same year, another young man had a serious skiing accident the day before he was scheduled to return home to Australia from the United States after several months of travelling. He'd delayed his trip home by a couple of days to fit in the ski trip, but had neglected to extend the medical insurance that he'd sensibly taken out prior to leaving home. It expired just before he strapped on his skis. The cost of medical treatment in the United States can be prohibitive, and once again the family ended up paying a very high price.

The expectations of Australians who have been arrested overseas can be particularly hard to manage. Many of those arrested plead ignorance of local law, or say they are innocent. They can't all be. The initial expectation is often that the consular service will intervene to negotiate their freedom. But it doesn't really matter how much people say, 'I'm an Australian, get me out of here!' When we travel abroad, we are all subject to the laws of the countries we visit. From time to time, there's an egregious case in which the continued detention or treatment of an Australian prisoner violates our national sense of justice and fairness, and the government decides to advocate strongly, or enter into negotiations, for release or a lesser penalty. But these kinds of interventions are very much the exceptions to normal practice. The normal consular role is to confirm that an Australian prisoner has access to local legal representation, to conduct welfare visits and to generally ensure that he or she is being treated fairly under local law.

The Australian media could sometimes encourage unrealistic expectations of the service. A particular consular case might send elements of the media into a frenzy, with journalists getting emotionally involved in what they see as a human tragedy and demanding to know what the department is doing about it. Fortunately for me, Lyndall Sachs joined the department as the leader of the small DFAT media team at about the time I took up the consular role. She'd spent seven years working as the senior media spokesperson for the United Nations High Commissioner for Refugees in former Yugoslavia, based in Belgrade and in London. She'd also been assigned by UNHCR to central Africa in the mid-1990s, in the wake of the Rwandan genocide. Lyndall was always focused and professional, but the media role was very demanding. There were only four members of the team – all on call on a twenty-four-hour roster basis. In the early 2000s, government ministers still held that the department should be ahead of the media in their knowledge of what was happening on the ground in any given international situation. This was extremely difficult, given relative resourcing and the advent of instant communication. The *Australian Privacy Act* also imposed serious constraints on the department's ability to explain its side of the story – it requires the department to keep individual cases confidential to the fullest extent possible, unless the clients give consent or go to the media themselves.

The service I inherited in early 2000 was built on decades of experience. Other senior members of the branch, and many of our overseas consuls, had helped manage serious crises and dealt with very difficult individual cases over previous decades – including the extraction of Australians from Egypt in 1973, the conviction and execution of Australian men Kevin Barlow and Brian Chambers on drug-smuggling charges in Malaysia in 1986, and the evacuation of Australians from Jakarta as recently as 1998. But there was an obvious need to review and modernise the operation, particularly in light of the communications revolution that was gathering pace across the globe. I could also see that there was a need for some cultural change. The service could be overly rigid in its application of the rules, and could quickly become defensive if it received criticism from aggrieved consular clients or their next of kin. It needed to be more active in keeping ministers informed about cases likely to attract public attention. And, importantly, there was still scope for improvement in the quality of communication with clients' families back in Australia.

None of this was lost on most members of the consular service – in fact, they were generally impatient to get on with it. They could see the gaps for themselves. And in early 2000, when I joined them, they were conscious that the Australian parliament itself had recently focused its attention on the service and come to the conclusion that change was necessary. It had taken tragedy in Cambodia to bring this about.

Things looked promising for Cambodia for a brief moment in early 1994. The Khmer Rouge, the hardline communist movement that had inflicted deep trauma on the country in the 1970s, was still in control of some regions. But a national coalition had been elected the previous year, and a UN peacekeeping mission was winding down. Meanwhile, Cambodia had become a travel destination for the more adventurous members of the Lonely Planet generation. Some intrepid travellers were drawn to the sleepy coastal village of Sihanoukville, on a little peninsula in the Gulf of Thailand. It was about five hours from the capital by taxi, bus or train.

In April 1994, Kellie Wilkinson from Queensland was on her way to Sihanoukville by taxi with two British friends when they were intercepted by guerrillas and marched into the jungle. Consular staff were despatched to Sihanoukville to liaise with the local police and military, Foreign Minister Gareth Evans raised the matter with his Cambodian counterparts, and police agents flew in from Canberra and London to supplement the Australian and British embassies' efforts. Over the next several weeks there were unconfirmed sightings of the hostages, and reports of ransom demands. Then reports slowly began to filter through that one or more of the hostages had been killed, and in early July, following the forensic testing of remains found in a Khmer Rouge–controlled area, the families' worst fears were confirmed.

The sickening pattern was repeated only days later. On 26 July, David Wilson from Melbourne and two travelling companions from Britain and France were on a train to Sihanoukville from Phnom Penh when it was attacked by the Khmer Rouge. This time the insurgents were intent on using their windfall to advantage. They removed the foreigners to a remote location, demanded a million-dollar ransom, allowed messages to be exchanged with the families and distributed video appeals from the hostages. Meanwhile, concerns grew that the Cambodian military would be prepared to sacrifice the hostages' safety in order to inflict military defeat on the Khmer Rouge. The media also began reporting on tensions between DFAT and the Wilson family, who were critical of the government's public opposition to ransom payments and believed that the embassy should be taking a more active role in the hostage negotiations. David's father, Peter, and other family members also felt that the embassy was keeping them out of the loop. Reports emerged in October that the hostages had been killed, and in early November their graves were identified and bodies exhumed.

The Wilson family refused to consider the matter closed, and, with some media support, campaigned for a full inquiry into the handling of David's case. The Australian Senate eventually responded by launching an inquiry into the consular service. Public hearings commenced in September 1996, having been delayed by the Australian federal election earlier that year. The inquiry probed the appropriateness and effectiveness of DFAT's consular work, focusing on the handling of more difficult and complex situations – including the David Wilson hostage case. It also considered DFAT's responsibilities to provide timely and accurate consular travel advice. The senators heard testimony from departmental officials, the general public and the families of victims. While the inquiry examined the management of a number of other cases, it was the Wilson family who stated their concerns most forcefully and whose testimony dominated media coverage.

The Senate inquiry raised questions that go to the heart of the consular conundrum. One of them was what we should really expect of our government beyond our own borders. The department sought to explain that there were real, practical limits to what it could do in another, sovereign country. Another key question was where personal responsibility should begin and end. Why, some asked, did David Wilson and his friends choose to board a train to Sihanoukville when Kellie Wilkinson's abduction and murder in the same area had been a matter of very recent public attention? DFAT observed that its advisory notice for Cambodia had identified the dangers of travel outside Phnom Penh and urged travellers to seek advice from the embassy. I can't help reflecting, though, that David and his friends had been backpacking around South-East Asia for a few months and would have had very limited access to English-language news. In those days, too, travel advisories were simply issued to the media and travel agents, trusting that they would be disseminated further. Sometimes they were but often they weren't.

The Senate did not support the Wilson family's assertions that the Australian government should have taken a tougher stance with the Cambodian authorities over the aggressive behaviour of its military, or that it should have pressed them harder on the ransom negotiations. The committee found that many Australians had unrealistic expectations of DFAT's consular services, given international convention and the laws of other countries. The senators saw scope for the department to improve its performance in distributing travel advice, but their suggestions were limited to the dissemination of the *Hints for Australian Travellers* booklet we all still receive with our newly minted passports, and ignored entirely the potential of emerging modern communication tools such as the internet. The inquiry did, however, signal that the department needed to lift its performance in its dealings with media about consular cases. There was some criticism of DFAT for being 'unprepared to guide and work with the media'. But the clearest message was that the department needed to focus more strongly on the needs of anxious family members. The inquiry recommended strongly that 'the provision of information to families, in such distressing circumstances, be a high priority for DFAT and any mission abroad'.

The consular service I inherited from my predecessors had taken the Senate's message about the primacy of family communications to heart, and this was reflected both in amended guidelines and in practice. But the impact of the Senate inquiry extended well beyond this. A spotlight had been focused on a challenging area of DFAT's operations, and ministers and secretaries alike could see the vulnerability. Consular work might be routine much of the time, but it was the element of the department's work that was best known publicly, and most likely to get you on the front page of the newspapers – for the wrong reasons. It required more focus from the top, and needed to be understood by career diplomats as something integral to the department's broader purpose. Ashton was not the first head of the department to emphasise the importance of the work, but he moved deliberately to change internal attitudes. He did this by signalling that ambitious policy officers should regard a consular rotation as a positive step in their careers. At the same time, he made it clear to ambassadors designate that he would judge their performance both on the quality of their missions' overall consular operation and on their personal engagement in high-profile or difficult consular cases.

The organisation had several opportunities to put these principles into practice between 1997, when the Senate handed down its findings, and when I assumed leadership of the service in early 2000. The catastrophic failure of a pedestrian bridge in Tel Aviv in July 1997 killed four and injured more than sixty Australian athletes during a ceremony for the Maccabiah Games. Ian Wilcock, Australian ambassador to Israel at the time, watched helplessly from the crowd as the tragedy unfolded, but worked tirelessly and conscientiously to provide comfort to the anguished relatives afterwards; he needed no Senate inquiry or departmental secretary to tell him this was the right thing to do.

Another awful incident took place in June 1999 at Interlaken, Switzerland, when a group of young adventurers canyoning in a gorge were hit by a two-metre flash flood. Fourteen of the twenty-one who lost their lives were Australian. The experienced consul-general in Geneva, Mal Skelly, moved quickly to the scene. In fact the Australian governor-general himself, William Deane, also flew to Switzerland to participate in a memorial service after the disaster. My new colleagues in the consular branch were still assisting the families of these victims when I came on board the following year. Several were wrung out by the experience.

The department's relationship with the Wilson family would never be restored. Peter Wilson still believed the department was withholding information that would explain what had happened. Soon after I joined the branch, I decided that we needed to show Peter literally everything we had on file about his son's case. We declassified almost everything and sent it to him. With the approval of Foreign Minister Alexander Downer, I then flew down to Melbourne with a locked briefcase containing the very few items we had excised (on the grounds that their public release would compromise intelligence sources). I drove to Peter's house in the suburbs and sat in his kitchen drinking tea while he read them all. Over the next year or so, I spoke to him on the phone from time to time when he had a question. He was a decent man. I don't know that I actually helped.

CHAPTER FOUR

Baptism by Fire

THERE CAN BE AN ASSUMPTION, particularly by younger people in the first flush of their professional lives, that the path to the top simply involves building one successful experience upon another. In recent years, though, as I have listened to my own career achievements described in flattering terms to a public audience prior to a speech or some other kind of presentation, I have thought to myself, *Ah yes, but what about the setbacks?* I don't mind admitting that my first steps as head of the consular service were marked by a serious stumble.

When I started formally in the consular role, trouble was flaring in the South Pacific, which Australians commonly think of as a region characterised by white sandy beaches and swaying palm trees, and populated by a gentle people who value a laid-back lifestyle. The Pacific has, in fact, had its fair share of serious conflict over time. The Bougainville Civil War saw conflict throughout the 1990s between the state of Papua New Guinea and the secessionist Bougainville Revolutionary Army, killing thousands. The previous decade had seen a sustained independence struggle by indigenous militants in French-ruled New Caledonia, and a short-lived civil conflict in Vanuatu around the time of its independence in 1980.

On 19 May 2000, only three days before I commenced in the consular position, a gang led by bankrupt businessman George Speight stormed the parliamentary buildings in Suva, the capital of Fiji, and kidnapped the prime minister and thirty-five other parliamentarians. This was the country's third coup d'état in thirteen years. Speight, who'd studied in the United States and lived for an extended period in Australia, claimed to be a champion of local Indigenous rights. His actions appealed to elements of the Fijian population who'd been affronted by the election the previous year of a multi-ethnic government led by the country's first Indo-Fijian prime minister, Mahendra Chaudhry. The Australian-accented Speight held regular press conferences to justify his actions and rally support, and we all watched on as the drama unfolded on our television screens.

Tensions increased in Fiji over the following days and weeks, and our concerns grew for the security of the Australians who were either visiting or living in Fiji. Approximately 200,000 Australians visited Fiji on holiday each year at that time, and about 2000 more lived there. Speight held Prime Minister Chaudhry and his colleagues hostage for about two months as he wrangled with the president, Kamisese Mara, who had been quick to denounce the coup, and then with a military administration that stepped in under the leadership of Commodore Frank Bainimarama at the end of May. Some soldiers defected to the Speight group, gunfire was exchanged between the two camps and violence broke out across several of the country's islands.

In my first few weeks in my new job, people in the corridors sometimes smiled at me sympathetically and commented that I was having a 'baptism by fire'. In fact, it was nothing compared with the crises we would later face, but it certainly was an extended lesson in contingency planning and crisis preparation. With our support, the high commission in Suva conducted a campaign to ensure that all Australians in country were registered. I asked a couple of the more experienced hands in the branch to deploy to Suva to support the consular operation on the spot at this difficult time. We elevated the travel advisory to recommend strongly that Australians should not visit Fiji, and that those who could leave should do so.

The High Commission in Suva supported Australians to travel by convoy from Suva to Nadi, where they flew out from the country's international airport. Meanwhile, we began a series of meetings with the Department of Defence to ensure we were prepared if a large-scale emergency evacuation was required. We formulated contingency plans for both air and sea evacuations. The Royal Australian Air Force were put on standby, while the Royal Australian Navy positioned some of its vessels in the Pacific closer to Fijian waters.

Of course, this was not the only issue we were working on at the time. One of the things about consular work is that the new cases don't stop rolling in. We might have been preparing for a massive evacuation operation in Fiji, but things kept happening to Australians around the world that also required careful management. There had been an air crash in the the Papua New Guinea highlands on 29 April, and two Australians were among the dead. We spent time helping Australians caught up in local hostilities in the Philippines and India, and continued to respond to the daily deluge of 'routine' arrests, deaths, hospitalisations and whereabouts inquiries.

The stand-off in Suva was resolved by the Fijian military in the end. The temperature dropped, and the Australian Defence Force was stood down. The commander of the Fiji Military Force back then, Commodore Frank Bainimarama, is today the prime minister of Fiji, having led a further coup himself in 2006. Speight remains in jail for treason.

As it turned out, our evacuation planning did have some practical use, although it was not necessary in Fiji. Trouble had been simmering for some time in Solomon Islands, north-west across the sea from Fiji. The capital, Honiara, only a three-hour flight from Brisbane, had become the scene of serious inter-ethnic tensions. Honiara is on the island of Guadalcanal, which since the 1970s had become home to thousands of economic migrants from Malaita, the most populous island in the country. Since 1998, these people had been subjected to a campaign of intimidation led by Guadalcanese militants. Things took an abrupt turn on 5 June 2000, when the 'Malaita Eagle Force', formed to protect Malaitan rights, took Prime Minister Bartholomew Ulufa'alu hostage and forced him to resign. These events led to the outbreak of full-scale civil strife between the two ethno-nationalist groups. With the security situation deteriorating, DFAT moved quickly to advise Australians not to travel to Solomon Islands, but our parallel advice to those actually in the country – that they should leave – hit a snag when the fighting shut down the Honiara airport.

It's a big call for a diplomatic head of mission to formally request a full-scale military evacuation. Such operations involve a major commitment of national defence and military assets, civilian and logistical support, and money. They expose the government to potential criticism from the Australian community, the media and the political opposition if things are mishandled, or if the evacuation is subsequently viewed as unjustified. Most importantly, it needs to be determined if an evacuation is in fact the safest option for our citizens. There are some situations where the better call is to advise people to stay at home and keep their heads down.

It's very important to respect the call of the head of mission if a consular evacuation is under consideration. The ambassador on the spot is, after all, best placed to judge. And it's rare for a diplomatic head of mission to overreact to unrest or violence on the streets. In fact, ambassadors more often have to restrain headquarters from overreacting to perceived threats to Australians overseas. Ambassadors in Australia's neighbouring countries – those within the ADF's region of operational capability – sometimes have to guard against military contingency planning developing a momentum of its own. If a government knows that its forces are well positioned to intervene, it becomes more likely that it will actually do so unless it receives persuasive counsel to the contrary. I have experienced this myself when, as Australia's High Commissioner to Papua New Guinea, I had to push back against an urge on the part of some officials in Canberra to deploy the ADF to safeguard the Australian community, during what were admittedly troubling clashes between rival political factions and their supporters.

Back in Canberra, we'd been meeting regularly with the Department of Defence to refocus our contingency planning efforts on Solomon Islands. After the closure of the country's only international airport, a 'Landing Ship Heavy' of the Royal Australian Navy, HMAS *Tobruk*, had been positioned closer to Honiara as an additional precaution. Yet even after all this planning, the cable we received on the morning of 7 June 2000 took our breath away. The message from High Commissioner Martin Sharp was short and simple: he was requesting an immediate seaborne evacuation of Australian citizens, along with the nationals of Canada, New Zealand and other partner countries. There were a few raised eyebrows at the hastily arranged interdepartmental task force meeting in Canberra that morning, but the eventual consensus was that if this was the head of mission's call, we had better get on with making it happen.

A couple of years previously, the Australian cabinet had endorsed the principle that DFAT should pursue 'cost recovery' from Australian nationals who were evacuated at the government's expense. In other words, if Australians were evacuated by the Australian Defence Force, or on charter flights contracted by the government, they should contribute the equivalent of a commercial economy airfare home. This seemed only right in circumstances where people had been given ample opportunity and encouragement to get to safety by commercial means, and had either ignored the government's warnings or delayed their departure until it was too late.

On 8 June, HMAS *Tobruk* docked in Honiara and the consular team on the ground worked overtime to encourage Australian residents to take up the evacuation option. We were also offering evacuation, on a space-available basis, to citizens of our consular partner countries – starting with New Zealand. Where necessary, the local team assisted with safe transport to the embarkation point. The mission also obtained assurances from the Malaita Eagle Force that they would not interfere with the operation.

We were working at breakneck speed in Canberra, too. The team in Honiara needed guidance and support, and the Canberra-based twenty-four-hour Consular Emergency Centre had picked up Honiara's telephone load, screening all incoming calls from the Australian community there. Phone calls and messages flowed back and forth between our team and senior levels of the Department of Defence, and we also had the media to deal with, not to mention Australian government ministers. Both groups were hungry for information. I spoke to senior members of the consular team at the High Commission in Honiara about how we were planning to implement the cost-recovery principle. We all knew that the standard way of doing this was to ask each individual, at some point, to sign an 'undertaking to repay' the costs of the evacuation. Some experienced team members in Canberra and Honiara were asked to sort out the 'choreography' of the cost-recovery initiative, and I moved on to other pressing matters.

As the senior accountable officer, I made two mistakes that day. First, I failed to check for myself exactly how this delicate issue was going to be handled on the ground. I felt that it was all in good hands. To the extent I thought about it, I assumed it would be handled early in the registration process, perhaps at the High Commission itself. I should have 'trusted but verified'. Second, I neglected the equally important principle of 'no surprises'. I went home at the end of a long day without picking up the phone to inform someone more senior in Canberra – my line deputy secretary, Ashton himself or the foreign minister – that we would be implementing cost-recovery consistent with the government's requirements. Strictly speaking, we had covered off on the issue in our written briefing notes for the minister, which we also shared with the senior hierarchy of the department, but these were emailed out at the end of the day as the evacuation was progressing in Honiara. In retrospect, we had buried the warnings too deep. I should have made those calls.

Ashton rang me when I was still in the shower the following morning. His assistant's tone of voice prompted Roxanne to bring the phone immediately into the bathroom, and I quickly wrapped a towel around myself before taking the call. It was the secretary, after all – to speak to him on the phone dripping wet and naked was unthinkable!

Ashton had already seen that morning's media clips, and had just come off the phone with the defence minister, John Moore. Ashton was furious. The ABC and other media outlets had been present in Honiara the previous evening, and had captured the spectacle of Australian women and children being asked to sign 'undertakings to repay' as they were boarding an Australian military vessel in a conflict-torn country. It was a very bad look. The story was running on all television channels and in the newspapers, and was to become the subject of furious commentary on talkback radio by the end of the day. The department's public image took a hit, and Ashton took it very personally.

And so, within months of taking on the consular leadership role, I found myself being held responsible for a serious public relations stuff-up that was dominating the nation's headlines. Yes, others had been involved and the lines of communication and hierarchy were complicated, but I was the accountable senior officer in Canberra. Everyone, from the prime minister down, expressed their displeasure in my general direction, and I was told not to underestimate the impact this would have on my career.

This experience was actually a baptism of fire in the *personal* risks associated with leadership. The department's embarrassment didn't amount to a crisis in the real world. No one had been hurt, and everyone had been trying to do the right thing. Even in Honiara it wasn't really that big a deal – some passengers had been put out by the cost-recovery requirements and had complained, but the Navy reported that the overall mood on board the ship was good. Back in Canberra, however, the department was on the defensive in the face of extremely negative media reporting about the way things had played out in Honiara, and our political masters were deeply unimpressed. Ashton had been working to strengthen DFAT's standing in the eyes of the government, and it was clear he saw this as a serious setback – for the department and for me.

I found the next several days very difficult, but I had help. When I got out to my car the morning after this private and public disaster, demoralised after a sleepless night, I found a note

Roxanne had placed on the dashboard. It was a quote from Ralph Waldo Emerson:

> Finish each day and be done with it. You have done what you could. Some blunders and absurdities no doubt crept in; forget them as soon as you can. Tomorrow is a new day. You shall begin it serenely and with too high a spirit to be encumbered with your old nonsense.

This thoughtful intervention, along with messages and good wishes from friends and colleagues back in the office, lifted my determination. I reflected that this new job would provide plenty more challenges, and that these would also be opportunities for me to prove my mettle. I pressed on with my job and began to plot a wholesale reform of the government's systems for responding to disasters affecting Australians overseas – a process that equipped us well for the far more serious challenges that my team and I would face in the coming years.

In a professional sense, it became clear to me that people were watching to see how I dealt with the setback – that it was an important character test. I am sure Ashton didn't even want to hear my name for a few days in June 2000, but my relationship with him developed strongly over subsequent years. I came to regard him as an important mentor.

The passengers on board HMAS *Tobruk* had a difficult five-day passage to Australia in June 2000. The seas were rough, and most on board were sick. When asked how the 'customers' were faring at a daily joint task force meeting, a naval officer replied deadpan: 'It's the old rule – when one kid chucks, they all do.' To add insult to injury, by the time the ship reached Townsville, the airport in Honiara had been cleared and flights to and from Australia had resumed. Some Australians who'd refused to board the ship now flew back to Australia in comfort, and were home sooner than they would have been if they'd joined the official evacuation. It may not have been our proudest moment, but there were a lot of people trying to do the right thing and making the best judgements they could.

As it happened, the next crisis was actually in Australia. A backpackers' hostel in Childers, Queensland, was razed to the ground by fire in an arson attack on 23 June 2000, and fifteen young travellers were killed. Seven were British, three were Australian, two were Dutch, and there was one each from Ireland, Japan and Korea. Technically, it was a kind of 'reverse-consular' crisis, in which the victims were (mostly) foreign nationals in Australia, but the Queensland government needed help managing the international dimensions and our team had relevant experience that positioned us well to assist. We stepped in to advise the Queensland officials responsible for directing the response, and some of our staff were despatched to the scene to work with foreign consular officials as they sought to identify survivors and victims. It was an awful human tragedy, which certainly put my personal career concerns into proper perspective.

The Solomon Islands evacuation wasn't the only time things went off the rails under my watch. Given the risks in consular work, and the sheer number of cases on the books at any given time, it's surprising that there aren't more such situations. Almost three years later, our embassy in Phnom Penh, Cambodia, was monitoring an arrest case involving an Australian citizen, Clint Betteridge. He was accused of raping a fourteen-year-old girl, his passport had been confiscated by the Cambodian authorities pending his trial and he was prohibited from leaving the country. Even so, he managed to obtain a replacement passport from the embassy and quietly flew out to Australia, which has no extradition treaty with Cambodia. The media was onto it like a flash, and public outrage naturally followed. DFAT stood accused of helping an alleged paedophile evade justice; the embassy noted that it had warned the Cambodians that he was a flight risk, but this came across as a weak defence. We questioned those responsible in Phnom Penh, and any officials in Canberra who had been aware of the decision. They all genuinely believed that they were applying a longstanding and fundamental principle of the passports world – that unless an Australian citizen has been convicted of a crime, they have a legal right to be issued a travel document. It's hard to explain how deeply held this understanding was. Experienced passport officers would tell consular training course participants that, under the *Australian Passports Act*, an application simply could not be refused if the applicant had not been convicted, even if a judicial process against them was underway. The only problem with this strongly held belief was that it was wrong – as a quick check with the lawyers revealed.

Minister for Foreign Affairs Alexander Downer made it clear to me that a DFAT official needed to address the media to explain things. So I found myself stepping in to front a jostling, aggressive media throng for the first – and I hope, only – time in my life. It was amazing how quickly things calmed down when I opened the press conference with a clear admission: 'The decision to issue a passport to Mr Betteridge while he was on bail was a wrong call. This department is certainly not going to compound one wrong call with another, and his current travel document has therefore been cancelled.'

In response to follow-up questions, I repeated that a serious mistake had been made and emphasised that I had since sent instructions out to the global network about what should be done in similar circumstances in future. The media throng soon packed up and left, and by the following day the story was over. It was an interesting lesson in media management – owning up to the mistake and outlining what had been done to prevent a recurrence left the press with nowhere to go. Clint Betteridge was sentenced to twenty years' jail in absentia, and was arrested by the Australian Federal Police pending extradition to Cambodia, under regulations designed to get around the absence of an extradition treaty, but I understand from media reporting that he was released a couple of years later because the Australian government wasn't satisfied that he would receive a fair trial in Cambodia.

Now, when I see an organisation stumble publicly, I can't help but feel sympathy for the individual responsible – as happened in 2020 during the Covid-19 pandemic response, when someone in the consular area provoked a media storm by bungling a mass email with information about loans available to stranded travellers. Instead of blind-copying all recipients, DFAT accidentally made all email addresses visible to everyone on the mailing list, provoking a Twitter storm and widespread accusations of incompetence. I can only hope that, like me, the person concerned was able to learn the lesson and move on. I also hope that he or she received the right kind of personal support.

CHAPTER FIVE

Plying the Trade

'A FUNNY THING HAPPENED OVERNIGHT, boss,' said the consular operations manager as I arrived at work one morning. So many of my working days in the consular branch started like this.

It was mid-2000, and an Australian adventurer had been climbing an escarpment overlooking the Mediterranean Sea. The man was in his early twenties, and had gone rock-climbing on his own. He hadn't told anyone about his plans. He didn't speak the local language and hadn't given any thought as to whether a climbing permit was required.

Hundreds of feet above the base of a cliff, his rope had snagged, and try as he might, he couldn't clear the jam. He couldn't go up, and he couldn't go down. There was nobody else in sight – or within earshot. He rested for a while on a small ledge and tried again. No luck. So he did what any sensible young man would do in such a situation. He carefully leaned back on the ledge, gently extracted a mobile phone from his backpack and called his mum.

Woken in the middle of the night in Adelaide, his mother listened with rising alarm to her son's sorry tale. She quizzed him on his location and noted down what she could. They hung up and she rang 000, the Australian emergency number. The operator couldn't help directly – the emergency was on the other side of the world – but patched her through to the Consular Emergency Centre. Despite the grand name, this was just a corner area on the third floor of the DFAT building in Canberra, where one or two officials worked the phones on a roster day and night.

The duty officer took note of the situation, wrote down the young man's number and rang him. After a small delay the phone was answered. Following a friendly chat, the duty officer told the climber to 'hang tight' – he claimed in the debrief later that he hadn't intended the pun! – and then rang the consul at the nearest Australian embassy. After a flurry of calls, an emergency services helicopter was despatched to the scene by the local authorities. Our hero was winched to safety within about an hour of that first call to Mum.

This incident seemed doubly amazing to those of us in the consular area at the time. Our friend was very fortunate that he was carrying a mobile phone; they were by no means universal in 2000. I was the only one with a mobile in my family, for instance, and that had been issued to me because my consular job required it. We were also proud of the response of the Consular Emergency Centre (CEC), established only the year before. Before then, it had been nearly impossible for a member of the general public in Australia to access consular support after hours.

We'd taken the idea for the CEC from the Canadian Department of Foreign Affairs and International Trade, who at that stage were the 'first movers' among like-minded governments in reforming their consular operation. The idea was to provide an around-the-clock service to Australians abroad in genuine need of urgent assistance, and to their families in Australia. It was staffed on rotation by members of the operations team in my consular branch. They were all very good at what they did.

There were so many warm, professional women and men among them. One of them in those very early days was a man called Rowland Pocock, whose kind and patient style struck a real chord with the clientele. He was among the small group I despatched to Fiji in my first month in the job. He was a mainstay of the branch and popular with all his colleagues. I have since met a number of people outside DFAT who have told me about the kindness Rowland showed them at moments of great distress for their families.

The CEC had not yet been fully 'rolled out' in 2000. We were proud to note in DFAT's annual report that year that forty of Australia's 100 overseas posts were connected to the centre. What that meant was that the switchboards at these forty posts had the facility to transfer calls to the centre in Canberra, at no cost to the caller, when they pressed the appropriate number in response to a recorded message. It's the kind of service that most Australians today would take for granted, but it was quite an initiative at the time.

The experiences I had in my first year as the head of the consular service were real eye-openers. My perspective was not that of a 'frontline' consular officer. My role as leader of the global network was to lead the management of large-scale consular crises when required, and otherwise to guide and support staff, lead reform efforts, make decisions on cases which the consular guidelines hadn't envisaged, help manage media and political interests, and generally direct traffic. But I made a point of travelling regularly to engage with the far-flung members of the consular network so I would have a better sense of what our people were dealing with. We held consular conferences every two years in each region of the world as a way of staying connected with our global workforce. I would often add a busy consular post to my travel itinerary on my way to or from one of these conferences. This provided me with the opportunity to meet the 'clients' in some of our more difficult cases.

There was always something interesting or dramatic happening, and it was satisfying to be able to draw a 'straight line' between my own work and the 'real world'. It not only led me to appreciate my new colleagues, but gave me a window into the human realities that sit behind the headlines, and insights into some key themes that were playing out in Australian society more broadly. It was always fascinating, even if it was sometimes sad.

In Australia and other Western societies, the last decades of the twentieth century saw a growing trend towards 'deinstitutionalisation' for people suffering from mental disorder or disability. Long-stay psychiatric hospitals were replaced by more accessible community health services, and patients were increasingly supported to maintain independent lives. Mental health care focused progressively on reducing the awful sense of hopelessness felt by the unwell, and the helplessness experienced by their families. These positive reforms were made possible by the availability of new medications that helped people manage psychiatric episodes, and meant that confinement was often no longer necessary. By the early 2000s, many people who would once have been institutionalised felt confident enough in their ability to manage their lives that they were travelling independently overseas. If they could apply for a passport and buy an air ticket, there was nothing stopping them from leaving the country.

There are no statistics that can tell us how many Australians with mental illness make a real success of travel. I suspect – and I certainly hope – that most of them do. As with the broader travelling population, there are also cases where it doesn't work out. Drug addiction and mental illness are, sadly, common challenges that consular officials must contend with. Australians sometimes turn up at an overseas mission, or are brought there by the local police, in the middle of a psychiatric breakdown. The foyers of these missions are usually fairly calm places, but they could sometimes be the scene of alarming situations. It is confronting, for example, to see a grown man urinating in the pot plants of an embassy waiting area.

Experienced consular staff were already reporting a rising trend in such cases by the 1990s. Often the person involved had arrived very recently from Australia, and the first thing they'd done, in the excitement or perhaps confusion of finding themselves in a rich new cultural environment, was to stop taking their medication. It seemed to be particularly common in large Asian cities, such as Bangkok – destinations that were relatively accessible to Australian travellers on a budget, and where the local cultural environment was giddyingly different. The priority for our staff, of course, was to make the client safe and to ensure they received proper care. We'd also need to trace their next of kin and perhaps arrange repatriation back to Australia. Sometimes this would lead us to parents or siblings back home who would do everything they could to help. In many other cases, however, the family just didn't want to know.

The people at the centre of very difficult consular cases – arrests, long-term whereabouts inquiries, mental health breakdowns – often seem to come from broken families. This is most obviously true with the many child custody disputes that play out over international borders. These are among the most challenging situations that Australian consular officials have to deal with. They often have contact with parties on both sides of the dispute, and the exposure to two wildly different perspectives can be bewildering.

I witnessed an international custody dispute firsthand when I became the personal case manager for an Australian woman whom I will call Leanne. Years previously, Leanne had fallen in love with a man who, like her, had grown up in Sydney. Unlike Leanne, his family had emigrated from Lebanon in the 1970s and he was a dual Australian-Lebanese citizen. He was of Muslim heritage, but she felt that they shared core values despite their differing cultural backgrounds. She converted to Islam to please his family, and they married and had two children – a boy and a girl. The marriage broke down when the children were both still of early primary school age, but the couple remained on reasonable terms and were able to agree on custody arrangements in Australia without involving the courts. When her husband proposed that he take the kids on a short trip to Beirut to meet his family, Leanne hesitated, but after a few weeks she agreed. He and the children left Australia and never came back.

The inherent difficulties in child custody cases such as these would receive considerable public attention in 2019, when another desperate Australian woman, Sally Faulkner, was encouraged by the *60 Minutes* 'current affairs' program to take part in a ham-fisted attempt to abduct her own children back from Lebanon.

Child custody cases straddle many international boundaries, of course, not just those between Australia and Lebanon. But the situation with Lebanon is doubly complicated because it is not a signatory to the Hague Convention on the Civil Aspects of International Child Abduction. The convention provides legal procedures for abducted children to be returned to their home country. It allows many Australian children to be returned home each year, but it also cuts the other way. For example, the Family Court of Australia ruled in 2012 that four girls should be removed from their mother's home in Queensland and returned to live in Italy with their father. Like Leanne's husband, the mother had brought the children 'home' under the guise of a holiday, and had then refused to return with them. These cases highlight the risks parents need to consider before permitting children to travel or live overseas with their current or former partners.

When I first met Leanne, it had been eighteen months since her husband had left Australia with the kids. She'd been to Lebanon once in that time and had won the grudging agreement of her ex-husband's family to see the children briefly. She'd been told that joint custody arrangements could be agreed in Lebanon if she relocated there, but finding a home and establishing a life in Beirut without local connections was not really a practical option for her. There were many legal and bureaucratic obstacles in the way of her obtaining residential status in Lebanon, for instance, and there was no guarantee it would lead to a satisfactory custody arrangement.

I had the opportunity to visit Lebanon myself in early 2001, when I was on the way back from a regional conference in Warsaw. This gave me an opportunity to discuss Leanne's case with our embassy staff and local authorities, and better understand its complexities.

I remember a lot about that visit to Beirut: the bay laid out in a curve beneath us as the plane approached in the early hours of the morning; the incredible landing, seemingly only inches from the rooftops below; the Mediterranean light; and the 'green zone' dividing the city along religious lines, so reminiscent of the cities I knew in Bosnia. But three encounters dominate my recollections.

The first was with Stella Sultan, Leanne's formidable lawyer, who has represented many women in similar custody battles. Stella was passionate, well respected and well connected, and she sympathised strongly with her clients. She had very occasionally managed to convince a court to rule against the father in a custody case, but it almost always went the other way. What I learned from our discussions was that, under Lebanese law, the dice were largely loaded against mothers from the start. The legal code amounts to a 'law of deprivation' from a mother's perspective. A standard 'age of custody' is set for each religious sect – this means the age at which the mother should surrender custody of a child to the father. A Shiite mother can lose custody of a girl when she turns seven, and of a boy when he turns two. In the Sunni sect and for Protestant Christians, it is when the child turns twelve, irrespective of gender.

The second conversation that sticks firmly in my mind was with Sheikh Mohammed Kanaan, a judge of the Ja'afari court in Lebanon, which adjudicates matters of personal status – things such as marriage, divorce, child custody and inheritance. He struck me as insightful and genuinely sympathetic about Leanne's plight – not at all what many Australians might expect of an Islamic judge. He clearly believed there should be legal reform to prevent husbands from taking advantage of the law to intimidate the mothers of their children. He also believed that there were cases where the judge should rule against the father. However, cultural resistance to change remains strong; as far as I am aware, little has changed in this area of Lebanese law since the early 2000s. As a result, pursuing her cause through the courts was getting Leanne nowhere. Instead, she had to focus on reaching an accommodation directly with her husband. They were communicating again, which was at least something.

The third encounter in Lebanon that left an impression on me was with one of DFAT's own – a young woman named Kerin Burns, who was posted as vice-consul to the embassy in Beirut. She was in her mid-twenties and it was her first overseas posting. Watching her at work led me to reflect on how remarkable it was that young Australians with relatively little life experience could prove so capable in managing workloads full of very confronting situations. Kerin did have some more experienced people at the embassy who could provide guidance, but for the most part she was on her own. Like everyone else, she found the custody cases heartbreaking. She could see that, in countries that were not Hague signatories, the system benefited the abductor, and that women were almost always the ones left vulnerable. The same could be said for the prison visits she had to make.

Kerin was one of many across the network supporting Australian citizens in prison. She found that visiting a Lebanese jail was a surprise in many ways – it was completely unlike the Goulburn jail, near Canberra, which she had visited as part of her consular training course. One striking difference was that there was no separation between prisoners and visitors, unlike in Australia. Despite this, she never felt unsafe – the Lebanese guards and prisoners were both chivalrous and respectful in their approach to her.

I accompanied Kerin on a jail visit and could see some of this dynamic at play. I could also see the public relations value of this young Australian woman at work in the rough and forbidding prison environment. Using images of her and others at work in our public information material would help underline a point that the consular service was changing, and that a new, more diverse generation was coming through. I asked Kerin to take a camera along the next time she was there to get some photos of herself at work. The prisoners and guards alike showed huge enthusiasm for the project, lining up like grinning schoolkids against a wall for a 'class photo' with the Australian vice-consul.

I have seen the inside of prisons in many different countries and, like Kerin, was surprised by the experience. For example, the jails in Bangkok were not at all what I expected. I attended both the men's and women's jails in that city in 2001, as Australia was negotiating a prisoner transfer treaty with Thailand. Granted, I was at liberty to leave any time, yet the atmosphere seemed tranquil. Prisoners smiled in that shy, respectful way that you might experience at a cafe or temple. Prisoners and guards seemed to treat each other gently. There was none of the abusive cat-calling or the anti-authoritarian and threatening behaviour that can confront you when visiting Australian, British or American prisons.

The Australians I met were all incarcerated for drug-related crimes, were working on their Thai language skills, appeared to be on comfortable terms with the prison staff and shared private jokes with their fellow prisoners. I remember the Australian women seemed, at least on the surface, remarkably resilient and well adjusted. They were only just a little younger than I was at the time, and came from towns and places I knew. They were bright and personable, and reminded me of my friends back home. They were pleased to have visitors, obviously knew our consul well, and were keen for a good chat.

I don't for a moment think that my fleeting encounters with these prisoners gave me a real insight into their lived experience. It was clear that the Bangkok jail was overcrowded – the inmates slept like sardines on the floor, and the proportion of people to toilets was unacceptable by any standards. I can't imagine how it must have felt when the lights went out at night. All this, along with health concerns, communication difficulties and dislocation from home, must have made the experience a very difficult one, giving the Australian prisoners plenty of reasons to regret their actions. At least two of the people I met that day were transferred back to Australia during the following year to complete their terms. I suspect they had to adjust to the harder, edgier atmosphere of Australian jails, but I'm also sure that they would have welcomed the greater personal space, as well as the higher food and sanitation standards and the opportunity to be closer to family and friends.

Back in May 2001, I also visited a twenty-two-year-old Australian man in jail in a Middle Eastern country. He had grown up in Australia but was also a citizen of the country where he was imprisoned. He was actually being held for a crime committed in Australia – he'd allegedly committed a murder there four years earlier, when he was just eighteen, and he had immediately fled the country. He'd calculated that his other country of nationality had no extradition treaty with Australia, yet its government also claimed his victim as one of their citizens and believed they had jurisdiction over the alleged crime. The young man was polite and respectful, had a baseball cap on backwards and was 'wired for sound'. I met his father by chance on the way out – he was delivering his boy's lunch. Without this kind of family assistance, things could be pretty grim. We stopped and spoke for a while. He was both ashamed of his son but also fiercely protective. I often saw parents waiting outside, tortured by the crimes their beloved child had apparently committed, and by the penalties they had incurred.

The Australian deaths which our consular staff dealt with on a daily basis were all, by definition, tragic. Many could be attributed to natural causes, but they still came as a shock to the families concerned. Often they involved older Australian couples on their long-awaited retirement trips overseas, or migrants to Australia visiting their families abroad in retirement. While consular staff can help make the arrangements if someone has a heart attack or is involved in a road accident, the ones who are left behind often find themselves responsible for the very high costs associated with repatriating the body, on top of all the funeral arrangements, if there is no travel insurance. These costs can come as an awful jolt to the newly bereaved.

More generally, dealing with the death of a loved one overseas can be a nightmare for the next of kin. As well as being emotionally and financially draining, the process of repatriating a body can be dauntingly bureaucratic. Every year consular staff help many grieving families navigate unfamiliar foreign agencies to bring their loved ones home. South-East Asian countries, such as Thailand and Indonesia, generally record more consular death cases than other regions – this partly reflects the relatively high levels of tourist traffic there, but Australians are more likely to need help there than in, say, Europe or North America, where English is generally spoken and the local systems can be easier to navigate.

If all this sounds like difficult work, that's because it is. And yet there are people working away in DFAT's consular service who would not consider doing anything different. They find it fulfilling to be working in a field that involves supporting others in distress; for some there is also something slightly addictive about the immediacy of the work. Many are left feeling that their time working in the consular field is among the most fulfilling experiences of their lives. As one long-termer put it to me, 'Once the consular bug bites, no other role seems quite as attractive.' Another, now retired, responded dismissively when someone told him on his last day that he would miss the work. But sometimes, he admits now, he gets 'itchy feet' when a crisis is unfolding. 'You want to be part of it,' he says.

CHAPTER SIX

Some Cases Are More Equal than Others

AN AUSTRALIAN WOMAN IN HER early thirties, her eleven-year-old daughter and seven-year-old son sat anxiously in the vehicle as their driver sped them towards the 'Friendship Bridge' border crossing between Laos and Thailand. The children must have been confused, upset and full of questions. Their father, Kerry Danes, had just been detained by the Lao authorities. Now their mother, Kay, was rushing to get them out of the country. It was 23 December 2000, two days before Christmas, and their home town of Brisbane must have seemed a long way away.

When they arrived at the bridge, they handed their passports and declaration forms to the border guards. There was a delay – too long – and then a police contingent arrived, accompanied by a senior government representative who oversaw foreign investors. Kay had last seen him at her workplace only an hour or so earlier, questioning her husband about some missing gems. The police searched the family luggage ruthlessly. They did not find the gems they were looking for, but they did find what they thought was a large sum of money in Kay's bag.

In the middle of all this, the consul at the Australian embassy in Vientiane, Louise Waugh, materialised by Kay's side. It's not a standard part of the service for our consuls to arrive like the cavalry, at critical times of need. But Vientiane is a small community, and Louise had been tipped off by Kay's sister-in-law. Louise acted with the impeccable judgement and good sense that she was well known for within DFAT. Her presence sent a useful early signal that the Australian government was taking an interest in the proceedings. She was also able to take responsibility for the children when Kay was taken away to the Lao Department of Immigration. Louise visited Kay in detention the following day, and they agreed that Louise should arrange for the children to fly home to stay with their grandparents in Brisbane. After putting them on a plane on Christmas Day, Louise delivered Christmas dinner to Kay in the detention centre.

Kerry and Kay Danes were destined to become a major and protracted preoccupation for me and for others, including Foreign Minister Alexander Downer. About eight months after their arrest, my family and I were taking a short weekend walk in the bushland south of Canberra – a rare break from what was an enormous year for the consular service, and for me. My thirteen-year-old daughter, Annabelle, ripped a piece of loose bark from a scribbly gum. In May Gibbs' *The Gumnut Babies*, one of my daughters' favourite books from their early childhood, the wriggly lines on the bark of the gum tree were the newspapers of the Australian animal world. 'Oh, look,' Annabelle said in sardonic tones. 'It's a newspaper article from 2025! The Danes case is still going and my dad is still working on it!'

The story of Kerry and Kay Danes has dimmed in the collective memory over the years. Even I have had to remind myself of some of the details by re-reading Kay Danes's own accounts of the experience. But the whole episode provides some insights into why some consular cases attract significant media and public attention when others don't. Those that assume a media profile do so for a range of reasons. In some cases, the charges are patently absurd, and Australians are outraged by what they perceive as an injustice. In other cases, public opinion might be more divided on the question of guilt or innocence, but there are other, less tangible factors that help build momentum.

The Danes case had quite a few things going for it as far as the Australian media was concerned. One was its timing – the story hit the Australian headlines five days after the couple's arrest, on 28 December, in that quiet period between the start of the Boxing Day Test match and New Year's Eve. There was little else around at that time of the year to compete with what was also a compelling narrative. Australian children had been ripped from their mother, who was now imprisoned by an authoritarian communist state, in what seemed to be dark and corrupt circumstances. To give the storyline an additional whiff of excitement, Kay's husband, Kerry, was a member of the Australia Army's elite Special Air Service Regiment.

There was a sense that the couple had been duped and set up by others. Kerry was on extended unpaid leave from the SAS, working as the general manager of Lao Securicor, a security company, and Kay was their contracts manager. They provided security to a company called Gem Mining Lao, which held the concession to mine the country's main sapphire deposit in the 'golden triangle' region where Laos, Myanmar and Thailand meet. GML's owners had fled the country earlier in 2000, when the Lao authorities terminated their concession and accused them of embezzling funds. Before doing so, the GML owners had signed over formal control of the company's business affairs to Kerry on a 'caretaker' basis.

Consular clients and their families can themselves play a major role in determining the media and public attention afforded to a case. For many, stimulating media interest is instinctive. It is regarded as a time-honoured way of getting political attention. At the crudest level, the underlying assumptions can be that without public pressure, the Australian government will not take an interest in the case, and that the government of the other country will buckle if the blowtorch of international condemnation is applied.

By Boxing Day 2000, Kay Danes' father, Ernie Stewart, was making repeated phone calls to the Consular Emergency Centre, demanding immediate action to secure his daughter's release. He was of the firm belief from the outset that the surest road to success was through the media. We told him that he was, of course, free to take his story to the press, but that the foreign minister was fully aware of the situation and it was the embassy's top priority. Our view at the time was that no amount of media coverage would change that; indeed, Australian media criticism might harden the Lao government's resolve and make it more difficult for them to back down. We argued that public attention didn't always lead to prompt resolutions. In several previous cases, quiet background diplomacy, unaccompanied by public scrutiny, had led to quick and satisfactory outcomes. But Ernie was not convinced, agreeing only to delay by a couple of days. Meanwhile, the embassy pressed on with its efforts, with Australian ambassador to Laos, Jonathan Thwaites, making direct representations to the Lao authorities for Kay's release on compassionate grounds, and for consular access to Kerry.

In fact, the story broke in the Australian media the next day thanks to an alert from an investigative reporter based in South-East Asia. By that stage we'd already decided that the situation needed to be elevated, and so we implemented an agreed coordinated plan. Foreign Minister Downer played an active part in this plan, ringing the Lao ambassador in Canberra to demand consular access. The ambassador was then summoned to the department to have the message reinforced by officials. Ambassador Thwaites made representations to the deputy foreign minister in Vientiane on the same day. All this happened amid a blare of television, radio and newspaper reporting about how an Australian family had been 'torn apart' at Christmas. It was media gold, and Ernie burnished it on 31 December by holding his own press conference in Brisbane, calling for immediate Australian sanctions against Laos. In fact, both Kerry and Kay had received consular visits the day before this media blitz – from the ambassador, the consul and the embassy doctor. Thus began a pattern of weekly visits, during which the couple were also able to use an embassy mobile phone to make calls to their children.

Our engagement with the Lao government over the following weeks and months left us with the distinct impression that they wanted to find a way out of the situation, but the public profile of the case was hindering, rather than helping. From their perspective, it was important that the Danes were not seen by their own people to be receiving 'special treatment' because they were foreigners; the Lao authorities felt backed into a corner and were intent on allowing their own prosecutorial processes to unfold.

The media can sometimes become a key instigator and intermediary in the matter, amplifying the pressure for governments to act or 'do more'. This can encourage political intervention, which can sometimes be helpful but can also create further challenges. In a 2013 report for the Lowy Institute of International Policy on the 'consular conundrum', Alex Oliver, a long-term observer of the Australian consular service, went so far as to say that a 'vicious cycle' can be created: 'public expectations, already high and sometimes unrealistic, are stoked by political acts that override departmental protocols and service charters to provide ever increasing levels of consular service'.

I am not suggesting that this was quite the situation with Kerry and Kay Danes, but expectations were raised early in their case, when Foreign Minister Downer associated himself publicly with DFAT's efforts by speaking personally to the Lao ambassador amid the initial media storm. We all thought this was the right thing to do at the time. Acting on our advice, he continued to engage as time dragged on, signing several letters to Kay's parents in the first few months of 2001 to outline everything that he and his officials were doing to resolve the case. He also wrote to his Lao counterpart, Foreign Minister Somsavat Lengsavad, and then took the case up with him in person on the margins of an APEC meeting in Santiago in late March. As the weeks and then months passed without progress, Downer's credibility and effectiveness began to be questioned by the Australian political opposition and media, who were not letting go of the matter. For good measure, Ernie Stewart made occasional public statements, helping keep the media warm. Some of the press coverage verged on the hysterical, including excited reporting that Kerry's SAS colleagues were planning to 'bust him out'.

It took a lot of effort to 'right the ship'. In Laos, Jonathan Thwaites raised the case with every minister and senior official he met, sending daily reports detailing his conversations. His Lao counterpart in Canberra was called in again, and at one point the deputy secretary of DFAT, John McCarthy, was despatched to Laos as a special envoy to seek a resolution. Prime Minister John Howard spoke to his Lao counterpart, as did the governor-general. In February, the campaign was joined by Ted Tzovaras, a Sydney-based solicitor whose experience was in commercial dispute resolution.

Another risk with cases that assume a public profile is that they can attract people who, for egotistical or self-interested reasons, claim that they can 'help'. In this case, our interest was piqued when the Danes' legal team began hearing from 'local sources' that the Australian government should desist from making further representations, because they were confident from local 'sources' in Vientiane that Kerry and Kay would soon be released and the charges dropped. These confident predictions were completely inconsistent with our own analysis, and were never borne out by events. Predicted release dates came and went. These 'sources' would then advise that there had been a complication, that it had been overcome and that release was again imminent. Even when, in late June, the court sentenced the Danes to seven years' imprisonment and imposed heavy financial penalties for embezzlement and tax evasion, these sources predicted that the sentence would be overturned on appeal and the couple released. All of this created unrealistic hopes for both the incarcerated couple and their family.

It finally reached a point where the Lao government decided to try and make it easy for us. In July 2001, Alexander Downer met his Lao counterpart in Hanoi, where they were both attending a regional summit. Foreign Minister Somsavat Lengsavad came to the meeting with a proposed deal. He suggested that the quickest way of finalising the legal process would be for the Danes' legal appeal to be withdrawn, thereby discontinuing their formal assertion of innocence. He highlighted the financial penalties as the main obstacle, and said he recognised that the Danes could not afford to pay them. But if the Australian government issued a statement to the effect that we would encourage the Danes to pay the financial 'compensation', he suggested, face would be saved and the couple would be released. He noted that there was no extradition agreement between Australia and

Laos. He had all but spelled out that once the Danes were back in Australia, there was no way the financial penalties could be enforced. The content of these discussions was held closely at the time – DFAT officially relayed Somsavat's 'terms' promptly to the Danes themselves, but the details only became public months later, when the media gained access to the couple and their lawyer.

The Danes' legal team was reluctant about the 'Hanoi deal' (as the Danes themselves came to refer to it) and pressed ahead with the appeal. Their clients might have had misgivings, but they went along with this strategy. The situation seemed stuck. A couple of weeks after the Hanoi meeting, I ran into Ashton in the corridor. He'd just come from a meeting with a frustrated foreign minister. Ashton asked me what I thought could be done. I replied that we needed to put someone fresh into Vientiane for a while to replace Jonathan temporarily as ambassador. He had been working the case for seven months without a break. I said it should be someone sufficiently experienced who could speak clearly to the Danes about what was required to get them home. Ashton looked at me for a moment and replied, predictably, 'When can you leave?'

And that's how I came to be chargé d'affaires at the Australian embassy in Laos.

It didn't start well. The following Monday morning, as my Thai Airlines plane was on its last approach to Vientiane airport, it suddenly banked sharply to the right. The engines roared as the pilot worked to maintain distance between us and the ground. I had a window seat on the starboard side of the aircraft, so found myself looking directly down, at close range, into the paddy fields of Laos. I had experienced a 'go round' a couple of time before – when the pilot pulls out of a landing at the last moment – but this seemed a bit extreme. About a minute later the plane steadied, the vertigo lessened and I began to relax. After completing a full turn the crew brought us safely to the ground. No explanation or apology was offered, and my fellow passengers – all of them Lao or Thai – seemed to just accept what had happened without question or comment.

Louise Waugh was there to meet me at the gate. She looked at me curiously and asked, 'Are you okay?' She had seen what happened – a military helicopter had taken off suddenly, directly in front of the incoming plane, leading our pilot to swerve dramatically. It was the kind of incident that would probably lead to sensational news coverage and a high-profile investigation in Australia. But not here. We'd survived and life moved on. I was no stranger to South-East Asia, but it was a salutary reminder that norms and expectations were different here.

Later that day I joined Louise Waugh on a consular access visit with the Danes. Suddenly, there they were, sitting in front of me in their dark-blue prison uniforms. I handed over some gifts and letters from family that I had carried with me from Australia. The bulk of this was a Father's Day package for Kerry, including sporting paraphernalia from the Brisbane Broncos rugby league team, which pleased him immensely. They were clearly anxious and living in very difficult conditions, but they had used their interpersonal skills to establish respectful relationships with their Lao guards, even exchanging banter with some of them and with each other. They obviously trusted Louise completely. They had been told I was coming, and had heard a little about me from their family. I had a sense of being appraised.

I told them I had serious doubts about whether the current strategy was going anywhere, explained in my own words how I thought the Hanoi deal might work, and left them to think about it. I did the rounds of Lao ministers and senior officials over the next few days. The more I talked to people on the ground, the more it became abundantly clear that the Lao government was looking for a way to preserve face. A week later, back with the Danes at the immigration centre, I told them it was my considered view that they needed to drop their appeal, which had no hope of success. With their support, I would negotiate a statement of 'contrition' on their part, which would fall short of an admission of guilt. I said I knew that that this would be hard for them to take. Kerry said something like, 'My oath it is!' But I walked out of this second encounter with their agreement for the Australian government to re-engage the Lao authorities in these terms. I returned to Australia the following day, on 1 September 2001, with the expectation that I would return two weeks later. But the unprecedented crisis that hit the world on 11 September meant that the Danes would have to wait a few more weeks.

That I was back in Vientiane again by 25 September, when my team was still working on the aftermath of the 9/11 terrorist attacks in the United States, was a sign of the priority we had come to attach to this case. During my absence, and as expected, the Danes' appeal had been formally rejected by the Lao Supreme Court, confirming that there really was only one path to take: the Hanoi deal. The Danes had come to recognise the reality of their situation and agreed. Kerry's comment was simply, 'Let's get on with it.' He made it clear he was only agreeing for Kay's sake, and for the children. There was nothing fake about this.

It was amazing how smoothly things went once the Australian clients and their legal team were on board. Within twenty-four hours of my return to Vientiane, I had obtained the Danes' agreement to a statement of contrition, which expressed their willingness, in very general terms, to take note of the compensation requirement. In a series of meetings with government officials over the next few days, I was able to secure the Lao authorities' agreement to the wording. The Danes' statement was supplemented by a note from the Australian embassy to the effect that it would encourage the Danes to respect the compensation 'requirements'. It was all smoke and mirrors, and we knew it. They were transferred to the ambassador's care four days later. They lived at the ambassador's residence with Jonathan and his wife, Eve, for a month before the Lao president signed off on their pardon.

There was quite the media scrum when Kerry and Kay flew into Brisbane on 8 November 2001, more than ten months after they had been detained. They had to be spirited through a back exit by a member of the Brisbane DFAT office, and were then moved to an undisclosed location to be reunited with their family. The story was once again front-page national news, and more in-depth coverage followed over time – including an *Australian Story* episode on the ABC. Kay did not forget the less fortunate friends she had made in prison, and went on to become a public champion for them.

For the most part, the media and public assumed that Kay and Kerry were victims. But there were some who questioned whether the Danes had truly been innocent. After all, why did Kay run that day if she really had nothing to hide? Other aspects of the story – the missing gems, the cash Kay was carrying – sounded a bit murky to some Australians. I spent considerable time with them (and later read Kay's book about their ordeal), and I think the explanation lies in the Danes' deep mistrust of the Lao authorities. They were confident that they had done nothing wrong, but had no faith at all that the rule of law would be followed: in their minds, official questioning was bound to presage serious trouble. To be fair, that perspective was rooted in some reality. Laos is low on most international transparency indices – corruption is a real problem, and justice can be arbitrary. In any case, the balance of opinion in Australia was that Kerry and Kay's release was a good result.

There have been other high-profile arrests and detentions of Australians in more recent years that have provoked an even more significant public response, because our society comes to a unified view that the individual concerned is undoubtedly the victim of an injustice. Journalist Peter Greste, arrested in 2013 by the Egyptian military regime for 'falsifying news' and 'damaging the country's national reputation', was one such case. Another was academic Kylie Moore-Gilbert, detained by the Iranian authorities in 2018 on trumped-up 'espionage' charges. And there have been several Australians who have been detained in very dubious circumstances by China amid the serious downturn in the relationship between Canberra and Beijing. In the minds of almost all Australians who follow the news, these are unquestionably cases of arbitrary detention.

There have also been other high-profile cases where Australian opinion has been more divided. Many were sceptical about Schapelle Corby's assertions of innocence when she was arrested in Bali on drug-smuggling charges at the end of 2004, but there were countless others who accepted her protests of innocence without question. There was something about Schapelle that many Australians seemed to identify with. The case generated numerous media polls, and 'Free Schapelle' merchandise was everywhere to be seen for a while – hats, stubby holders and bumper stickers. For me looking on from a distance, it seemed that little thought was being given to how this was going down in Indonesia. In comments reported by *The Sydney Morning Herald* on 12 May 2005, Dr Jason Sternberg, a lecturer in media and communications at the Queensland University of Technology, went so far as to assert that some elements of the public campaign 'spoke to a deeply racist undercurrent that runs through Australian culture at the moment'. The Indonesian authorities and media certainly saw it that way. As Sternberg reflected: 'It plays on the fear that we are suddenly, somehow unexpectedly under threat from Asia again ... All these transnational tensions are being played out through this one poor woman stuck in prison, facing life in jail.'

This is a real risk. A public debate with little strategy can lose sight of the person in question, and no thought is given to the potential consequences of ill-expressed public anger for that individual. Corby was found guilty by the Indonesian courts in May 2005 and sentenced to twenty years in prison. Her supporters could even watch it all unfold, because most Australian television channels carried the proceedings live. Over the years that followed, when the media interest had subsided at least a little, the Indonesian government progressively exercised some clemency and reduced the sentence. She was freed in 2014 and deported to Australia three years later.

Not all Australians would agree about the merits of Julian Assange's case either, but that didn't prevent it from making headlines all over the world from 2010, when the United States launched a criminal investigation into Wikileaks, the website founded by the Queensland-born Assange, after it published heavily classified communications and other material belonging to the United States and its allies. From a media perspective, Assange's story was the gift that kept on giving. It was loaded with controversy from the start. For some, Assange was a traitor who had participated in the theft of secret information and exposed innocent agents' lives in the process. For others, he was a whistleblower and journalist dedicated to exposing ugly truths about the world's greatest military power.

The story offered twists and turns at every stage. Sweden issued an arrest warrant for Assange in November 2010 over allegations of sexual assault, and requested his extradition from the United Kingdom, where he was based. Assange then breached the bail conditions associated with this extradition request and moved into the London embassy of Ecuador, which had agreed to grant him asylum. He spent almost nine years there before the Ecuadorian government revoked this decision and Assange was dragged from the embassy by the British police. By then the Swedish authorities had decided not to proceed with their prosecution, but Assange remained in British custody pending an extradition case from the United States for the original theft of classified material. Since 2020, as the matter has slowly progressed through the British judicial system, each new development has been the subject of intensive media and public interest.

Another differentiating factor in this case was the concerted international campaign for Assange's freedom. As the case dragged on, his well-organised supporters called on successive Australian governments to demand that the United Kingdom release its citizen. The campaign was backed by Amnesty International and Human Rights Watch, and enlisted the support of a wide range of public figures – from Australian human rights barrister Geoffrey Robertson to one-time US vice-presidential candidate Sarah Palin and rock musician Roger Waters of Pink Floyd. But over the years both Labor and Coalition governments were fully prepared to push back. They were no doubt assessing the merits of the case, but they judged that there was insufficient Australian public support, or any other basis, to provide more than the regular consular treatment for Assange.

Over time, Australian foreign ministers from both sides of politics expressed their confidence in the capacity of the British legal system to deal with the matter fairly. In 2021, Foreign Minister Marise Payne noted: 'We have made nineteen offers of consular assistance to Mr Assange since 2019 that have gone unanswered.' Of course, she meant the standard consular assistance that is offered to everyone – welfare visits in prison and ongoing monitoring to ensure fair treatment under local law. Assange and his supporters wanted more than that.

By April 2022, Julian Assange had spent three years at Belmarsh maximum security prison awaiting judgement about his future, and he'd already experienced seven years of isolation in the Ecuadorian embassy before that. His detractors would argue that much of this has been self-inflicted, but increasingly I have the sense that Australian public opinion is consolidating around a view that he's been punished enough.

There are many factors that can influence the public to swing behind certain cases, but it helps a lot if there is an appealing and consistent public narrative. And those whose loved ones are locked up overseas will naturally do whatever they can to secure their release – especially, but not only, if they truly believe them to be innocent. Some individuals are fortunate that their families are well connected, or have access to a circle of advisers with expertise in public advocacy, international relations and the law. Kay Danes' father, Ernie Stewart, didn't have any of these advantages but left nothing on the table as he pushed publicly for his daughter's release from her Lao prison in 2001. I always admired him for that.

CHAPTER SEVEN

Getting Ready for the Big One

WE KNEW, IN THOSE EARLY years of the twenty-first century, that we needed to build a more robust consular system, one capable of responding to whatever new pressures the coming decade would bring. It was pretty clear that our operational arrangements, which had evolved slowly over previous decades, were no longer fit for purpose. While we could not imagine how dramatically the international operating environment would be transformed on 11 September 2001, we had assessed the implications of the rapid growth in Australian traveller numbers, along with the new expectations and opportunities arising from the communications revolution that was underway.

There were also some unexpected events in my first year running the consular branch that shaped and stimulated our reform efforts.

We recognised that we had an important obligation to advise Australian citizens about serious risks in the international environment, and we worked conscientiously to put the travel advisory system on a more professional footing. Until the late 1990s, Australia only issued travel advisories for countries where there were specific, serious risks – a civil war, natural disaster or widespread violent protests, for example. Under this model, the existence of a travel advisory was effectively a black mark against the country concerned. We were progressively changing this thinking, extending the system to provide some form of travel advice for all countries of the world, even if it was only very general or benign. We kept our focus on the risks to Australians overseas, and would not be swayed by diplomatic considerations. This led to difficulties from time to time. An upgraded travel advisory can invite serious blowback from the foreign government concerned – it's rarely appreciated by another country if you tell your citizens it is dangerous to go there.

Terrorism and other militant activity featured in our thinking as we framed travel advice prior to September 2001, but our advisories were often focused on other risks. As well as civil unrest or war, we noted health or security dangers, recommended caution in visiting, suggested that travel be deferred to a particular location in some circumstances, or even urged people to leave.

In preparing travel advisories, we drew on assessments from Australian missions overseas about the security conditions in which they operated, and on our experience of the common or recurring consular problems Australians were experiencing overseas. We also consulted intelligence reports and the advisories prepared by our consular partners – the United States, the United Kingdom, New Zealand and Canada. We often reached different conclusions from our overseas counterparts, but it was a useful 'benchmarking' exercise. In some cases – where the risks or sensitivities were great – the foreign minister would also be asked to sign off on them. When I arrived in the consular branch, there was already a requirement that Alexander Downer authorise every change to the travel advice for Indonesia, for example. He took a sensible and careful approach to this responsibility, often ringing me to talk about the wording and how it related to what we knew through our intelligence channels.

It was not enough for travel advice to be accurate and timely. It also had to reach its intended audience, and by today's standards the distribution of advisories in 2000 was very basic. We were only just beginning to make them available via the internet, and we relied heavily on the mainstream media and travel agents to relay our advice to the public. When I authorised a new travel advisory, it was sent out through a combination of fax and email messages to mainstream and travel journalists, and to every registered travel agent on our books. While many passed it on, there was nothing to compel them to do so. Travel agents were sensitive to any official recommendation that Australians not travel to a country or region – an insurance policy would automatically lapse if someone ignored this kind of warning. But many of them were reluctant to burden their clients by passing on other advisories.

Mindful of this, DFAT's public affairs efforts focused on promoting our travel advice at every opportunity. As the department's main 'talking head' on these issues, I spoke at travel industry conferences, briefed politicians and gave media interviews. I drew on our rich collection of dramatic stories, trying to hammer home the importance of taking travel advice seriously. I was twice a radio guest of John Laws, our country's greatest 'shock jock', and survived well enough on both occasions. I even flew down to Melbourne once to appear on Bert Newton's daytime television show, only to find myself squeezed into a ninety-second segment between a report about the Eurovision Song Contest and an advertisement for ab-blasters.

Through 2000 and the first half of 2001, the consular team also systematically started to upgrade our crisis response systems. It was an almost-forgotten incident in the Greek islands that first revealed a serious weakness in their systems. In hindsight, this pivotal event helped prepare us, inadvertently, to weather the coming storms.

The ferry MS *Express Samina* had 473 passengers and sixty-one crew members on board when it left Piraeus, the port of Athens, on the evening of 26 September 2000. It was late summer, and many of the passengers were foreigners touring the Aegean islands – including, inevitably, several Australians. The ship was on autopilot, and the first officer was reportedly watching a football match when it struck a rock just before midnight. The water inrush from a gash in the ship's hull destroyed the generators. Safety experts have observed that the kind of damage the *Express Samina* sustained would not normally sink a ship of its size, but nine of the eleven watertight compartment doors were open, despite legal requirements that they be locked and closed, causing the ship to sink.

The crew's conduct during the evacuation came in for heavy criticism in subsequent investigations, which also led to calls for improvements in safety standards for Greek shipping. The captain and first officer were both to receive long prison sentences, while the manager of the shipping company took his own life. Local fishermen led the initial rescue response, dragging survivors from the dark water. They were aided over time by larger ships, including from the British Navy, diverted to the scene from a nearby NATO exercise.

When he was alerted, Ross Burns, Australia's ambassador to Greece, led Australia's coordination efforts with the Greek authorities. His team worked amid the confusion to establish how many Australians had been on board, and to determine their safety and whereabouts.

News of the tragedy broke in the Australian media on the afternoon of 27 September. In keeping with established protocols, the embassy focused on its local operational response, referring inquiries from the Australian public and media to the Consular Emergency Centre in Canberra. Thousands of Australians were travelling in the Greek islands at the time, often having left only vague itineraries with their families back home. The team took a total of 2800 calls from Australian relatives and friends anxious about their loved ones, and our systems were overwhelmed. People were forced to wait far too long to speak to someone, and some didn't get through at all. It wasn't good enough. We were able to ramp up the number of phone operators from within the branch's resources, and gradually brought the situation under control.

Initially, the ship's manifest took some time to be made available, and it was also unreliable, so there was little information about who was on board. As the pieces of the puzzle were gradually put together over the following twenty-four hours, in consultation with families and the local authorities, we and the Athens embassy team were able to identify and then progressively contact the fourteen Australians who had been passengers. Two had been injured, but all had survived. Eighty-two others were not so fortunate that night.

Few Australians may remember the MS *Express Samina*, but it had a significant impact on the Australian consular service. The deluge of calls we received was a useful reminder that public anxiety at home could be disproportionate to the number of Australians actually involved. We conducted a frank and robust 'lessons learned' exercise following the incident. Crisis planners are often accused of spending too much time preparing for the last crisis, but this impulse is not always wrong. Any self-respecting organisation appreciates that a properly reflective process can reveal systemic weaknesses, staff training deficits or connections that need to be developed further.

In the weeks and months following this event, we increased the capacity of our telephone systems substantially, introducing a phone manager system with a queuing and messaging facility for the first time. We trained a reserve cadre of DFAT volunteers serving in other areas of the organisation, who could be enlisted to help manage future crisis events. We also began to roll out a global online consular management information system – a shared database for the entire network. Until then, consular case information had been exchanged by emailing documents or spreadsheets, which carried a significant risk of error and slowed things down. We were also connecting more and more of our posts to the Consular Emergency Centre via free-call or reverse-charges arrangements, giving more Australians around the globe immediate access to the service at no cost. We expanded our global consular footprint by appointing honorary consuls, and extended the remit of our consular sharing agreement with Canada, whereby we step in to help Canadians in countries where they have no diplomatic presence and vice versa.

There were some important personnel changes within the branch at the beginning of 2001. The pivotal role of Consular Operations Director had fallen vacant at the end of the previous year, when the incumbent retired. The holder of this position had oversight of all of our casework, liaison with families and the management of our operational staff. It was effectively a deputy position within the branch. I was very pleased that we were able to appoint Keith Gardner to the role in January that year. He had extensive consular experience, with postings in India, Poland, China and Jamaica under his belt. He was fresh from his role as head of the DFAT office in Darwin, at a time when the city had served as an important logistics and military hub for Australia's participation in the East Timor peacekeeping operation. He had operated with scant resources and shown that he was an all-rounder with the right attitude. We were also fortunate to recruit Warren Macilwain, a strong and steady figure, to oversee the CEC's operational work. These appointments gave me confidence that we were well set up for whatever was to come.

We also put a lot more effort into crisis contingency planning. The experts will tell you that this is a sophisticated business. It involves analysing scenarios, designing procedures, building robust systems, training responders and leaders, ensuring the right equipment is on hand and conducting practice drills. It also involves developing methods to adapt rapidly to events you haven't anticipated. But for me the most useful thing to do is to imagine that your worst nightmare is about to unfold. It all starts with the nightmare. To focus the mind and stimulate urgent, serious preparation, there's nothing like contemplating a situation that would leave you horribly exposed and unprepared, and then acting like you only have a very short time to get ready for it.

The worst thing we could think of in the very early 2000s involved an airliner full of Australian passengers crashing in a neighbouring country where there was limited local capacity to respond effectively. Imagine QF1 – the daily Qantas flagship flight from Sydney to London – coming down in central Borneo. Planes carrying up to 350 passengers were regularly flying in and out of Australia to Indonesia, Papua New Guinea and several other regional nations. If they were on their way to or from an Australian city, the majority of the passengers would likely be Australian. Even if they weren't, as the nearest developed nation with the required logistical capacities, Australia would have an obligation to lead the response effort.

Thankfully, this specific scenario has never occurred – although it came close in 2014, when Malaysian Airlines Flight 17 was shot down while flying over eastern Ukraine, on its way from Amsterdam to Kuala Lumpur with 298 souls on board, including thirty-eight Australian citizens and residents. In contemplating our horror crash scenario back in the early 2000s, we thought some kind of freak accident – mechanical failure or a midair collision – was the most likely scenario. We never imagined missiles fired from the ground, or terrorist attacks on aircraft.

Hijackings were thought of differently at that time: they were attempts to bargain for the release of militant prisoners in return for the lives of hostages – a dangerous situation, to be sure, but one in which police negotiators and trained special forces units usually had oversight and control, not DFAT. Back then, the world had not yet experienced suicide hijackings, where the objective is simply to use an aircraft as a weapon to destroy lives. The perpetrators of the hijackings that lay ahead not only accepted their own martyrdom but were actually intent on it.

Our anxieties about an air crash led the consular service to bolster our relationships with a range of airlines that flew in and out of Australia, from Singapore Airlines to Qantas. We visited each other's crisis centres, shared information about our contingency and crisis procedures, recorded relevant emergency numbers in our respective manuals, established protocols for the sharing of data, and built personal links between relevant staff. As the national carrier with the most substantial international network of flights, Qantas was a particular focus of our attention, and there was a longstanding pattern of engagement to draw from. The work we did to build our links with the national airline meant that a useful supplementary capacity was available when we came to evacuate thousands of Australians from Bali – once after the collapse of Ansett in September 2001, and then after the terrorist bombings of October 2002. The partnership would also prove useful for the evacuation of Australians from Lebanon in mid-2006. The relationship has continued over the years – Qantas became heavily involved in the government's effort to bring stranded citizens home following the Covid-induced collapse of commercial air links with Australia.

A scenario in which misrule and chaos boiled over in Papua New Guinea was also one we considered seriously. Our nearest neighbour was emerging from a difficult decade, in which the Bougainville Civil War had combined with serious underlying economic difficulties and social challenges, leading to sporadic outbreaks of unrest in Port Moresby and some regional centres. There were tens of thousands of Australians living and working in PNG. We knew that Australia, with all its defence and other resources either in the country or nearby, would be expected to take charge of any general evacuation of foreign citizens. Traditional cultural arrangements were under serious strain, and it was important to have plans in place for a worst-case scenario.

We had built on the experiences we'd had in Fiji and Solomon Islands in mid-2000 to develop our capacity to respond to outbreaks of conflict across the broader region that might impact the safety and security of Australians. That's the real point about contingency planning: the nightmare you can think of may never happen, but an organisation's preparations for that scenario can help strengthen its capacity to manage unanticipated events. A joint Consular Planning Assistance Team was established to connect our Australian Defence Force colleagues with consular personnel, and regular meetings were established across a range of locations in the Indo-Pacific region, including in PNG, in an effort to ensure that we were in a position to respond to conflict or natural disasters – from cyclones in the Pacific to earthquakes in Japan.

Our contingency planning did not take full account of the terrible ambition and capability that was building within the international terrorist movement at the time, but we were certainly aware of a growing general threat. Terrorists led by Osama bin Laden had planned a triple attack in January 2000 to coincide with the millennium celebrations, which included bombing the Radisson Hotel in Amman, Jordan, popular tourist sites at Mount Nebo and on the Jordan River, and the sinking of an American naval destroyer, USS *The Sullivans*, in Yemen. The plot was foiled, but by October 2000 al-Qaeda had recovered sufficiently from this setback to succeed in bombing another American naval vessel, USS *Cole*, while it lay at anchor in Yemen's Aden harbour, killing seventeen US Navy sailors. Closer to home, a series of explosions in Jakarta churches killed seventeen people and wounded about 100 on Christmas Eve 2000 – these attacks were tied to the Jemaah Islamiyah movement, which was in turn linked to al-Qaeda. Only six days later, five different blasts killed twenty-two people in Metro Manila, the largest city of the Philippines. It would be another eight years before three members of the Moro Islamic Liberation Front were sentenced to life imprisonment for these bombings, which are understood to have been carried out under instruction from, and financed by, Jemaah Islamiyah.

We also knew that Australia's leadership role in the international humanitarian and security intervention in East Timor had attracted the negative attention of South-East Asian militants, and awareness was building in Western intelligence circles about the links between Jemaah Islamiyah and al-Qaeda. These were matters of public discussion at the time, and were reflected in our travel advisories. So we were alert to the possibility of Australians being killed in a terrorist attack, but at the turn of the century, the balance of probability seemed to be that Australians were more likely to be caught up by mischance in terrorist activity that targeted others.

In many ways this perspective mirrored the other arms of the Australian government. The biggest event in Australia in 2000 was the Sydney Olympic Games, and this was naturally a strong focus for Australian security and intelligence officials. Declassified Australian cabinet documents show that ASIO advised in the lead-up to the Olympics that it had no information that anyone was planning to attack the games. The organisation hedged its bets by noting that this situation 'could change quickly depending on the international situation'. Security concerns were apparently confined mainly to the possibility of a team being taken hostage, as had occurred in Munich back in 1972. ASIO assessed the threat to the games as 'medium', balancing low likelihood with the significant consequences if something actually were to happen.

Meanwhile, global political attention was largely directed elsewhere. The spirit of the times remained obstinately optimistic – this was reflected in the September 2000 Millennium Summit, which drew world leaders together at the United Nations in New York to discuss the values, principles and aspirations for the international agenda of the twenty-first century. The goals they agreed to included eradicating poverty, promoting gender equality, reducing child mortality, combating disease and ensuring environmental sustainability. The summit also set deadlines for collective actions to achieve these goals – which have fallen by the wayside, unfulfilled, in the years since.

A close-run election in November 2000 brought a new president to power in the United States. George W. Bush had no experience – and apparently little interest – in international affairs, and while he promised a less interventionist foreign policy than his predecessor, he also distanced himself from multilateral organisations, including the United Nations.

The security and intelligence agencies reporting to the new US president actually had an increasingly sophisticated understanding of the danger posed by the global jihadist movement, at least in broad terms. It's clear from the evidence that came to light after

September 11 that the Central Intelligence Agency had been targeting Bin Laden since the bombings of the US embassies in Kenya and Tanzania back in 1998. In the wake of those attacks, President Bill Clinton had ordered missile strikes against training camps in Afghanistan, where Bin Laden was believed to be attending a meeting, but the terrorist chief had evidently moved on by the time the missiles struck. Other operations had been contemplated involving Pakistani commandos and helicopter assaults, but were abandoned as impractical or too dangerous – either for the special forces involved or for the women and children in Bin Laden's entourage. George Tenet, who had served Clinton as CIA director and been kept on by Bush, was heavily focused on the threat represented by Bin Laden, but his organisation was unable to ascertain, or articulate, when and where the danger would manifest itself.

The question of who knew what and when ahead of the 9/11 attacks by al-Qaeda has been the subject of much vigorous retrospective debate. But for whatever reason, the concerns of the US intelligence establishment did not translate into the kind of political focus required to mount a concerted defensive response. The early months of Bush's presidency saw almost no public commentary about the emerging dangers on the international scene. The administration was focused instead on important domestic issues, such as social security and education.

In the midst of all this, Bush's Secretary of Defense, Donald Rumsfeld, gave vent to his personal convictions in a speech to a military and defence industry audience at the Pentagon. He opened the speech by warning of an adversary that posed a 'serious threat to the security of America'. This adversary, he warned, 'attempts to impose its demands across time zones, continents, oceans and beyond. With brutal consistency, it stifles free thought and crushes new ideas. It disrupts the defense of the United States and places the lives of men and women in uniform at risk.'

With an ideological flourish, Mr Rumsfeld revealed this enemy to be none other than red tape at his own Department of Defense, which he said was stifling innovation and letting down American taxpayers. Rumsfeld's speech peaked with the line: 'Today we declare war on bureaucracy.' The speech was silent about real enemies to the security of the United States people.

It was a strange speech, and in retrospect its timing makes it seem stranger still. The Secretary of Defense was speaking on 10 September 2001.

CHAPTER EIGHT

The Turning Point

THE ATTACKS THAT TOOK PLACE on September 11 were to change the international paradigm. As the world's largest military power, the United States would be propelled into new conflicts in Afghanistan and Iraq, drawing Australia and other allies with it. Five years later, President Bush would characterise the 'war on terror' launched in response to these events as 'the decisive ideological struggle of the twenty-first century, and the calling of our generation'. All over the Western world, insecurity became the 'new normal'. A sense of perpetual, impending doom seemed to be confirmed by attacks over the following years in places as diverse as South-East Asia, Madrid and London.

September 11 was also a defining moment for the Australian consular service and for me.

The attacks that day led Australians to understand that our alliance with the United States positioned us, along with other citizens of the 'free world', as terrorist targets. We would be told to be 'alert but not alarmed'. According to a Newspoll published more than two years afterwards, on 21 April 2004, 68 per cent of Australians believed that Australia was under threat of an imminent terrorist attack. These anxieties changed the cultural landscape at home, with Australia's Muslim community being portrayed in some media, and perceived by many, as alien, culturally incompatible and threatening. The Australian government would find itself confronted with new complexity overseas, as the international coalition's reprisals against Afghanistan flushed out a series of unusual Australian consular cases.

September 11 brought terrible human tragedy, especially for the United States. We in the Australian consular service also had our hands full, managing an enormous wave of anxiety back in Australia and supporting the families of Australians who were killed.

We now know that ten Australians died in the 9/11 attacks. Alberto 'Pocho' Dominguez, a sixty-six-year-old grandfather from Sydney, was on board the first plane that hit the North Tower at 8.36 am local time. Working high in that tower was Andrew Knox, a twenty-nine-year-old environmental architect from Adelaide, who managed to speak briefly to his twin brother before the end came. Also in the North Tower were thirty-seven-year-old Craig Gibson from Sydney, who was working with an insurance firm; Elisa Ferraina, twenty-seven, from Sydney, who was attending a financial technology conference; Steve Tompsett, a thirty-nine-year-old IT expert from Sydney, also attending a conference; Lesley Anne Thomas, forty, from the New South Wales Central Coast; and Kevin Dennis, forty-three, from the Gold Coast. Lesley and Kevin were stockbrokers working for the same company. Two more Australians died after the second plane hit the South Tower sixteen minutes later: thirty-one-year-old Leanne Whiteside from Melbourne, who had just started working for an insurance company there, and forty-four-year-old Peter Gyulavary from Geelong, another environmental architect. Like Andrew Knox, Peter left behind a twin brother. On board the third plane that hit the Pentagon in Washington thirty-five minutes after that was sixty-two-year-old Red Cross coordinator Yvonne Kennedy from Sydney. She was on a holiday that had been a retirement gift to herself.

Half a world away, many Australians had either gone to bed or were thinking about doing so. It was 10.46 pm on a Tuesday night in Canberra when the first plane hit, and I had fallen asleep in front of the television. *The West Wing* was on – we were addicts of that program. Roxanne reached across from where she was sitting and poked me in the leg. 'Come on, you love this show,' she said. I sat up, and just as I did so the first news flash came on the screen. We looked on in confusion at the images of a smouldering aircraft embedded in one of the World Trade Center's towers. The phone rang almost immediately – it was the duty officer from the Consular Emergency Centre checking whether I had seen the news.

I think that, like many, I wanted to believe this was a terrible freak accident. There was 'only' one plane involved at that point, and the damage to the building seemed localised. My main thought in those initial minutes was that, going on experience, at least one Australian was likely to have been on board the plane. As I spoke to the duty officer, the CEC was already reaching out to the Australian Consulate-General in New York, and was putting into place the standard communication protocols to sustain what at that stage looked likely to be a 'mid-sized' consular response. This all seemed appropriate. I asked the duty officer to enlist the help of some additional senior Canberra-based consular staff to support and guide the work of the consulate-general during the Australian night. The priority would be to determine whether there were any Australian victims.

When the second aircraft smashed into the South Tower soon after, it was immediately clear that a very different response was required. I rang for a taxi – it would be a while before I could get home, and I figured that I might not be in the best condition to drive by then. On the drive from my home to the office, the taxi driver and I listened together to the rolling news from New York on his radio. In response to his questions, I explained what I would need to do when I got to work. He flatly refused to accept payment when we arrived at the department.

Soon after I arrived at work, news came through that a third jet had smashed into the Pentagon. I don't remember exactly when, but sometime that night we also learned that a fourth aircraft had come down in a Pennsylvanian field, and stories began to emerge of the passengers on board that plane whose heroic efforts had prevented further loss of life.

The consular operations crew dealt with quite a few telephone inquiries from concerned family members and members of the public late that night, but the flow of calls was manageable – just. The timing was on our side – most Australians were asleep and oblivious to what was going on; with no smartphones or social media, you really had to be watching television or listening to the radio to be aware that something had happened. We knew, though, that the situation would change dramatically when Australia woke up to the news, and we planned to ask the breakfast news services to publicise our free-call number for anyone concerned about family members. About 15,000 Australians were living and working in Manhattan and the New York district at the time, and it was our role to bring clarity to people calling about a loved one or friend whom they couldn't contact themselves. We calculated that we'd need to release the number to the media by 6 am.

As the night progressed, the Canberra consular team and their colleagues in the United States were sharing what information they had with each other. Our people in New York and Washington were among many thousands of people urgently seeking word about victims and survivors, and the US emergency authorities were in no position to manage these inquiries. They were too busy trying to save lives. A group of the department's senior leadership had found each other in the room adjoining the crisis centre, where we sat open-mouthed in front of television screens as the towers burned, and then toppled. Calls were made and answered from time to time, to colleagues and to ministers. There was no real need to advise Prime Minister Howard, who was in Washington himself. But we dutifully copied in 'Prime Minister Abroad' in the flash cable advising the global diplomatic network that the crisis centre was being activated in response to the attacks.

As it happened, Howard had met with President Bush for the first time the previous day. Their discussion had been on economic issues, not terrorism, but events were to redefine the leadership of both men – and the relationship between them. Howard responded to the attacks with a clear message of Australia's solidarity with the United States, addressing the House of Representatives' emergency session hours after the attacks; a few days later he symbolically invoked the ANZUS alliance for the first time in its fifty-year history.

Back in Canberra, like so many others around the world, my colleagues and I looked on grimly as poor, desperate souls jumped to their deaths to avoid incineration. Speculative reports came in about further hijacked aircraft streaming across the Atlantic. A trans-Pacific flight out of Australia was turned around because a passenger was behaving suspiciously. Such was the anxiety that swept the world that night.

We were all very conscious of the telephone onslaught that would come the next morning, and knew a significant number of DFAT volunteers would be needed to help manage it. The full-time consular operational staff in Canberra could be pivoted to the task, but that would not be enough. Consular operations director Keith Gardner, who'd arrived at work at about the same time as me, had shown typical forethought by stopping at a service station on his way to buy plenty of instant coffee, tea bags, milk and biscuits. He knew already that we would soon be playing host to a large number of volunteers from across the department.

The head of the corporate management division had one question for me: 'How many do you want and when do you want them?' His personnel team would need to take up the challenge to summon reinforcements. We spent some time trying to 'scope' the crisis that was to come. This involved monitoring how things were going for the CEC, and trying to sift through the reports to work out exactly what we were dealing with. There was no science to it – just instinct and a bit of experience. I then turned to my corporate management colleague and said: 'Thirty – I need thirty people at 0500.' The personnel team hit the phones and I met with my staff to plan setting up the call centre.

I struggle to remember the details of the rest of the night. An enduring memory from around dawn is of the nervous faces of the volunteers who turned up to answer the phones. We stepped them through their lines and the information we needed them to collect. We explained that their role was to try to screen out the many general calls they could expect about people who were simply travelling or living somewhere in the United States, and to identify the cases where there seemed genuine reason for concern. We asked them to make every effort to be polite, no matter how difficult some emotional and stressed callers might be.

Another task was to reclaim the department's main crisis coordination centre for its intended purpose. Two weeks previously, my branch had put it at the disposal of the DFAT division, which dealt with legal and people-smuggling issues, to serve as a 'watch office' for what had become known as the '*Tampa* affair'.

In late August, the Australian government had denied permission to a Norwegian freighter, MV *Tampa*, which was carrying 433 asylum seekers and five crew members rescued from a distressed fishing vessel, to enter Australian waters. When the skipper decided to proceed to an Australian port because his passengers were in such desperate condition, the Australian government deployed SAS troops to seize control of the ship and turn it away. These events precipitated a new Australian approach to the management of incoming asylum seekers, including the establishment of various asylum seeker processing centres in the Pacific.

By 11 September, the '*Tampa* crisis centre' was still operating extended working hours, but it was closed overnight. I took possession of the centre that night and told the relevant deputy secretary that I was doing so. There was no argument. When Rod Smith, an assistant secretary from the International Organisations and Legal Division, turned up to open the *Tampa* watch office he was told that he'd been evicted because there was now a higher-priority crisis. 'That's entirely appropriate,' he replied. 'Not only is it a real crisis; it's also one that isn't of our own making.'

Australia woke to the news of the terrorist attacks in the United States, and as expected the DFAT phone lines were hit hard. The waiting times for many callers were too long, particularly in the first few hours, but we managed. The first shift of volunteers was replaced by another mid-morning, and by 3 pm we had taken about 15,000 calls. Of these, 8000 callers had chosen to register with us the details of the friends or relatives they were worried about. This information was provided in turn to our people in New York and Washington, who did whatever they could to check the whereabouts of each individual. By the end of that first day there were about fifty people on our 'special' list – those Australians for whom we held very serious concerns, because the information supplied indicated they could well have been on the scene at one of the attacks.

The staff of the Australian embassy in Washington DC swung strongly behind their colleagues at the consulate-general in New York as they worked to respond on the ground. The team in New York was led by Ken Allen, a former businessman who had only recently been appointed consul-general, a role which usually focuses on trade and investment matters. He responded conscientiously and with energy to the situation. As the hours turned into days and then weeks, he hosted the families of the victims in his home.

Managing the fallout from September 11 was a brutal experience for the consular operations team. Tracey Wunder's story was typical. Tracey was on the roster of the CEC in Canberra. She'd returned from a posting as consul in Jakarta a year previously, and before that had served in Rangoon, Baghdad, Lagos and Warsaw. Tracey left home for her rostered morning shift in the early hours of 12 September, oblivious to what had happened late the previous night. We'd woken up a lot of people during the night, but it had made sense to let the next shift of consular professionals sleep on. But as soon as she found her way to work impeded by police roadblocks around the US embassy, Tracey knew something was up. She sized up the situation when she arrived, was given a snap briefing by the team manager and caught a few glimpses of the shocking media coverage. But there was no time to dwell on the horrific images.

Tracey plugged in where it made sense, and began dealing with the most difficult callers and guiding the less experienced operators. It wasn't until almost three days later that she finally went home, after one of the most challenging experiences of her working life. She sat in front of the news for a while trying to process it all. It was only when she turned off the television that she collapsed in tears. She went to bed and turned up for work again the next day.

The detective work continued intensively through the first week after the attacks. Within a few days, the number of 'cases of serious concern' had been whittled down to the mid-twenties as contacts were progressively made with people who turned out to be safe and well. In many cases, people who'd called the CEC to register their concerns rang back or emailed to let us know when they made contact with their loved one, but in too many cases they didn't. Some didn't even respond to our follow-up attempts. Time and effort was wasted looking for people who were known by their friends and family to be fine. These cases distracted not only the consular teams in Canberra, New York and Washington, but also hard-pressed police officers and others trying to trace the missing in the United States.

The first prize for irresponsibility, though, went to an Australian man whose office was on an upper level of one of the World Trade Center towers. The information provided by his distressed family and friends made him an almost certain victim. Nobody was known to have survived from his floor, and all efforts to contact him came to nothing. Ten days after the attacks, just as his family was arranging a memorial service for him, we tracked him down in London. He was working there on temporary assignment, and had been there – an ocean away – on the day of the attacks. If he had a mobile phone, he hadn't been checking it. He certainly hadn't thought to be in touch with anyone.

It was a couple of weeks before we could say definitively that 'only' ten Australians had died. Consular staff continued to support the families concerned over the next several months as they stepped through the traumatic process of identifying their loved ones' remains.

The thing about crises is that the more routine consular work doesn't stop. And we were also managing what was a very significant 'crisis within a crisis'. On 14 September 2001, less than three days after the attacks, Australia's second-largest airline, Ansett, was grounded because it could not pay for fuel, catering or employee wages. Thousands of people were left stranded – across Australia, but also at international locations such as Japan, Hong Kong and Bali.

It was particularly chaotic in Bali, one of the airline's high-traffic destinations, and the Australian consulate there was besieged by anxious Australians who had no accommodation or had run out of funds, and who all wanted to get home. In the ordinary course of events, this would have been an 'all hands on deck' situation, but because we were so preoccupied with the 'main' crisis, I had to delegate its management to a small group of consular hands. They set about the work with diligence, liaising with the consulate, with angry families and with Ansett's competitor, Qantas, which was only too pleased to help out with a series of additional charter flights.

One of the fundamental rules of the consular world was turned on its head in the aftermath of the September 11 attacks. As I've explained, it had been a longstanding principle that Australian travellers or their families should bear the costs of any emergency or humanitarian support that might be required because of accident or misadventure overseas. This remains the case today – in 'ordinary circumstances'. If an Australian is seriously unwell overseas, or dies in a traffic accident or the like, the government will not cover the costs of compassionate travel, medical evacuation or the repatriation of remains. This is a private responsibility, and it's why travel insurance is so strongly recommended. Australia's conservative government of the time was philosophically attracted to the principle of self-funded support, but it had actually been a bipartisan position since the dawn of time. As I had come to understand through my searing experience with the Solomon Islands evacuation the previous year, however, the commitment to 'cost recovery' could crumble quickly when politics came into play.

It was Tony Blair, the British prime minister, who started it. Within the first several days after the attacks, the British government announced that it would lay on a charter aircraft, at government expense, for the families of the British victims to travel from London to New York. Alexander Downer's office was immediately bombarded with questions from the Australian media: would we match this response and support travel to the United States by the Australian families? This would not be the last time the department faced this kind of dilemma. Dennis Richardson, who was running ASIO at the time, summed up the dynamic years later, after being appointed as secretary of DFAT, in a speech in August 2011: 'In a crisis, people and the media understandably look at what different countries are doing. So, you almost get yourself into a competitive space, where if Country A is doing more than you, then you have to ask yourself whether you shouldn't be doing the same thing.'

Downer held out for much of the day, and I spoke several times to his staff, recommending that he think very carefully about the precedent we would set for the hundreds of Australians who died abroad each year. What, I asked, should we say to the family of a young Australian who had recently been killed in a bomb blast in an incident in the Middle East, and who had covered all the associated costs themselves? Was that life worth less to the government than the lives lost on September 11?

The deeper truth was that I was torn myself. I could see what this looked like from a public point of view – never mind the families of the Australian victims.

To his credit, Downer rang me before he announced his decision. He had made his mind up, but wanted me to understand his reasoning. 'You won't be happy with me,' he said. He felt that the British government had left him no choice, and so he would shortly be announcing that the government would cover the costs of travel to the United States by two family members of each Australian victim.

When I relayed the news to one colleague, he shook his head grimly and said, 'It's a black day for the consular service.' Perhaps it was my optimistic nature, or just pragmatism, but I couldn't see the point in succumbing to this gloomy view. In retrospect, I've come to believe that there are moments of national solidarity when it becomes appropriate for the government to extend an additional level of assistance to its citizens. It's not a perfect answer, and it doesn't resolve the problem I was so keen to share with the minister at the time, but it's the best I can do.

There were several thoughtful articles and reviews written in the years that followed about how the crises of this period reshaped the relationship between the consular service and its clientele. Some commentators judged that the government's reaction to major events and disasters had encouraged an attitude that 'someone will look after me if I get into trouble'. According to this line of argument, an impression was created in people's minds that the Australian government would always respond to crises, big or small. Writing for the Lowy Institute, Alex Oliver has commented that the trend for successive governments to gradually 'bid up' consular services had the potential to create a 'moral hazard', by discouraging Australians from assuming personal responsibility. She depicted the resulting dilemma in stark terms: 'The reality is ... that the bureaucrats' rule-book will continue to be thrown out of the window regularly and haphazardly by governments seeking to display a muscular approach on consular services to impress domestic audiences.'

I agree that it would be much better to have greater consistency, but I have also seen for myself how difficult it is for governments in the modern era to navigate public opinion and expectations. Their political response to consular events often stems from a defensive impulse, as they try to avoid 'political damage' by being seen to do everything they can. The dilemma then, as now, was that an effective response to a crisis would raise the bar higher for the future, but a poor one could result in heavy criticism.

There was an imperative for DFAT, along with Australia's intelligence and security agencies, including the Office of National Assessments (ONA), ASIO and the Australian Secret Intelligence Service, to take stock again in the wake of September 11 – to review our state of readiness for this frightening new world in which terrorists armed with box-cutters could strike so successfully at the heart of global economic power. We conducted our own internal review exercises, but it was also important to come together with our international partners to share our various responses and determine what had gone wrong, as well as what had gone right.

The natural focus of these international exchanges was what I liked to call the 'mutual therapy club'. Heads of the Australian, US, British, Canadian and New Zealand consular services came together annually to share their experiences and reform efforts, taking it in turns to host the group. I'd met the others once before September 11, at a meeting hosted the previous year in New Zealand. It was already clear to me from that encounter how our services were subject to similar pressures. We all faced growing, and sometimes unreasonable, expectations from the steadily increasing travelling public; we were contending with increasing numbers of our fellow citizens presenting with mental health difficulties; and we were grappling with difficult child custody cases that straddled both national and cultural borders. We were also, to varying degrees, working to capitalise on the new communications technologies as we reformed our respective services.

My British counterpart, James Watt, Director of Consular Affairs at the Foreign and Commonwealth Office in London, was forced to cancel his plans to host us all in the United Kingdom in late September 2001 – we were all far too pressed with our respective national responses to the terrorist attacks. It wasn't until mid-November, as we came up for air after the first emergency phase, that we attended a two-day meeting at Admiralty House in central London.

I had my own preoccupations as I stepped off the plane at Heathrow into the cold and grey winter weather. Diana Thomas and Peter Bunch – two Australian members of a Christian humanitarian organisation called Shelter Now – had been imprisoned by the Taliban government of Afghanistan in August, along with two Americans, two Germans and sixteen Afghans. They'd all been accused of seeking to conduct religious conversions. We became even more concerned for their safety as the US-led coalition of armed forces began its offensive against Afghanistan in the wake of the September 11 attacks. The Taliban seemed set to lose control of the capital, and were likely to hold the hostages to ensure their own safety.

Our concerns evaporated the night I arrived in London. We all went out to dinner together, and early in the evening, as I was talking to Mary Ryan, American Assistant Secretary of State for Consular Affairs, our mobile phones rang simultaneously. We looked at each other and smiled as we listened to the news from our respective home bases: the hostages in Afghanistan had been picked up by the Northern Alliance and transferred to the safe-keeping of US special forces.

We all had something to share over the next couple of days about how we'd managed public anxiety and supported victims' families after the recent attacks in the United States, even if our respective national death tolls varied widely. Sixty-seven British citizens, twenty-four Canadians, ten Australians and two New Zealanders had been killed, but of course the Americans had lost 2605 of their own. James's team at the British Foreign Office had activated an arrangement with the London Metropolitan Police to help field the thousands of public calls they received. Gar Pardy, the driving force of the Canadian consular service, said that the September 11 response had exposed shortcomings in their global case management software, which he was moving rapidly to fix. As we listened to Gar speak with urgency about improvements to his arrangements, I thought about how the Australian team had resorted to emailing casualty lists back and forth between headquarters and the United States. I resolved to move much faster to upgrade and roll out our systems, to put us in the strongest position possible when the next major crisis inevitably came along.

Mary Ryan updated us on the status of the US disaster victim identification process. Not that you would know it from talking to her, but when we gathered together that November she was dealing with another kind of crisis. The US consular service was different from the rest, in that it had responsibility for issuing US visas overseas at the time. Mary was under sustained political attack at home over the twenty-two visas that had been approved for the September 11 hijackers and their co-conspirators. As she told Congress, consular officers had not been provided with the necessary intelligence to identify terrorist suspects, because the FBI had not been prepared to share that information. She left the State Department in September 2002 in what was characterised as a routine personnel change. She had many admirers who thought it was wrong that she had been 'let go'.

There were a few bright moments from those brief days we spent in London. An update of the Australia–Canada Consular Sharing Agreement was ready for signature, and Gar and I had brought with us the formal copies prepared by our staff. Gar insisted that we sign them on the bar of a London pub, so we gathered at a tavern in the St James area to seal the solemn moment. It's possible we'd had a few to drink, because when I inspected my copy of the agreement when I got back to Canberra a few days later, I noticed that Gar had signed for Australia and I'd signed for Canada. I'm pretty confident no one else ever noticed.

CHAPTER NINE

The Ones Who Lost Their Way

TODAY, THE TERM 'AUSSIE JIHADI' brings to mind the scores of Australians who flocked to join Islamic State from 2014, as that newly emergent military organisation rapidly expanded the territory it held in Iraq and Syria. The image of the Australian-born Khaled Sharrouf and his son brandishing a severed head stands as an appalling motif for this group. The death of Sharrouf, his wife, Tara, and their sons – along with the determination shown by Tara's mother, Karen, in bringing her surviving grandchildren home – lingers in the public mind as a cautionary tale about the high human cost of falling in with terrorism.

In fact, Australian 'home-grown terrorists' first emerged as a phenomenon much earlier, in late 2001, following the invasion of Afghanistan by the United States and its allies, including Australia. Australians with al-Qaeda or Taliban associations seemed to be popping up regularly in Afghanistan and neighbouring countries for a while. Some were picked up by the US-led coalition forces in Afghanistan. Others approached Australian officials in the region in an effort to get home, or at least reach safety. And back in Australia, many families turned to the consular service, asking for help to track down loved ones who had 'lost their way', in more than one sense. Responding to these cases in the context of the 'war on terror' required us to write the rule book as we went. Their stories illustrate the complexity that can be involved in delivering consular assistance in the face of competing security imperatives, and the delicate balancing act that is sometimes required.

Some Australians would probably say that if an Australian citizen joins a terrorist organisation and then finds themselves in difficulty overseas, they should be left to rot. Many would at least say that our national security interests should come before any obligation to provide consular protection. Others would argue that support should be provided to all Australians, irrespective of any presumed guilt. From a strictly legal perspective, the Australian government is entitled to withdraw consular protection for any reason. It is nation-states, not individuals, that enjoy 'rights' to consular access and protection under the Vienna Convention on Consular Relations, which governs international practice and consular relations between sovereign states. And there is no Australian law that says citizens are entitled to consular support overseas. So, whether to provide such assistance is essentially a political judgement, based in great part on society's expectations.

The Australian government responded to the most recent generation of Australian jihadis in Iraq and Syria by stripping them of their citizenship wherever possible, thus removing entirely any obligation to provide consular support – or indeed the right to return home. This was possible because so many of them were dual citizens, which meant, theoretically at least, that revocation of their Australian citizenship did not render them stateless. Even so, these people could not be dismissed completely as 'Australians of convenience'. Many were at least second-generation Australians who were well integrated in our society, with most tracing their heritage to the Middle East. The human cost of Australia's policies was highlighted as recently as April 2022, when the UN Human Rights Council expressed concern about forty-six people, including thirty children, who had been deprived of Australian citizenship and were still among those in Syrian detention camps enduring conditions that 'meet the standard of torture'.

It would be harder still to argue that the first cohort of Australians to join the global jihad back in the early 2000s were people whose Australian identity was never fully formed. There were five people in this group who came to public attention. With one exception, these Australians who found their way to Afghanistan prior to the September 11 attacks were from unremarkable Anglo-Celtic families and had grown up without any connection either to the Middle East or to Islam.

The first of them, and the one to show the most enduring commitment to the cause, was Robyn Mary Hutchinson. She was born in Mudgee, in rural New South Wales, in 1953. As a teenager in the 1960s, Robyn embraced the hippie counterculture, drifted to Indonesia, converted to Islam and changed her first name to Rabiah. She married and divorced three Indonesian men in succession; the third was a leading figure in Jemaah Islamiyah.

Hutchinson told her story to Sally Neighbour for the latter's book *The Mother of Mohammed*, and key extracts were published in the news media, including in *The Weekend Australian* on 2 May 2009. She travelled to Pakistan in 1990 with five of her six children, apparently intent on finding an ideal Muslim community in which she could raise them. She found her way to Afghanistan in the early 1990s, established her family in Kandahar and ran a hospital there. She reportedly came to be referred to as 'the Elizabeth Taylor of the jihad' by some in Western intelligence circles – a reference to her total of eight marriages. The last of these was with Abu Walid, a member of al-Qaeda's governing council.

Jack Thomas was a generation younger than Hutchinson. He was an outgoing kid from a loving home in Melbourne's western suburbs. After finishing school, he enrolled to study dance at the Victorian College of the Arts. He left college to join a punk rock band, volunteered with St John's Ambulance at a soup kitchen, and became an apprentice chef. He was introduced to Islam by a schoolfriend, and has said that his 'whole world came together' when he converted. Drawn sympathetically to the worldview that Muslims were being suppressed, he adopted the name Jihad, which can denote either a spiritual or military struggle. He decided to find a Muslim wife, and someone suggested Maryati, an Indonesian woman who'd studied in Melbourne. She was in South Africa, so he flew there and married her.

Thomas spoke to the media several times about his experiences, including for the *Four Corners* program 'The Convert' in February 2006 and for the *Herald Sun* in May 2013. Through his new wife, he built strong connections with the Indonesian community in Australia, some of whom were followers of JI. He went on camping trips with Abdul Rahim and Abdul Rahman Ayub, twin brothers who were JI's leaders in Australia, playing paintball and sometimes firing live weapons. On his way to Mecca on pilgrimage in 2000, he met Abu Bakar Ba'asyir in Kuala Lumpur – JI's spiritual leader and a friend of Maryati's family. In early 2001, Thomas set off with his wife and daughter for Kabul, to join the Taliban's struggle against the Northern Alliance in Afghanistan. They arrived in Kabul in March 2001, where he was vetted by the Taliban and sent to al-Qaeda's training camp in the mountains.

David Hicks grew up in Adelaide. His parents separated when he was ten years old. He got involved with alcohol and drugs as a teenager and drifted for years, working on remote cattle stations and in city factories. In 1998 he moved to Japan to work as a horse trainer. While there, he became engrossed with television coverage of the struggle by the Muslim Albanian Kosovo Liberation Army for independence and survival against Serbia, and in 1999 he decided to head to the Balkans to lend them a hand. After completing military training with the KLA, he returned to Australia and converted to Islam. In an interview with *The Sydney Morning Herald* published on 10 December 2010, Hicks described this decision as ill-considered: 'In my youth I was impulsive. Unfortunately, many of my decisions of that time are a reflection of that trait.' David set off for Pakistan in November 1999, at the age of twenty-four, and began training with Lashkar-e-Taiba, the Pakistan-based terrorist group dedicated to fighting Indian control of the contested region of Kashmir. He then found his way to al-Qaeda's stronghold in Afghanistan, where he received further training.

Mamdouh Habib was not an adult convert like the others. He was born in Alexandria, Egypt, to middle-class parents and raised in the Muslim faith. According to him, he left Egypt after completing his national military service and worked across the Middle East and Europe. He then decided to join his brother and sister in Australia. He arrived in 1982, still in his mid-twenties, got married and after a few years became an Australian citizen. Mamdouh retained his Egyptian citizenship and became involved in the carpet cleaning industry. He has claimed – in several media interviews and in his book, *My Story: The Tale of a Terrorist Who Wasn't* – that he was harassed by Australian security agencies for years over alleged terrorist links, and that ASIO even tried to recruit him to spy on the jihadist movement. According to *Four Corners*, Habib was interviewed by the police in early 2001. A threat assessment concluded that he was a 'repetitious and vexatious complainant' with little credibility, and that there was no basis to believe he would commit an act of violence. Shortly afterwards, Habib travelled to Pakistan. He has claimed that he was seeking to explore a commercial opportunity with a Saudi figure called Mr Qahtani, but that shortly after they met, Qahtani was murdered and Habib himself was abducted by a group of Pakistanis. He then somehow managed to flee his captors and make his way into Afghanistan.

Matthew Stewart was the last of the five to arrive in Afghanistan. He grew up on Queensland's Sunshine Coast – in Mooloolaba, where my family had spent many summer holidays. Having been to Afghanistan myself, I can tell you that it is as far from Mooloolaba as it gets. Stewart has been described by those who knew him as 'quite a sensitive kid' with a stutter. According to his family, he never once exhibited any interest in Islam. He was a keen surfer. He worked in construction, drifted a bit and then joined the Australian Army. Stewart served as an infantry soldier with the Australian intervention force in East Timor from 1999, and by all accounts was traumatised by his grisly experiences there. His friends say that Stewart was also victimised by individuals who had authority over him, and that he struggled with a drug problem. He had some kind of breakdown, received treatment and left the Army in the first half of 2001. One of his friends recalled that in his last encounter with Stewart, in mid-2001, he seemed calmer, like someone who had settled on a plan. He departed Australia in early August on a flight to Kuala Lumpur, without telling his family.

It was at Al Farouq, al-Qaeda's training camp, that Jack Thomas, the former dance student and charity worker from Melbourne, met David Hicks, the horse trainer from Adelaide. Thomas was impressed by the hardwired and practical Hicks. They did their training together. Thomas says that he didn't know that it was an al-Qaeda camp until Osama bin Laden visited for the first time. And even then, he says, he didn't really know who he was dealing with. Hicks, for his part, says that he did not hear the term al-

Qaeda until much later. Both men acknowledge that they met and spoke with Bin Laden, and Thomas has spoken about the leader's charisma and appeal. Both deny suggestions that they were close to the leadership or involved in any real terrorist planning.

The 9/11 attacks sent a frisson of excitement and jubilation through the Islamic movement, but it quickly became apparent that the United States and its allies would be seeking retribution, and that this would involve the invasion of Afghanistan, where al-Qaeda had for years enjoyed freedom of operation. Operation Enduring Freedom, a campaign of aerial bombing and ground operations led by the Americans but supported by almost thirty countries, including Australia, commenced in early October. Australian special forces personnel were among the first to enter Afghanistan.

The orders went out that the al-Qaeda leadership should disperse, and the movement quickly came under enormous pressure. Each of the five key Australians in Afghanistan emerged over the following several months to confront the consular service, in one way or another, with a new kind of complexity.

Rabiah Hutchinson was in Kandahar when she heard about the September 11 attacks from BBC Radio. Her immediate priority was her family. She somehow arranged for her two daughters and granddaughter to be collected from Kabul and taken to Herat, near the Iranian border, where she, her eldest son, and her husband Abu Walid (the senior al-Qaeda figure) met up with them. They had their first terrifying experience of the international coalition's carpet bombing there. Hutchinson and the children were separated from her husband, and fled across the country in the other direction, to the border region with Pakistan. Over the next few months, the Afghan National Alliance and its foreign allies progressed across the country, wiping out Taliban and al-Qaeda forces and destroying their facilities. In November,

Hutchinson abandoned her resolve to stay in Afghanistan, and after a further perilous journey she crossed the Iranian border with the children and travelled to Tehran, where they were reunited with Abu Walid. The couple then fell out: Abu Walid had by now become a prominent critic of Bin Laden, and Hutchinson saw this as a betrayal. She moved back to an Iranian town near the Afghan border for about six months, before deciding that enough was enough. She presented herself at the Australian embassy in Tehran in mid-2003 with the four children in tow. She asked to see the consul, but the embassy receptionist tried to direct her to the visa office – presumably because the little group looked more Afghan than Australian. Hutchinson says that she went to the shops for a while, and that when she came back a couple of hours later the penny had dropped and the embassy moved promptly to make arrangements for her and her family.

Jack Thomas says he was shocked when he heard about September 11. However, as the US-led counter-offensive began in Afghanistan, he sent his wife and daughter home to Indonesia and stayed to fight the Americans, who he'd heard were mercilessly slaughtering his fellow Muslims. As the temperature rose, he joined a convoy of fighters going to Pakistan, and along the way asked one of the top al-Qaeda lieutenants how he might help the cause in the future. He lived for many months in Karachi, before making plans to travel home. While in Pakistan, he told *Four Corners*, he was visited by Khalid bin Attash, an associate of Osama bin Laden, who proposed that he help mount an attack in Australia similar to those conducted against the US embassies in Africa back in 1998. By this point, Thomas says, he had had enough, and he did not agree to anything because he was focused only on returning home. Thomas was arrested in January 2003 trying to board a flight at Karachi airport and delivered to the Pakistani security services. Two weeks later he was flown to

Islamabad and received the first of five consular visits at his place of detention from the Australian High Commission.

David Hicks was in Quetta, Pakistan, when news of the September 11 attacks came through, apparently on a mission to sort out a visa issue and talk to some contacts about funding his return flight to Australia. His reaction was to turn around and head back to Afghanistan. He has claimed subsequently that he was shocked by the attacks, and that his only intention was to retrieve some personal property, including his passport. In his later US military trial, it was asserted that Hicks had been inspired by the attacks and reported for duty with al-Qaeda. He did join an al-Qaeda force near Kandahar, was assigned to a Taliban group and then travelled towards the frontline with the Northern Alliance forces. Hicks has explained his actions by saying that, once back in Afghanistan, he found his return route to Pakistan blocked; his safest option was to align with an armed group that could offer him some protection. Hicks was picked up by the Northern Alliance near Kunduz in early December 2001, and handed over to the US forces in exchange for a US$5000 reward.

Mamdouh Habib says that when word got around about the attacks in the United States, he rang home to find out what had happened. The security authorities later cited his comments during that telephone call to support their charge that he had prior knowledge of the attacks. An Appeals Administrative Tribunal later determined that there was no evidence to support these charges, but observed that he had been untruthful about his activities and still constituted a threat to national security. Habib is believed to have entered Pakistan on 4 October 2001, just before the international offensive began in Afghanistan. He was identified as a foreign national when he crossed the border and was detained by Pakistani intelligence on 5 October, while on his way to Karachi from Quetta by bus.

Matthew Stewart's story reveals the limits to the government's ability to establish the 'welfare and whereabouts' of an Australian who is determined not to be found. As Stewart's family has noted publicly, they approached the consular branch in Canberra in late 2001. They were very concerned about the welfare of the troubled young man and sought our assistance in establishing his whereabouts. We asked several of our embassies to enlist the assistance of their host governments to track him down, including in places like Russia, Pakistan and Iran, but we were unable to locate him through this network. As Foreign Minister Downer later indicated publicly, we came to the conclusion on the basis of all the information available to us, that by the time the family sought our help, Stewart had already been in Afghanistan for several months. This has been corroborated by some of the others, including Mamdouh Habib, who says that when he was in Kandahar in early September, Stewart arrived there after a long, dusty ride from Iran in a sheep truck. According to Habib, Stewart was highly agitated about his experiences in East Timor and claimed that Australian forces had committed serious atrocities.

The wake of September 11 saw a period of unprecedented pressure on the consular service on a range of fronts. At headquarters in Canberra, the small group of consular officers managing these new complex cases were the same people who were still supporting the families of the Australian September 11 victims. The Australian mission in Islamabad, which was at the centre of the action for several of these cases, was dealing with considerable turmoil. The situation in Pakistan was deteriorating rapidly, and the High Commission was being downsized to remove non-emergency personnel and families. The head of mission, Howard Brown, and his consul, Alistair Adams, were working to encourage the local Australian community to return home without delay.

As we grappled with each of the new, unusual cases that had popped up in the wake of the US invasion of Afghanistan, it became clear that they would require delicate handling. Protocols needed to be established to ensure that the consular and law-enforcement arms of government acquitted their responsibilities properly and did not get in each other's way. We did not always get it exactly right; an inquiry by the Inspector-General of Intelligence and Security found, ten years later, that the consular service could have done better in keeping Mamdouh Habib's family informed. For my part, I know that a dedicated group of consular officials did the best they could, in highly unusual circumstances, to provide these individuals and their families with advice and support.

There was a war on, and this affected the mindset of some. According to the public report of the IGIS inquiry, a senior government official responded to a briefing outlining our plan to seek welfare access to Mamdouh Habib as follows: 'Security considerations override everything else in this case. Whatever Habib's original "consular" status, it has been overridden by his current situation and detention by the United States on suspicion of al-Qaeda links.' It might have been the view of some that the consular people should take a step back, but it didn't affect my approach to the job, or our determination to do what we thought was right from a consular perspective.

As the public IGIS report also notes, ASIO was informed of Mamdouh Habib's detention through intelligence channels on 6 October 2001. I heard about it from a senior official of that agency shortly afterwards and got in touch with the mission in Islamabad. Alistair Adams approached the Pakistani foreign ministry in Islamabad about access, but concluded that the authorities were going to give preferential access to Australian security officials alone. So he sought to obtain whatever information he could about Habib's welfare from the ASIO officials who were permitted to visit Habib soon afterwards. We also relied on these officials, for a time, to facilitate exchanges of messages between Habib and his wife in Australia. This 'consular outsourcing' arrangement, as it might be called, came in for some criticism in the IGIS report. I still fail to see what the practical alternative was, and take some comfort that at least one Australian government official was able to check on Habib's welfare and report back.

As the public IGIS report also noted, in late October 2001 ASIO was approached by the United States to sound Australia out about the option of sending Mamdouh Habib to Egypt. As has become well known since then, US government agencies engaged extensively in the practice of 'extraordinary rendition' – that is, transferring prisoners to other countries for the purpose of 'enhanced interrogation'. ASIO made it clear at the time, and then to the IGIS inquiry, that they had informed their US counterparts that Australia would object strongly if this was contemplated. A couple of weeks later, in mid-November, we were informed through the intelligence network that Habib had already been moved to Egypt.

We put our hearts and souls into obtaining welfare access to Habib in Egypt. I summoned the Egyptian ambassador in Canberra and told him that I had reliable information that an Australian citizen was in detention in his country, and sought immediate access by our ambassador in Cairo, Victoria Owen. The Egyptian asked me how I had come by this interesting information, and I replied that he had no doubt already worked that out. He courteously promised to look into it. Victoria Owen bailed up most of the Egyptian cabinet, including the prime minister, about the case, and pushed her way into almost every government office in Cairo in her quest to obtain access. In the end, we were denied access to Habib in Egypt. He was transferred in early May 2002 to the Guantanamo Bay detention camp in Cuba. David Hicks was already there.

Hicks has provided a detailed account asserting that he was violently mistreated by US military and intelligence officers after being handed over by the Northern Alliance in early December 2001. He has said he was moved repeatedly by air between US naval vessels and military bases in the region, before ultimately being flown to Guantanamo Bay.

Our consul-general in Washington DC conducted regular visits to Hicks and Habib in Guantanamo Bay over the next several years. The cases dragged on and attracted the attention of the media, human rights organisations and the Australian Greens party. I and others were repeatedly questioned about Hicks and Habib by the Australian Senate. David's father became a regular voice on the airwaves. Over time, as September 11 receded into the past, Australians' sense of social justice asserted itself and the Howard government became keen to see the cases resolved. The unique system of military commissions established by the Bush administration was not to be rushed, though, and it became a point of frustration between the two governments.

The situation was far from what many Australians considered just, but our officials were at least visiting these prisoners to check on their welfare, and sending information back to their families. The consular service did what it could to facilitate contact between these two prisoners and their families, as it seeks to do with every prisoner held overseas. We had no option but to accept the rules that applied within the jurisdiction where the individuals were held – in this case, US military jurisdiction. We worked to ensure that, within the parameters allowed by the 'host' authority, the prisoners were aware of their legal entitlements and received support equal to that received by anybody else.

David Hicks told our consul-general in 2004 that his treatment by the Americans had been 'fair and professional' since arriving in Guantanamo Bay. As I reported to the Senate in June that year, Habib was a different kind of prisoner: 'Mr Habib is not communicative and ... can be belligerent in discussion with our consul-general, but for the most part, he's simply reluctant to communicate.' Ultimately, the US government dropped its case against Habib in 2005 and he was repatriated to Australia. He sought compensation from the government for his alleged torture and reached a confidential settlement with the Commonwealth in 2010. In March 2007, Hicks was sentenced to seven years in jail by a US military tribunal, with all but nine months of this term suspended, given time already served. He saw out the remainder of the sentence in South Australia.

The Hutchinson case was also eventually resolved, following endless meetings in Canberra during the second half of 2003 to determine how the unusual situation should be managed. Here was someone who was apparently an avowed supporter of the al-Qaeda leadership, and who had been married to one of its top lieutenants, looking to travel home to Australia in an aircraft full of other passengers. It was, of course, for ASIO rather than DFAT to come to a judgement about whether she would constitute a security risk. From a consular perspective, I remember emphasising in our advice to ministers that Australia was obliged to provide Hutchinson, as an Australian citizen, with the 'right to abode'. We had to take her back. This position was accepted, and limited-issue passports were provided to the group to allow their return. The escort arrangements were made by the relevant security agencies. They flew home to Australia in October 2003, escorted by two air marshals. I suspect the consular team in Tehran were relieved to see them go.

From our point of view, Jack Thomas was the most straightforward of the five cases. Alistair Adams, the busy consul in Islamabad, got into a proper pattern of welfare visits over the five months Thomas was detained there. He was also, however, being interviewed by ASIO and the AFP. We confirmed to Adams that he should not share any information gleaned from his welfare visits with the enforcement agencies. We did our best to maintain 'walls' between the two governmental operations. Things can be tricky in these circumstances for the diplomatic head of mission, who often has some personal knowledge of what is happening in both areas. I was often in the same situation back at headquarters. But we tried to compartmentalise information, and to maintain proper standards.

After two months of detention, Jack agreed to do a formal record of interview with the AFP and, in the course of an extensive recorded session, told them everything he had done and everything he knew. In June 2002 he was allowed to return to Australia, where he was placed under a control order. He'd told the police enough to get himself charged with receiving money from a terrorist organisation, but there was one problem: the Pakistani authorities had failed to arrange legal representation for the AFP interview. The case was quashed on that basis, and on the basis that Thomas had previously been subject to duress by his captors.

Matthew Stewart, the former Australian soldier, was never found. But it was not the last we would hear about him. In 2002, news reports – evidently based on documents found in former terrorist training camps in Afghanistan – began to emerge that Stewart had joined the jihadist movement. In 2005, an al-Qaeda propaganda video was released featuring a balaclava-wearing man with an Australian accent. Mrs Stewart denied that the man was her son, but several of his former Army colleagues were sure that it was. Foreign Minister Downer confirmed publicly that the government believed Stewart was one of a number of Australians who had turned to al-Qaeda. A Turkish journalist reported having spoken to him in 2010, and rumours surfaced that he had been killed in an air strike. The trail went cold again, and then in 2015 an al-Qaeda online magazine ran an interview with a man known as Usama Hamza Australi, who was training fighters in Syria on behalf of al-Qaeda. He said he was originally from Queensland and had joined the movement after serving in the Australian military. The article explained that he'd first been taken in by the Taliban in Afghanistan, before joining al-Qaeda in 2002, and that he had spent the following several years in Afghanistan and the Pakistan border region.

Stewart's ability to move among the shadows in the region, and his success in evading capture following the destruction of al-Qaeda's safe haven in Afghanistan, leaves me guessing that he probably escaped again when the movement suffered setbacks and scattered in 2019. I suspect he is still out there, and that the 'welfare and whereabouts' consular file opened back in 2001 will remain open indefinitely.

CHAPTER TEN

Bombings in Bali

BALI IS NOT AN EASY gig for a DFAT consular officer. It is an affordable and nearby holiday destination for Australians, and around a million of them visit each year – more than any other nationality. While all demographics are represented, many visitors are young or have little experience of the world beyond Australia. Bali is a popular place for football teams marking the end of season, for brides-to-be and their girlfriends, and for young singles looking to get their hair braided and party. Some believe Bali is an independent country, and are surprised to learn on arrival that they have come to Indonesia. Our consular staff always have a very full caseload, whether it be lost or stolen passports, motor scooter injuries or arrests. Supporting long-term Australian prisoners has been a major aspect of the work over the years; it has sometimes even involved supporting those facing execution, as Indonesia takes a very tough approach to drug crime in particular.

On 12 October 2002, the Australian consul-general in Bali was Ross Tysoe. Ross had been managing the busy consular post with distinction for two years. He and his wife, Helen, were finishing dinner at the home of friends when the table started to rattle. Ross recalls that they all thought it was an earthquake at first – seismic activity was common in Bali – but Ross soon took a phone call from a local staff member that corrected this impression. There had been at least one massive explosion somewhere around Jalan Legian, a crowded street in the busy nightclub area of Kuta. We came to understand later that there were three explosions – at the Sari Club, on Jalan Legian, at Paddy's Pub, just down the road, and outside the United States consulate. The staff member who called Ross, an Indonesian woman, was concerned about her husband, who had a business next to the Sari Club – she did not know it at the time, but he had just been killed. Ross jumped in a car with a friend and drove to Kuta to investigate.

On the way, they took a call from an expatriate they knew who advised them strongly against proceeding – if there had been more than one bombing already, it seemed highly likely there would be more. But they kept going. The scale of what had happened became clear as Ross neared the scene: Jalan Legian was littered with wrecked vehicles containing incinerated human remains, and the buildings in the vicinity were all damaged or destroyed. At some point Ross phoned his colleague, vice-consul David Chaplin. They agreed that David should go to the Bali International Medical Centre, reasoning that many of the injured would make their way there to get help.

By the time David reached the medical centre, about forty casualties, stunned and bloodied, had already arrived. It was clear from what they told him that many others had not survived. David spoke to Ross on the phone. 'We've got a real problem,' he said. By then, Ross had reached the location of the nightclubs. He asked David to round up all the local staff and volunteers on the consulate's lists, and then rang our ambassador to Indonesia, Ric Smith, in Jakarta. Ric then rang me. It was around 3.00 am in Canberra, and about ninety minutes had passed since the first explosion.

While I hurriedly dressed, Ross and his team were dealing with absolute chaos. David soon found his way to Sanglah Hospital, where the Indonesian medical staff were besieged by burns victims, and bodies were beginning to pile up outside the morgue. Identifying the injured was extremely difficult, and impossible for the dead. Two Australian doctors, on holiday in Bali themselves, turned up and helped the beleaguered Indonesian medical staff establish a basic triage system. David moved among the injured, passing people his mobile phone and asking them to call home. He asked volunteers to sit with the seriously injured and talk to them. At one point, he decided that the best way he could help was to assist in mopping the blood from the hospital floor. In these early hours of the crisis, and during the many difficult weeks that would follow, Ross and David were the backbone of the local consular response.

Before I left home, I spoke quickly to Bill Jackson, who had been promoted to become Director of Consular Operations only the day before. Bill was a very experienced consular hand with several overseas postings behind him, and had been working in the number two position, as Manager of Consular Operations, for several months. In his new role he had accountability for our engagement with consular clients and their families. Bill had been up for a little longer than me, having been woken by the team on duty at the CEC soon after the blast. He told me what he knew so far, and we agreed that his priority should be to summon several experienced consular staff to the centre. Bill rang Tracey Wunder, who had also just taken on a new role, replacing Bill as operations manager, which gave her direct oversight of the CEC and day-to-day case management. Tracey was on leave on the South Coast, and, as she put it, 'drove straight back smelling of seawater and campfires'. Bill and I agreed that he needed the staffing branch to help ensure that twenty-five volunteers from other areas of DFAT were available from 5 am to help field the onslaught of public calls we knew would come. Around 20,000 Australian tourists visited Bali every month in 2002, and all would have friends and relatives who would be anxious when they heard the news.

Fortunately, we had spent the year since the September 11 tragedy upgrading our phone network, and had expanded the terms of our agreement with the Centrelink-run passport information call centre in Hobart so that they could step in and help manage calls if it looked like the CEC was going to be overwhelmed. These reforms had been spurred by the flood of calls we'd received after the terrorist attacks in the United States, but they also reflected a broader motivation to modernise the consular service. We had bedded down the global consular management database and trained more DFAT volunteers in the use of our communications systems. We had also delivered refresher training for consular staff overseas through a series of regional workshops, and every newly appointed head of mission was now required to attend the consular training course prior to taking up their position. The consular service had taken several important steps towards professionalisation, and was coming to be regarded as a central DFAT function.

I also spoke with Tracy Reid, who was acting director of the crisis management and consular information section. This was the group of people who were responsible for opening the department's main crisis centre, where they would rally an interdepartmental task force from across government to coordinate the overall response, as well as coordinate communications across the DFAT global network and with other agencies. They were also responsible for drafting our travel advisories. Tracy was in the chair because her immediate boss, Jeff Roach, had been blessed with his first child only a day or so previously and was on parental leave. He ended up back at work too early, despite our efforts to protect him at such a special time. When Tracy answered the phone, she feared it might be bad family news, as her husband was on a twenty-four-hour solo bike ride at the time. When she realised it was 'just a consular crisis', she initially felt some relief, but of course that didn't last long. She tells me that she has never forgotten my words to her over the phone that morning: 'I think we just had our own September 11.'

I caught a taxi to work and went straight to the CEC. It was bedlam. They had already been reinforced by one or two others, but the phones were completely out of control. They had spoken to both Ross and David in Bali a couple of times by then.

This crisis was already different from September 11 the previous year. It was playing out in 'live time' for the Canberra team, because the victims themselves were ringing in from the scene of the devastation. Mobile phones had recently become a standard personal item for Australians, particularly for young travellers. Survivors were calling us to let us know what had happened, to ask for help or guidance about what to do next, or to say that they couldn't find their friends, siblings or partners. They were also calling their parents in Australia, who in turn reached for whatever official numbers they could find. Police stations across the country had already started transferring calls to us.

As I walked into the CEC, one of the duty officers took off his headphones and said in exasperation, 'Oh my God, now I've got a radio station on the phone. They want a comment – what do you want me to do?' I told him to transfer it straight to my mobile phone. My intention was to tell them to bugger off and stop bothering us in the middle of the crisis, but when I answered I was immediately informed that I was on air, live on Perth radio. 'Yes, we are aware of the problem,' I said in response to some breathless question. 'We are working on it urgently right now – you'll have to excuse me because I have work to do.' I hung up.

I managed to reach Ross in Bali – he seemed as calm and steady as ever, speaking with disbelief about what he had seen. He was on his way back to the consulate, where work needed to start quickly on identifying the missing. The consulate team was tiny – just Ross, David and a couple of local staff – and the task was immense. But help was at hand – Australians and other English-speaking expatriates living in Bali soon started turning up and asking if they could do anything to help. These ex-nurses and local businesspeople had settled in Bali for the lifestyle, and although they had no consular experience, they were willing to volunteer. When they understood that a key task was tracking down missing people and identifying the dead and injured, they swung into it with determination. They set themselves up in the office and began phoning around the hospitals and hotels. They quickly developed comprehensive lists of Australians they could account for, building up a picture that would be a huge help to the consular professionals when reinforcements arrived. This volunteer effort was critical to the consulate's operations in the first thirty-six hours after the bombing.

Back in Canberra, more staff arrived and the main crisis centre was opened up. Slowly but surely, the team began to establish a slightly more coherent pattern of communication with the staff and volunteers 4500 kilometres away in Bali. The painstaking work to compile lists of the missing and injured began. Given the extent of the burns injuries, it was often not possible for those on the ground to tell if a victim was Australian, Indonesian or any other nationality. At some point in those early hours, it began to dawn on us that Australia, as the nearest developed country with a quality health system and the resources to manage a large scale aero-medical evacuation, would have to evacuate everybody requiring serious medical attention, irrespective of nationality. As it turned out, we would even end up evacuating Indonesians from Indonesia.

It was still dark when Bill Jackson put it to me that two International SOS air ambulances were available for immediate deployment from their base in Singapore, less than two hours' flight from Bali. We had an agreement with International SOS that dated back to the 1980s – it had initially been struck to cover emergency medical evacuations for Australian diplomatic staff. I authorised the immediate despatch of the two aircraft. This was a no-brainer – it was a commercial arrangement, at some cost to the taxpayer, but that was of no consequence in the circumstances. We would have asked for more, but two was what they had available. They would at least be able to help a few people, pending the ADF's arrival.

I had calls to make. At some point after 4.30 am I notified Alexander Downer's office – it might have been Peter Woolcott, the chief of staff, or Chris Kenny, the media adviser. Whoever it was telephoned the foreign minister and also passed the message on to the prime minister's office. John Howard received a call at about 5 am. I was ringing Ashton Calvert at about the same time. I gave him a quick summary, and his guidance was, as ever, crisp and clear. 'Throw everything at it,' he said.

Bill and I moved to where our volunteer call centre operators were assembling – all members of the reserve cadre of DFAT officers who had received some training in our systems, and who understood the basic principles involved in public crisis communications. We drew breath and began to step these willing but nervous colleagues through what was about to happen, how they should engage with each caller and what information they should seek to establish. Lyndall Sachs's team conveyed our free-call number to the media just in time for the 6 am news bulletins and morning shows. We asked the media to emphasise that only people with genuine cause for concern should call, and that families should appoint one person to ring in on their behalf. We hoped that this would limit the deluge. Most media outlets did as we asked, but it did not prevent our phones from being overwhelmed in the first few hours of the day.

Other critical players materialised as dawn approached. Chris De Cure, head of the parliamentary and media branch, appeared at my side. We would forge a real partnership through this crisis. He was effectively the co-cordinator of the crisis response in the first several days. He kept a sharp focus on the organisation of the CEC while managing our communications with ministers, members of parliament and the broader public. He was methodical and careful, a great foil for my own more instinctive and sometimes head-on approach.

Lyndall mobilised her media team to deal with the endless inquiries. What I didn't know at the time was that Lyndall's niece had been at the Sari Club in Bali, and was missing; Lyndall carried this anxiety with her for the first thirty-six hours of the crisis response as she coordinated the extremely challenging media relations effort, staying in touch with her distraught sister but keeping her grave concerns to herself. As it turned out, the young woman was safe – she had left the club just before the bombing. Lyndall only shared this with me two decades later, and I told her how surprised I was that I hadn't known about it before. 'I was being discreet,' she told me. 'You had enough on your plate.'

Paul Grigson, the head of the Indonesia political branch, was also in among it, working with the Jakarta embassy as it engaged with the Indonesian authorities. It would take firm and deft diplomacy for Australia to do what we were about to do – move in and lead a crisis response on sovereign Indonesian territory. Meanwhile, our staff were in touch with their counterparts in other agencies. The Defence chain of command was stirring into action, and the aero-medical teams and C-130 crews at RAAF Base Richmond, outside Sydney, were being woken up. We were also in early touch with the immigration service, given the looming imperative to evacuate large numbers of people into Australia, many of whom would have no travel documents.

We had never done anything on this scale before, but the team and I had enough experience by now to understand the core principles that needed to be applied, and to have a broad feel for what was to come. I knew the pandemonium would eventually settle, and that what seemed completely unmanageable would, over time, be brought under control. The trick was to progressively bring structure to our response by putting the right people in the right places, and to ensure that communication flowed smoothly. Then it was a matter of standing back and letting people do the jobs they were trained to do. At the personal level, there is a curious steadying that happens. It becomes very important to screen out the noise, and to make a special effort to be considered, calm and polite. When I think back over the crises I have been involved in, people were almost invariably very respectful with each other, even if this was not their normal style. I remember individuals being momentarily stunned due to tiredness and giving garbled responses to questions, but I don't recall people ever flapping or shouting.

Around 7 am I received a heads-up call from Miles Jordana, John Howard's international adviser. 'Mate, the boss wants to speak to you at eight o'clock if that's convenient.'

I was surprised. 'The prime minister wants to speak to me?' I replied. I was not at the top of the pecking order, and I hadn't dealt directly with Howard before.

'Well, he wants to talk to the person who is actually

coordinating the response, and that's you,' Miles said. 'He is very clear about that – he doesn't want a fuss, you don't need to prepare anything, and he doesn't need to speak to Ashton or a deputy secretary.'

I said I would be ready for the call.

John Howard's political friends and adversaries generally agree on one thing: the man is unfailingly courteous in his dealings with people, no matter who they are. I was an independent public servant and didn't associate with one side of politics or another, but my personal experience with Howard, starting that day, was always consistent with this view. I served five prime ministers in my time as a career diplomat, and the two heads of government who had most in common in this sense were John Howard and Julia Gillard. They may have occupied very different positions on the political spectrum, but they were both consistently thoughtful and respectful in their dealings with others. Many will be surprised that I associate these two figures with each other in this way, but it's how I found them.

I answered the call on a crisis centre phone line, as Miles and I had arranged. His personal secretary announced that she had the prime minister on the line and then put him on.

'Hello, it's John Howard here, Mr Kemish,' he said unnecessarily. We didn't really know each other, so he didn't want to presume by using my first name. 'I hope I haven't distracted you from your work too much – I'd just like a minute of your time.' He'd rung to impart one simple message. 'There is nothing more important than this right now,' he said. 'I'd be grateful if you could pass on to your colleagues from the other agencies that they should not think for a moment about cost as a limiting factor. Whatever can be done should be done, regardless of the expense. Funding will not be an issue.' He thanked me for my work and rang off quite quickly – an emergency session of cabinet's National Security Committee was about to convene, he explained apologetically.

This was an immensely empowering message from the head of government, delivered at precisely the right moment to the person best placed to relay it to others. I walked almost immediately into the adjoining room, where I was about to chair the first interagency meeting, and I began by passing on the prime minister's message. I could see the effect on the team – any questions or preconceptions they might have had about limitations on their room to manoeuvre dropped away.

The business of the meeting started with an update from Bali. The Department of Defence needed as much detail as we could supply about the extent of the injuries. The pooled information would all be fed into a regularly updated and comprehensive situation report for government ministers and relevant officials in Australia and overseas; this would in turn inform the government's public line, which Lyndall Sachs and her team would craft. Having established a shared understanding of the situation, the meeting worked through the operational decisions that were required. We then made a formal request for deployment of the RAAF. They were already at an advanced stage of preparations and almost ready to go, under instruction through their own chain of command from the chief of the Defence Force, General Peter Cosgrove.

We were relieved to receive word shortly after the meeting that two RAAF C-130 Hercules aircraft had taken off, each carrying seven specialists (an anaesthetist, surgeons and nurses), and were lumbering their way north. It had been six hours between the first sketchy notifications to Defence and take-off – that might seem a long time, but it was about half the time normally required to staff, equip and despatch a medevac operation of this scale.

The ADF let us know that they could find some space for a

few of our staff on a military aircraft that would be flying out to Bali that afternoon in support of the main deployment from Richmond. Bill Jackson rang two of our experienced colleagues from the consular operations team to inform them, laconically, that we would like to offer them a free trip to the tropics. I also rang Colin Rigby, the department's staff counsellor, who agreed readily to join the others. Colin was a senior member of his profession who had established DFAT's first global psychological support service and provided specialist advice on resilience to members of the consular service, among other staff. His primary role during the Bali deployment was to ensure that our staff received support, but as it turned out he would prove invaluable in supporting the families of the victims. Our colleagues were asked to report promptly to the RAAF air base at Fairbairn, in Canberra, with their passports and as little luggage as possible, but to assume that they would be away for about two weeks. Meanwhile, several members of Ric Smith's embassy team were asked to get themselves to Bali as quickly as possible on domestic commercial flights. So at least some reinforcements would soon be on their way for our colleagues at the scene. Many more would be needed.

As the day progressed, the broader Australian effort got into full swing. Three Qantas flights took off for Bali during the afternoon, carrying several medical teams. Western Australian business and media magnate Kerry Stokes sent his own plane to Bali that day with a medical team on board. Qantas also arranged additional charter flights to help bring Australians home. No one knew what would happen next, and anxious holiday-makers were very keen to leave. A number of the walking wounded from the nightclub bombings were so desperate to get home that they hid their serious injuries from the Qantas flight crews. Staff from the Darwin and Perth hospitals reported later that they had people walking into their accident and emergency centres back in Australia in the days after the attacks.

Meanwhile, the AFP, ASIO and other agencies met separately to launch a joint investigation, and began their outreach to Indonesian counterparts. Prime Minister Howard spoke to President Megawati Sukarnoputri early in the afternoon to secure an in-principle agreement that there should be full bilateral cooperation on both the humanitarian response and the criminal investigation into the bombings. The attacks were an absolute tragedy for Indonesia – it was becoming clear that a great number of innocent Indonesians had lost their lives, along with Australians and many others. As the coordinating government leader, John Howard also took calls from New Zealand prime minister Helen Clark, British prime minister Tony Blair and US president George W. Bush in the first twenty-four hours.

The relief must have been palpable for the staff and volunteers in Bali when the RAAF aircraft landed and the medical teams got to work. The consular crew were out at the airport to brief the incoming teams, and to help organise transport for the injured to the airport. By this time, more planes were on their way from Richmond – it was already clear that the number of serious burns victims would require a sustained response for several days. The first C-130 left Bali late in the evening, arriving in Darwin, the nearest Australian city, just after midnight. And so began a prolonged emergency military airlift, dubbed 'Operation Bali Assist' by the ADF, which saw the evacuation of hundreds of injured – Australians, South Africans, New Zealanders, Canadians, Brits, Americans, Germans, Hong Kongers and of course Indonesians. The seriously injured locals were from lower socioeconomic levels of Balinese society. They were rickshaw and taxi drivers, cooks and security guards. For them and their families, evacuation to Australia was a terrifying prospect. None had ever contemplated a situation where they would be taken away like this to another country.

We had some experience in dealing with international crises, but this was different. For Australia it was also a domestic crisis. It put immense strain on our health and other support infrastructure nationally. And, as it turned out, about a third of the victims would prove to be Australians. It required a broad, whole-of-government approach, and we found ourselves engaging very closely with domestically focused agencies that we had not worked with before.

As the Bali response progressed, a team of professional social workers from Centrelink, led by their national manager, Desley Hargreaves, began to work alongside us. Centrelink is better known as the agency responsible for pensions, unemployment, sickness and other benefits, but it also plays a role in the aftermath of floods, bushfires, cyclones and other disasters, administering disaster payments and providing other social care. Desley's team stepped in to provide an ongoing liaison service for the families of the Bali victims, to ensure that no one missed out on appropriate financial support and to help clients facing particular challenges and difficulties after their return to Australia. This filled an important gap, as in usual circumstances the consular remit ended when an individual returned to Australia.

It was also the first time I'd had any dealings with Emergency Management Australia, which until then we had thought of as an organisation dedicated to coordinating efforts to respond to, and recover from, disaster and emergencies at home. They worked with the various state emergency services to plan disaster responses and provide logistical support. The more we worked with them, the more we understood how helpful they could be. They were led strongly by their director-general, David Templeman, who was full of useful tactical advice, and could also be relied upon to procure equipment and supplies to support the team in Bali. Ed Tyrie, who ran the Protective Security Coordination Centre (PSCC) in the Attorney-General's Department, was also a very steady, helpful hand. His organisation was responsible for the coordination of protective security and counterterrorism arrangements between the Australian government and the various state and territory governments.

By the end of the first twenty-four hours, DFAT staff had handled 10,000 calls from the public. The consular team in Bali had done a first check of all hospitals, hotels and airports, and estimated the number of Australians seriously injured at 113. About 220 Australians were still unaccounted for at that point. We knew that many would be among the seriously injured, but also that many would certainly be dead. Over the next week, 420 DFAT volunteer staff were rostered on a twenty-four-hour basis through the department's crisis operations and call centres – in addition to normal consular and switchboard staff. This represented about half the DFAT staff based in Canberra, all putting in extra time on top of their normal duties.

I managed to get home for a quick shower and a change after the first twenty-four hours, and then, as the hours turned into days, Chris De Cure and I made an arrangement to spell each other when we needed to sleep. I left my mobile phone with Chris when I went home, on the understanding that he would ring my home number if he needed me. He rarely disturbed my rest – he used his own judgement in consultation with the senior members of my team, and always had a neat summary of outstanding issues and questions waiting for me when I returned. While there were roster arrangements to cover the more junior staff working in the crisis centre and on the consular lines, we had to watch the more senior members of the broader team carefully, and sometimes had to push them to establish similar arrangements to that which Chris and I set up. I've seen many people come dangerously close to losing their focus and judgement mid-crisis through lack of rest, and it's to be avoided at all costs.

I remember speaking to the foreign minister, Alexander Downer, late on 14 October, day two of our response. It was a quick and businesslike call, but he took the opportunity to congratulate me on the initial emergency response, and noted in passing that the media had so far been very positive. 'Thanks, Minister,' I replied, 'but let's not forget about day three syndrome.'

He knew well what I meant. We had discussed the phenomenon before, and had experienced a version of it in the aftermath of September 11. By the third day of a mass casualty event, the media generally grows tired of reporting positively about the government's 'heroic response'. Meanwhile, family members begin to find their way to the scene of the disaster, and the media is there to see, and report on, their natural anguish and confusion. And so the criticism begins, fanned by journalists eager to get on to the next phase of the story.

CHAPTER ELEVEN

Sticking with the Families

DAY THREE, 15 OCTOBER, ALSO happened to be my daughter Eloise's eleventh birthday. She remembers that birthday as being different, mostly because I wasn't there, although she does acknowledge that I made it home for cake at one point. She understood why I was hardly present, as my work was all over the news.

As expected, distraught relatives of the victims began to arrive in Bali that day. DFAT officers were assigned to meet them on arrival – or at least those we'd been told were coming. The team ensured they were booked into appropriate accommodation, and they were each assigned a family liaison officer. Our people established a consular help desk in the arrivals area of Denpasar airport to try to catch incoming families who hadn't let us know their plans. The pressure on the local team was building quickly, but further consular reinforcements, social workers and counsellors were arriving to assist. Disaster victim identification specialists and investigators were also making their way to Bali – about twenty AFP officers had arrived by the end of 15 October, and that number doubled twenty-four hours later. This was just the beginning of one of the most difficult and resource-intensive operations the

AFP had ever undertaken. They responded to the disaster with enormous energy and focus under the steady leadership of their quietly spoken commissioner, Mick Keelty, whose close working relationship with his Indonesian counterpart, General Da'i Bachtiar, paved the way for the impressive collaboration that would follow between the AFP and the Indonesian National Police on both the investigation and identification process. Other key AFP figures included national counter-terrorism coordinator, Andrew Colvin, and the operational commander in Indonesia, Graham Ashton. Colvin went on to become the AFP commissioner and Ashton the head of the Victorian Police.

The ADF under General Cosgrove was no less impressive, continuing to fly return sorties between Bali and Australia, transporting the seriously wounded. The logistical skills and can-do attitude of Australia's men and women in uniform, is second to none. Only three hours' flight away, and with a fully functioning hospital, Darwin was the obvious first Australian destination for the emergency evacuation, but within the first few days even its medical facilities began to be overwhelmed, necessitating a further domestic airlift from Darwin to Perth and other southern cities, conducted by the RAAF and the Royal Flying Doctor Service. The federal and state health departments stepped in to help us manage this process.

Family members arrived in Bali full of desperate questions. Many still held out hope that their missing daughter, son, sister or brother would turn out to be alive. Some had accepted the inevitable, and simply wanted to claim the body of their loved one. Because of the horrible disfigurement of the injured and the dead, though, there were no simple answers; in many cases a long and painstaking DNA identification process was required. This was not at all what families wanted to hear. Our officials were themselves only beginning to grasp the immensity of the process that lay ahead, and in some cases struggled to explain what needed to happen.

The understandable anguish and confusion of the families, and in some cases publicly expressed anger, gave the media outlets exactly what they wanted: a new angle. The tone of media and broader public commentary quickly became more critical. 'Why is it taking so long?' became the refrain, and media commentators began to make snap judgements about the adequacy of the resources we were putting in place. Politicians of all stripes started to get involved. The foreign minister's office was peppered with questions from local MPs whose electorate offices were under telephone siege from people desperate to locate their friends and relatives.

The victim identification process soon became a nightmare. Families started appearing at the hospital and the morgue, increasingly frustrated at their inability to locate their loved ones. This reflected both confusion at the hospital and the scale of the disaster. For the first couple of days, the focus had been on identifying and assisting those who were seriously injured. The dead had had to wait. Amateur photographs began to appear on noticeboards at the hospital, and this quickly became a particular point of friction. In one case, six different Australian families identified, with absolute certainty, the same corpse as their own kin. A consular officer we had sent to Bali from Canberra, Kim Lamb, when confronted by one particularly insistent husband, took him through the identification process one last time. She examined the body very closely herself, turned to the grieving man and asked: 'Did your wife have a navel ring?' He said that she didn't. 'I'm sorry,' Kim said, 'but this is not your wife.' As the days passed, the specialists came to the view that only half the estimated 180 bodies could be identified by means of fingerprint or dental records; families would need to provide DNA samples to help identify the rest.

Meanwhile, Bill Jackson and his consular operations team in Canberra, working closely with their colleagues in Bali, had done some impressive work to identify Australians who were safe, those seriously injured and those who had likely been killed. This detective work brought relief to several anxious families, but left many others distraught. It was even more complex than it sounds. Establishing who had actually been present at the two nightclubs was the first step. This was a little easier if an individual had been with a group of friends, and if one of them was conscious and in a position to speak to authorities. But this was not always the situation. The survivors with the worst injuries, and certainly the deceased, were generally unrecognisable because of their horrific burns. Despite these challenges, the team had managed to narrow things down substantially, by methodically staying in touch with families and friends, regularly scouring the hospitals, and checking flight and immigration records. By the end of the second day, the number of Australians feared dead had been reduced to 148.

But something was bugging Bill, and he kept returning to one of the names on the list. It was a young man from Perth; let's call him Bruce. He had been spotted early in the evening at Paddy's Bar by someone who knew him, but no one had seen him since. The hospital searches had unearthed nothing, and the mobile phone number provided by the family was all we had to go on. Bill had rung Bruce's mobile a couple of times himself, he told me, but kept getting a message that the number was unreachable. I replied that Bruce was likely among the rubble of the two nightclubs, which was still being picked through by forensic specialists. 'You're probably right,' Bill said, but added: 'I reckon I'm just going to keep ringing that number – just in case.' The team began arrangements to source a sample of Bruce's family DNA.

Ross Tysoe continued to play his role with dignity and

compassion. He was the lead interface with the victims' families and friends, dealing with them on both an individual and a group basis. He and other consular staff answered their questions patiently and bore the brunt of their anger. Their feelings were understandable. However, many also found quiet ways to express their appreciation to the team, generously setting aside time in the midst of their grief to write letters and emails to Ross and others.

The families were a representative slice of modern Australia, and some were easier to deal with than others. As with many other consular cases, we were reminded of how the traditional family unit was changing. Our liaison arrangements were sometimes complicated by recent divorce or remarriage, and blended families were common. Sometimes the most passionate and demanding family representative would be a former partner or step-parent who had no legally recognisable claim to information; in a few cases they were being denied information by the formal next of kin.

Ric Smith was working hard in Jakarta in support of the government's response, urgently engaging the Indonesian presidency and ministers on everything from medical supplies to the counterterrorist investigation. It was a few days after the attacks before he could fly to Bali to assume overall coordination of the burgeoning Australian response on the ground. The number of Australian officials in Bali swelled to just under 200 in the first couple of weeks, including about 100 police officers.

A key individual who joined the consular leadership team in Bali was John McAnulty, one of Australia's most experienced consular hands. He was working in another headquarters role at the time, but had recently completed a posting as consul-general at the Jakarta embassy, and prior to that had served at our missions in Suva, Honolulu, Riyadh, Geneva, Beirut, Belgrade and Manila. John was always among the first to come to my mind when a consular crisis emerged, but in this case he also had very recent and highly relevant Indonesian experience. When I rang to ask him politely if he could deploy to Bali, I soon understood that he had been waiting for the call and was already getting packed. Lex Bartlem, another very experienced and unflappable colleague, also joined the hard-pressed Bali team from Canberra in that first week. He calmly took on a pivotal administrative role – as Ross put it, the consulate was spending money like there was no tomorrow, hiring vehicles from across the island, booking out most of the hotels and procuring all sorts of equipment. There was an urgent need to provide guidance and leadership to the beleaguered accounts staff – to bring order to chaos. The ever-positive Ruth Stone, a young policy officer from the Jakarta embassy, accompanied Ross throughout each day, playing an executive officer role and gathering information for the twice-daily situation reports that the post needed to send out to the network.

Back in Canberra, the demand for information from the media and politicians was relentless. It was essential to 'feed the beast' – we would lose public confidence quickly if we were judged to be unresponsive. Some of it was just tiresome: for example, state premiers and parochial news outlets wanted regular updates about how many of the victims were from their respective states. Chris, Lyndall and the media team did a sterling job dealing with much of this, but I also had to respond personally to difficult inquiries and help 'put out fires'. I also spoke several times a day with Alexander Downer, who, as the accountable minister for the consular service, was the government's principal spokesperson about the crisis. Given the pace of developments and the intensity of the media interest, he needed frequent updates to ensure he was in a position to respond confidently to questions, and to help explain to the Australian public what was happening.

Media and public criticism about the management of the bodies, and the pace of the victim identification process, was peaking on the fourth day, 16 October. The ADF was rushing to get refrigeration facilities to Bali, given concerns about the potential deterioration of the bodies. Some began to call for all the bodies to be transported to Australia. This would have been a breach of international law, Interpol forensic protocols and Indonesian sovereignty, but all this was hard to explain to agitated families who had little confidence in the Indonesian system.

Coronial arrangements in Australia are managed at the state level, and a number of state coroners leaned in to try to insist that their particular standards should prevail for this complex offshore operation. There was a lot of ego involved and, according to several present, after a particularly insistent coroner called, one of the senior officials managing the victim identification process in Bali commented quietly that he now understood that 'coroners don't live in Australia – they live in jurisdictions'. Tracey Wunder remembers a near-abusive call from one of the state coroners knocking the wind out of her. She also remembers that I went quiet when she told me about it, and that I went off to give the coroner a call of my own. I'd completely forgotten this encounter until Tracey mentioned it to me almost twenty years later, and then I remembered all too clearly the feeling of protective anger that had consumed me at the time.

Prime Minister Howard evidently saw the distress all this was causing the families and the Australian public, and decided to consult an expert himself. On 16 October he spoke at length with Professor Chris Griffiths, a forensic medical specialist at Sydney's Westmead Hospital, who had been deployed to Bali. Based on Professor Griffiths' advice, the prime minister told parliament later that day that the work underway between the Australian and Indonesian authorities to establish proper disaster victim identification procedures could not be rushed. Addressing assertions that families could identify their loved ones themselves, Howard noted that Professor Griffiths had told him that 'the appearance of remains alters often very dramatically after death; and his very strong professional view as expressed to me was that if the Interpol protocol was not followed, there was a one in five possibility of an identity error'. Howard expressed his understanding about the anguish involved, but concluded that, in the circumstances, the Indonesian authorities could not be criticised.

This was a helpful intervention. We in the consular trenches were glad that Howard was helping educate the Australian public about the realities of disaster victim identification. We still feared, though, that the media were poised to relaunch their attacks, and that family anger would be the catalyst.

The prime minister was clearly determined to stay on top of the details. I found myself in his office later that same afternoon, along with Ashton Calvert. Howard wanted to discuss what we were doing to prevent the bodies from deteriorating further. He'd heard correctly (probably from Professor Griffiths) that the industrial refrigeration units flown in by the ADF had not been put into use. We were actively working on this issue at the time, and were able to report shortly afterwards that the situation was under control. The forensic experts on the ground had advised that the bodies would freeze unevenly inside these containers – some would rot, and others would be burned by the cold. The better solution, which was now in place, was to preserve the remains in body bags with large quantities of locally sourced ice. It was not the only time when officials in Canberra came to the wrong collective judgement about how to resolve an issue in the field.

It had taken strenuous efforts by the team in Bali to get to this point. The vehicles hired to transport the remains to where the bodies were to be stored had failed to show up, and John McAnulty had been forced to walk out into the street with fistfuls of Indonesian rupiahs to convince local drivers to overcome their superstitions about transporting the dead. Almost twenty years later, there is still wonder in Ross's voice when he describes how young Indonesian Red Cross volunteers showed up a couple of times a day to replace and re-stack the ice around the bodies. They were always ready and smiling; not one of them ever backed away from the grisly task.

Ashton rang me at about 10.30 am the following day in the crisis centre. He was with the prime minister again. 'Ian, the prime minister would like some background about the memorial service he understands is planned to take place in Bali later today,' he said. I confirmed that a service organised jointly by the families and our staff was scheduled to take place at the consulate at sunset, Bali time – around 6 pm. Ashton took note of this and instructed me to stay on the line. He was back again within a minute. 'The prime minister plans to attend the ceremony. Can you advise Ross Tysoe, please, and tell him that Mr Howard doesn't want any unnecessary protocol. It's to be a low-key visit.' He added that the deputy prime minister, John Anderson, and the opposition leader, Simon Crean, would also be invited; they would shortly be leaving parliament for the RAAF Fairbairn base.

I was stunned. First, it didn't seem practical for the Australian prime minister to decide, late in the morning, to attend a service in Bali that same evening. But I did the mental arithmetic and realised it was doable – it was a six-hour flight, and Bali was three hours behind Canberra, so in fact they had an hour or so to spare. Second, I thought a prime ministerial visit was the last thing the hard-pressed team in Bali needed. They didn't have a moment to rest, and no matter what the prime minister might say about not wanting a fuss, a visit by the head of government involves a lot of logistical support. People would inevitably be diverted from their work.

Still, I went ahead and rang Ross on speaker phone from the crisis centre. Chris De Cure was at my side, as he had been since the early hours of the first day. I gave Ross the news in a couple of short sentences. There was silence on the other end of the line. I started to say something else but Chris quietly intervened: 'Hang on, mate, I think he's still struggling to lift his jaw back off the ground.' Ross collected himself quickly, and didn't vent or object as others might have. He thanked us politely for the call, and went off to make the necessary reception, transportation and security arrangements for an incoming prime minister.

I have to concede, looking back, that Howard's visit to Bali was a game changer. I wasn't there, but many people I knew were. None were rusted-on Liberal supporters, but all agreed that he handled the situation very well. Howard himself later told me that if there had been any questions in his mind about the quality of DFAT's response on the ground, he set these aside as soon as he met Ross at the foot of the aircraft stairs. He could sense very clearly what the man had been through, and concluded quickly from talking to him that the situation was in very good hands. They drove straight to the consulate, and Howard walked into the crowd of relatives and friends assembled for the ceremony, putting his arms around many of them. His voice cracked with emotion as he spoke, without notes, of the nation's anguish. One young man collapsed into his arms after laying a candle to the memory of the mother he had just lost. While I'm sure that not every family approved of the visit, most welcomed the gesture. I read all the letters sent to us after the ceremony – including from lifelong ALP supporters. They could all see that the prime minister's sorrow was genuine. Those of us still working on the ongoing consular response felt the external pressure and criticism ease markedly in following days, allowing us to focus more clearly on the job at hand.

The day after the prime minister's return to Australia, there was a morning tea arranged at Parliament House in Canberra for those families of victims who could make it. A national memorial service was to take place in the Great Hall of Parliament House that weekend, and the government would cover the travel costs and accommodation for close relatives. Bill and I joined the morning tea in the prime minister's office. For me, it was the first of many personal encounters with those who had lost someone in the bombings. Some said they felt both awkward about and grateful for the attention they were receiving, although no doubt they all wished things were very different. Roxanne and I met many more of the families when we attended the national service.

Within a week or so, I flew to Bali myself to review the situation and check in on our staff, and I was also able to attend a Balinese cleansing ceremony with families who were still waiting for news of their loved ones. Most put on a brave face, and some even engaged in classic Australian banter during the ceremony. But they were all drawn and exhausted. And many spoke about their concerns for the Balinese.

While in Bali, I also had the opportunity to talk to some of the police specialists who had deployed there from all over Australia as part of 'Operation Alliance', the AFP-led operation established at the invitation of the Indonesian police force to assist with victim identification and the criminal investigation. I was deeply impressed by how officers from state police forces across Australia were working seamlessly with their federal and Indonesian counterparts to bring clarity to the victims' families, and to help bring the perpetrators to justice. For the AFP itself, Bali was a watershed moment that led the force into a new pattern of engagement with their counterpart organisations across the Indo-Pacific region, especially the Indonesians. I was fascinated then, and on several other occasions in the years that followed, to see how police officers from radically different cultural backgrounds quickly established trusting relationships with each other.

Not long after I returned to Canberra, Bill walked into my office with a big grin on his face. It was by now about ten days after the bombing. 'What are you smiling about?' I asked.

'I just spoke to Bruce,' he replied.

Bill had rung the phone number yet again that morning, and this time someone answered. After establishing that it really was Bruce he was speaking to, Bill asked him where he had been. Bruce confirmed that he had been in Kuta when the bombs went off, but he hadn't been injured, apart from a couple of scratches. He had been wandering for a while and had now returned to Australia. Bill said, 'Mate, your family think you're dead – don't you think you should call them?'

Bruce's reply suggested that the idea hadn't even occurred to him. 'Yeah, you're probably right,' he said. 'I'm not in touch with the family much, but I'll let them know I'm okay.'

When Bill told me this, we looked at each other and shook our heads. I'm pretty sure that, shortly afterwards, Bill rang the family himself – just in case.

The first month after the bombings was one long scramble. Things just kept happening – at one point, while the forensic efforts to retrieve the remains were still ongoing, a group of Indonesians arrived with bulldozers to clear the rubble. Ric Smith stepped in personally to prevent them from proceeding. Meanwhile, we had managed to carry out several formal identifications through fingerprint and dental checking. The next of kin had to be formally notified of the deaths, and arrangements made by our consular staff for the return of the remains. The majority of the Australian victims had to be identified with the assistance of DNA, and it seemed to take forever. A combined identification team, drawn from every state in Australia, toiled on as a nation waited.

The rest of the world hadn't stopped, of course. Australians continued to travel all around the world, and some continued to find themselves in serious trouble, or worse. We had another 'crisis within a crisis' only weeks after the Bali bombings. On 11 November 2002, a Laoag International Airlines Fokker aircraft plunged into Manila Bay. Six Australian surfers were among those on board. Only one of them, Steve Thompson from Sydney, was pulled from the sea alive. An air crash overseas involving five Australian deaths was a very serious consular incident for our team in Manila, and for the operations crew in Canberra. Such moments, when everyone is distracted and exhausted, can be dangerous – and with serious consular cases, the stakes are always high. But the families had to be supported, investigations managed and the bodies repatriated by those who could be spared, at least for a while, from the Bali response.

As the identification processes in Bali was almost final, we struck agreements with each of the Australian state police forces that the Canberra consular operations team would notify the relevant force headquarters when a cable was received from Bali confirming an individual's death. A team of two police officers – usually a man and a woman – would then be sent out to the home of the next of kin to break the news in person. While almost all the families expected the worst to be confirmed, there would be a moment when all hope was finally extinguished, and it was important that it be handled sensitively. It was Tracey Wunder who negotiated these arrangements, building trust with the police in the process. Regrettably, we were forced to abandon this arrangement at one crucial moment. For me, and for many of my colleagues, it was the worst moment of the entire operation.

It was mid-afternoon in early November, and the first batch of the Australian DNA-based identifications was expected that evening. It had been a long wait for many, the media knew it was coming and public expectations were high. The consular operations team in Canberra had been given an informal heads-up about which confirmations were expected, but we were yet to receive formal notifications. The relevant police liaison officers were on standby across the country. I was standing in the open-plan area of the consular branch when Tracey approached me. She was ashen-faced, and a couple of members of her team were behind her, looking as troubled as she was.

A knot formed in my stomach as she explained the problem. An Australian reporter snooping around the Bali hospital had obtained a list of the Australians whose deaths would be confirmed that day, and had started ringing around the families back home to get a reaction. It was a truly despicable act, and quite out of keeping with my overall experience of Australian journalists. A number of colleagues still remember that moment – standing there and looking at me expectantly. 'Ring them up,' I said to Tracey and her colleagues. 'Get on the phones and ring the families on today's list yourselves.' It was better, I reasoned, that they hear confirmation of their loved one's death from a compassionate professional over the phone than from some hack seeking a reaction. And I wanted to get to them first, if at all possible.

Bill and Tracey then had the job of explaining to her police contacts why we were suddenly abandoning what we'd all agreed was best practice. They were all shocked, but most expressed understanding for our actions. Ashton, Ric and the foreign minister also supported my decision when they heard about it. Ric just said, 'I don't think you were given much choice, mate.'

I know, though, that at least one state police force never forgave me for it.

It fell to our consular staff to confirm the deaths to those families who had chosen to base themselves in Bali. Many of those who had travelled there for the cleansing ceremony had decided to stay. Tracey flew in to support the team as the notifications really got going. She remembers working as a pair with her colleague Richard Jameson to approach the next of kin and give them the grim news. It was sometimes, literally, a matter of tracking them down at their hotels, in a cafe, a restaurant or a foyer, and trying to find a quiet corner in which they could speak. At one such meeting they were almost interrupted by an Australian group who wanted to complain to the officials about the charges they had received for drinks at the hotel bar; Richard managed to spirit them out of the way while she delivered the news to the couple they had come to see.

We thought carefully about the arrangements for the return of the victims' remains. Some in the ADF were concerned that the use of C-130 Hercules aircraft would make it look like we were treating the bodies as freight. We could see their point, so we asked Emergency Management Australia to source coffins and Australian flags to drape over them, so that the deceased could be boarded, transported and delivered home with dignity and respect.

DFAT has offices in each state capital across Australia, with staff who liaise with local businesses and media, provide passport services and handle other inquiries. Our staff in these cities bore a significant emotional load through the Bali crisis – this was where the victims' families lived, for the most part, and they moved quickly to show them whatever support they could. Philip Green, who had responded so well to the bombings in Nairobi as a young head of mission fourteen years earlier, was by now the director of DFAT's office in Sydney. He escorted one large family group through Sydney airport in the first days after the bombing, who were on their way to locate their much-loved missing daughter and sister, and were confident of finding her alive. He saw them again a couple of weeks later when they returned home, crushed and crumpled by grief.

When the bodies began to arrive home, DFAT staff arranged small, respectful ceremonies for the families in quiet corners of airport hangars. It seemed to help.

CHAPTER TWELVE

Recovery

FUNERALS AND MEMORIAL SERVICES FOR the eighty-eight Australians who died in the 2002 Bali bombings took place across Australia in the weeks and months after the attacks. The immediate consular work subsided, injuries began to heal and the families were left to grieve. As the end of the year approached, we in the Australian consular service asked ourselves what would be next. Experience told us that 2003 would present fresh challenges, and we also knew that it was not the end of the road as far as the Bali response was concerned. There would be more work to support the families as the perpetrators of the bombing were arrested and came to trial, and we knew the first anniversary of the bombings would be an important moment – primarily for the survivors and the families and friends of the dead, but also for the many volunteers, officials and carers who had thrown their hearts and souls into the response.

Our immediate priority, however, was to come together with the other agencies who had supported our efforts, and to share perspectives on what could be improved. This was no self-congratulatory exercise. We were already aware of areas where we might have handled things better – for example, as the coordinating agency, DFAT had been too slow in the first few days to engage domestic Australian agencies, including the Department of Health, to ensure proper follow-up once the survivors and the injured returned to Australia. There were all sorts of technical gaps that had been identified too, and we took a systematic approach in working to address them as quickly as possible. To be fair, though, we had got a lot of things right. We'd pulled off an unprecedented large-scale aero-medical evacuation from a neighbouring country, we'd supported families through a necessarily lengthy identification process, and we'd ensured the respectful return of the victims' remains. Firm relationships had been established with most of the families, and we had managed to maintain a collaborative relationship with the Indonesian authorities as we moved onto their sovereign turf to coordinate a major crisis response.

We at DFAT didn't spend much time considering the cultural ingredients behind the success of the consular response, but several of the Bali responders have told me in recent times that they believe, after years of reflection, that we were only successful because the working culture of the organisation at the time allowed them substantial autonomy in the roles they were assigned. There was no room for micro-management; the unprecedented nature of the crisis required all of us to think for ourselves, make the best judgements we could and get on with it.

Like most people, I have experienced micro-management in my working life, both in my government and private-sector careers. I have consistently found that it stifles creativity and holds an organisation back from being its best. I am left concerned today that, as a general rule, instant communications are encouraging a trend towards tighter control and regulation – organisations become less and less tolerant of risk when human error can so quickly become the subject of a Twitter storm. In my observation, ministers and top officials have become progressively more focused on 'controlling the message' in recent years, and this has drawn them into the detail of decision-making on operational issues. There can be a very fine line between absence and intrusion, and leaders need to get this right – especially during a crisis. I'm pleased that during the major crisis responses of the early 2000s, I was only one link in a leadership chain that was generally prepared to stand back and respect the judgement of those below. Ministers and more senior officials across all portfolios showed a remarkable level of trust in their subordinates.

It has to be said that not everyone was comfortable with this. At an early point in the Bali response, I was in a meeting with Ashton when one of his deputies popped in to tell him that a three-star general had rung from Defence headquarters to query the relatively junior level of the DFAT official chairing the daily interdepartmental task force meeting. This was a direct reference to me – on the formal table of Defence rank equivalence, I was on the same level as a mere 'one-star' brigadier, and this obviously seemed odd to this particular ADF officer, given that more senior military officers were participating in the deliberations. Ashton (who was the equivalent of a four-star general) sent a response back that I was the responsible lead and had his complete confidence, as well as the prime minister's. I'd come a long way since the fiasco of the Solomon Islands evacuation.

As it turned out, I was promoted one rung, to the level of division head, in the immediate aftermath of the bombings. I had applied as part of a regular DFAT promotion around a month or so previously, and had somehow squeezed the formal interview in during the crisis response. I have absolutely no memory of it. In the archaic-sounding language of the public service, I was now a First Assistant Secretary. But I was not leaving the consular field behind. I simply had responsibility for the broader division, which included my consular portfolio. I now had oversight of media relations, public diplomacy and the passports operation as well as the consular branch. I was replaced as Assistant Secretary for Consular Branch by Rod Smith, whom I had known since our early days with the department. It was an interesting challenge for me to step back and let someone else handle the branch on a day-to-day basis, but it helped that Rod was so competent, and we settled into a strong partnership very quickly. My new rank also opened up the possibility of taking up a range of more senior ambassadorial appointments in the future – if the department would ever let me go.

Things were not always positive in the wake of the Bali response. We had to defend ourselves, and the government we served, against baseless accusations that we had known about the risk of an attack in Bali in advance, and failed to warn the travelling public.

It started very early in the piece, three days after the bombings, and as we were working hard on myriad fronts. My mobile phone rang for the umpteenth time that day. It was the prime minister's office. 'Mate, are you on your way? The PM's waiting.'

'Um ... what?' I replied intelligently.

I'd obviously missed a message. The prime minister was asking for a personal briefing from me, before Question Time in parliament that afternoon, on what we had known through intelligence channels about potential terrorism in Indonesia prior to the attacks, how we had responded to that intelligence in framing our travel advice, and how our advisories compared to those of our 'Five Eyes' partners: the United States, the United Kingdom, Canada and New Zealand. The PM was available now.

I grabbed a folder from my desk and rushed to my car in the DFAT basement. Within fifteen minutes I was sitting in the prime minister's office at Parliament House with John Howard and his chief of staff, Arthur Sinodinos. It was the first time I had met the PM in person.

We'd known from the outset that questions would inevitably be asked by the media about what we had said in our Indonesian travel advisory prior to the attacks, and that the opposition would be ready to pounce on any suggestion that we had negligently failed to warn Australians about known threats. In the first early hours after the bombing, Tracy Reid had started pulling together a matrix showing how the Indonesian travel warnings had been updated and amended over the previous eighteen months, and also how our actions compared to those of our alliance partners, who had access to the same body of intelligence. An enormous amount of painstaking, intensive work had gone into producing this matrix in such a short space of time. It was only the dawning of the digital age, so Tracy and her small team had spent hours on the phone and hovering over fax machines as they pieced together a comprehensive history of all the changes made to travel advisories for Indonesia in the past few years.

Over the next hour, Prime Minister Howard quizzed me, courteously but methodically, on the detail underpinning each of our decisions in relation to the Indonesian travel advice and other related warnings. At one point he asked me a question on a point of detail to which I had no ready answer. As one must in such circumstances, I replied: 'I don't know, Prime Minister, but I can find out and get back to you.'

'Yes, please,' he replied.

There was a pause, and I looked at him. He looked back expectantly.

Oh, he means now, I thought to myself. I retreated to a corner of the room to phone Jeff Roach back in the branch, who had only recently returned from parental leave. I was praying that he would answer his phone – and know the answer when he did. He came through for me on both counts, and I returned to my seat to continue the conversation.

A little later, as I walked down the office corridor, mentally exhausted and relieved to have survived this polite but insistent interrogation, the prime minister's voice called out behind me: 'Oh, Mr Kemish!' I turned and he beckoned me back into the room. I trotted back again, heart in my mouth. He said earnestly: 'You do understand that I'm asking these questions because I need to defend the government's position in parliament, don't you? I wouldn't want you to think I was questioning the integrity and judgement of you and your colleagues.'

Not many people would have done that. I appreciated it.

Howard made a clear statement to parliament that afternoon, but it did not prevent months of questioning in the chamber and in the media. Our accusers – and that was how I came to think of them – seemed determined to make the case that we had seen the Bali attacks coming and failed to provide a warning. It was nonsense, of course. Four public statements issued by the government in the month leading up to the attacks had made clear the ongoing serious, general threat, and there was no gap at all between the advice we had provided and that of our major consular partner countries. The formal Australian travel advice for Indonesia, updated most recently a month prior to the bombings, stated: 'In view of the ongoing risk of terrorist activity in the region, Australians in Indonesia should maintain a high level of personal security awareness ... Bombs have been exploded periodically in Jakarta and elsewhere in the past, including areas frequented by tourists.' These warnings were echoed in a regional travel bulletin for Australians in South-East Asia, a notice from the Jakarta embassy and a worldwide caution issued the day before the bombings. None of these statements reflected information about Bali or any prior knowledge of a bombing attack on bars or nightclubs. If we had such information, we would have moved heaven and earth to prevent the attacks and warn travellers to stay away.

There was, however, one perceived vulnerability in the travel advice. It contained the following additional reference: 'Australians in … central Sulawesi, should avoid inter-provincial and inter-city bus travel and exercise caution following recent attacks on passenger buses. Tourist services elsewhere in Indonesia are operating normally, including Bali.' Our detractors asserted that this final sentence reinforced a perception that Bali was a safe haven. I think any fair reading leaves little doubt that this statement was simply to differentiate the transport services in Sulawesi from those in other parts of Indonesia, including Bali – and that it took nothing away from the first sentence of the advisory, which highlighted the risk of terrorism throughout the country.

A formal Senate inquiry was nonetheless established to 'get to the bottom' of the matter in March 2003, five months after the bombings. I spent eighteen months fronting this inquiry on behalf of DFAT, alongside the heads of intelligence agencies such as ASIO and ONA. I respected the Senate's role in reviewing the work of the government in this important area, particularly after so many Australian lives had been lost. I knew that it was all 'just politics' and that an election was coming. But the consular service was being targeted and as the lead official from the area that reviewed the threat assessments and drafted the travel advice, it was hard to avoid feeling that my integrity was being challenged.

As the incoming director-general of ONA, Peter Varghese, was to say later, the organisation never raised any actionable information in relation to Bali. Nor did anyone else. Over time, the senators were forced to acknowledge that there had been no clear warning in the form of specific intelligence which, if identified and acted upon, would have provided an opportunity to prevent the Bali bombings or to act to protect those there at the time. The truth was on our side.

So were the families of almost all of the Australian victims. I came to know many of them in the weeks and months after the bombings, and wondered how they were feeling about the constant suggestions that someone had known something and not passed it on. As the inquiry got underway, I wrote to them to explain factually the purpose of the hearings – it was their right to know. I will always treasure the generous response I received from Daniel Lysaght, whose son Scott had been killed in the tragedy. He wrote that he wanted me to know that 'neither I nor any member of my family consider that the Government's travel warnings were in any way inadequate. We do not feel that there was any lack of advice that contributed to Scott's death.'

I also remember updating a group of family members on the progress of the inquiry in Bali as it coincided with the first anniversary of the bombings. One of them, a young man who had been injured that night and lost both his brother and best friend, said to me: 'I shouldn't worry about all that bullshit, mate. Even if you had said something in the travel advice about Bali, we would still have been there that night. It wouldn't have changed our minds.'

Brian Deegan, an Adelaide-based magistrate, took a different view. He had lost his son Joshua in the attacks, and he held the Howard government responsible for his death. Brian wrote an open letter to the prime minister in November 2002, criticising the government's foreign policy and linking the Bali bombings to Australia's support for the 'war on terror'. He was also critical of the travel advice. I spoke to Brian several times through 2003, as I did with many of the victims' families, and flew to Adelaide to be present when Alexander Downer invited him to a meeting. Downer did what he could to reach out to Brian, but he was not to be reconciled. None of us felt anything but sympathy for him. He actually ran against Downer in the 2004 federal election. The foreign minister was re-elected, but Brian Deegan came a respectable second.

The domestic political debate about these issues took place against a tense international backdrop. The United States and its allies, including Australia and the United Kingdom, were by now fully engaged in the 'war on terror'. These governments were dealing with threats at home and abroad, and were resolved to work together to deny the jihadist movement a safe haven. As 2003 got underway, President Bush was building international support for a military offensive against Saddam Hussein's Iraq. The aims of this exercise, according to the president, were 'to disarm Iraq of weapons of mass destruction, to end Saddam Hussein's support for terrorism, and to free the Iraqi people'. As the international coalition prepared to launch its 'shock and awe' military offensive, our focus in the consular service was on ensuring that Australians in the Middle East received prompt and clear messages, through the travel advice, to avoid or depart from countries and regions of particular risk. As we now know, it turned out that there were no weapons of mass destruction, and the rapid military conquest of the country by US-led forces, including Australian troops, only led to an extended, frustrating and damaging period of military occupation.

We also used the travel advisory service to broadcast urgent public health messages from early 2003. In February that year, the Australian consulate in Guangzhou began reporting to Canberra about a local outbreak of an unidentified infection described as 'atypical pneumonia'. The embassy in Beijing reported cases in the capital the following month, by which time the name Severe Acute Respiratory Syndrome, or SARS, had been coined. Working closely with the Australian health authorities, we put out travel advisories recommending against non-essential travel to China and Hong Kong, and issued precautionary bulletins about how travellers should minimise their exposure. Around 7000 people would die before SARS was declared under control by the World Health Organization in July 2003, and cases were still being reported a year after that – by which time the international public health focus had shifted to an avian influenza (H5N1) outbreak in East Asia. These pandemic threats were very serious, but of course they paled in comparison with what would come more than fifteen years later.

Political attacks on the travel advisory service in the year or so after the Bali attacks made its management very difficult for a while. The system became so risk-averse that the default expectation of many observers, and even some national security insiders, was that every bit of 'intelligence chatter' should appear in the travel advice, regardless of how unreliable it might be. I seemed to be constantly on the phone to the foreign minister to resolve some burning issue that had arisen in the travel advisory for Indonesia or some other country because something was or was not mentioned. Alexander Downer was very sensible about it, but we were all under pressure and we had to make some very fine judgements together. Intelligence is rarely specific; I don't actually remember any instance where a specific target was mentioned and the purported attack came to pass.

As we moved to highlight new potential risks through the travel advisory system over this period, working more actively to review and update our public material, we were sometimes accused by other governments of being 'trigger-happy'. The Greek government reacted with fury when we changed the travel advice in the lead-up to the 2004 Athens Olympics because of credible security threats in Greece. The games would be the largest global gathering since global jihadism had declared its hand so clearly in 2001, but for Greece it was a historic moment in another sense: it was the first time the Olympics would be held in Athens since the modern games had been launched there in 1896, so there was great sensitivity about any slights to the country's reputation. The Greek ambassador in Canberra and senior government figures in Athens reacted badly, and there were claims in the Greek press that we were trying to spoil their Olympics because we were worried they would outshine the Sydney Games of 2000. I took the opportunity of a contingency planning visit to Athens prior to the Olympics to make peace with the city's mayor, Dora Bakoyannis. I underlined our obligations to the Australian travelling public and assured her that Australians wished Greece nothing but the best for its historic Olympiad. She accepted my assurances graciously and helped calm the press. And, to everyone's relief and delight, the Athens Olympic Games were a great success.

Amid all this colour and movement, we tried to learn the deeper lessons, strengthening our consultative arrangements with ASIO to provide further confirmation that all intelligence available to the government was fully integrated into our public advice, along with ASIO's expert assessments of this intelligence. This involved, among other things, the establishment of a joint threat assessment centre housed in ASIO, but with seconded personnel from DFAT and other agencies. These initiatives were informed by our own reflections about where the vulnerabilities and potential for communication breakdowns lay. We also worked to improve the presentation and the consistency of our travel advisories, to make them more straightforward and digestible.

It was also clear that there had been insufficient public awareness of the travel advisory program prior to the Bali bombings. It wasn't just a matter of achieving a slicker, reliable product – we also needed to get it read more widely. This was how the 'Smartraveller' program was conceived, an initiative launched at the Sydney Opera House by Foreign Minister Downer in 2003. As we said repeatedly at the time, our objective was to see all Australian travellers being responsible and well-informed 'smart' travellers. This website service continues to this day – having been upgraded over the years to carry much more traffic. We then went on a public relations offensive, emphasising that the new international environment presented substantial new security and safety concerns. We saw it as an important part of our role to help Australians understand this new international dynamic.

We also launched Smartraveller 'kiosks' in 2003 – portals placed in the international departure areas of all our major airports where Australians could access the Smartraveller website and print the latest travel advice before their departure. The concept lasted about as long as the PalmPilot and the BlackBerry. It was quickly eclipsed as the increasingly ubiquitous smartphone made such shared facilities – and printing – redundant. Foreign Minister Downer was from Adelaide, and the first kiosk was launched there. Rod Smith flew to Adelaide for the event and experienced a heart-stopping moment when Downer pressed the button for the cameras and the kiosk failed to function. As it turned out, a small boy had switched off the power at the wall. The minister took it all with good grace, readily accepting the embarrassed apologies of the lad's very charming mother.

The trials of the Bali bombers began in May 2003. Imam Samudra, the planner of the operation, had been arrested in November 2002, and many others followed. Abu Bakar Ba'asyir, the spiritual leader of Jemaah Islamiyah, was arrested that same month in connection with attacks on Christian churches the previous year, but he was also implicated in the Bali attacks, having provided the inspiration that the foot soldiers needed. Some family members attended the trials, watching steadfastly as the accused were brought to account; some were formal witnesses. The team of social workers from Centrelink who had been assisting the families at home in Australia were asked to deploy to Bali to support those who were there for the court proceedings.

This was the first time that the Centrelink team had been deployed offshore, which opened their eyes to the work agencies like the AFP and DFAT did regularly. Desley Hargreaves sensed that some of the police and consular staff initially viewed the arrival of her team with suspicion – they had developed relationships of their own with the families on the ground, and felt unsettled by the new team's arrival. Before long, though, a typically Australian common-sense attitude prevailed, agreements were struck and a sense of common purpose emerged. When I next flew into Bali a few months later, it all looked seamless. The Centrelink team were focused on the job at hand, supporting the families of the dead and injured, who sometimes struggled to manage their frustration with the perceived slowness and unpredictability of the Indonesian legal system.

As the first anniversary of the bombing loomed, I was asked to help coordinate the arrangements for the commemoration ceremony on behalf of the Australian government. I flew to Indonesia with an interagency delegation on a planning visit. We spent time in Bali with security specialists checking out the venues, before heading to Jakarta to talk to the Indonesian authorities. The situation in Indonesia remained fragile. We stayed at the Marriott Hotel in Jakarta, which was bombed the week after we left: twelve people were killed and 150 wounded.

We had to balance the imperative to hold an appropriate, dignified anniversary event with some very serious security considerations; the ceremony would be attended by leaders from both countries, and would be an attractive target for any terrorist with capability and motivation. The possibility that the families of the victims might themselves come under attack was an additional concern. It boiled down to a choice between a large indoor convention centre and the Garuda Wisnu Kencana outdoor cultural venue. When I say that the latter was located on the site of an old quarry, it will probably give the wrong impression. It is an immense, beautiful place with dramatic chalk cliff surrounds and has a traditional Balinese ambience. I came away convinced that this was where the ceremony should take place. The security types favoured the convention centre because they felt it would be easier to monitor access, but they conceded that the outdoor option was workable.

A group of us went to see the prime minister back in Canberra, and I showed him some photos of the two venues. He inquired about the families' preferences and asked a series of questions about security and wet-weather arrangements. He ruled in favour of the old quarry. He also asked, just as the meeting was breaking up, if we could invite John Williamson, the Australian country singer, to perform at the event. I have to admit that I inwardly rolled my eyes at what I thought was a corny choice.

The anniversary on Sunday, 12 October 2003 might have taken place in Bali, but it was a major Australian national event, covered live by all the television outlets back home. I was there with a large consular contingent, many of whom had been among the first responders twelve months earlier. I had also been appointed as the local emergency response coordinator if something bad happened. The prime minister, opposition leader and many other senior Australian figures were in attendance, and a broader team of government officials were there in support.

A sentiment that came through consistently in our conversations with the victims' families and friends was how sorry they felt about the impact of the bombings on the Balinese community. Many locals had been killed in the attacks, and the livelihoods of a significant number were heavily dependent on tourism. It would clearly take a long time to rebuild confidence in Bali as a tourist destination; the Australians who had lost someone were keen to find ways to show their appreciation and support. They made significant donations towards the establishment of an eye clinic in Bali, as well as to orphanages and other important local causes.

It was a hot, fine day and the anniversary event was noteworthy for the heartwarming speech by the Indonesian security minister, Susilo Bambang Yudhoyono, who the next year would become his country's president. He and John Howard formed an enduring personal connection that day. I was asked to co-host the ABC's coverage of the event, providing commentary about the family members and others involved in the ceremony. Once it was all over, I had the chance to sit back and watch as the families relaxed, chatted and sang along with John Williamson at the reception after the event. He was great.

My consular colleagues and all the other officials were in among it, enjoying a moment of lightness and relief. I was struck by how much of a connection had grown between the official carers and their clients over the previous twelve months. I will not call it a moment of closure – I don't really like the term, and I don't believe that grief can ever be 'closed'. But it was an important moment of healing for many.

CHAPTER THIRTEEN

All Right for Some

THE MAN STEPPED OUT OF the lift in central Brisbane and came to an abrupt stop. He stared at the sign on the locked door of the Australian Passport Office: *The passports office is open to the public from 8.30 am to 4.00 pm.* It was about five o'clock in the afternoon, and I was leaving a meeting with the staff who were still working inside. As I stepped into the lift, I heard the man roar an expletive and then shout, to no one in particular: 'Second time I've come and they've been closed – no wonder everyone hates public servants!' It remains a mystery to me how he came to be surprised twice by the advertised office hours, but that's not really the point. The incident has stayed with me because it typifies a common view about those who work in service of the Australian government: that public servants have well-paid and comfortable jobs, don't like to get their hands dirty, and are somehow separate from the broader community of 'real, hardworking Australians' whose taxes pay their salaries.

The truth is that Australian foreign service officers, like other public servants, are Australians like the rest of us, people who have grown up in our neighbourhoods – our country towns, suburbs and cities. They do not come into the world fully formed as 'bureaucrats'. They generally have a strong sense of personal connection with the community they serve.

Many Australians go through their lives without ever really engaging with a federal government official. For some, their first encounter is with a member of the consular service, and comes amid a personal crisis. No one in these circumstances could be expected to stop and reflect on what the situation might be like for the consul, but I do think there should be greater appreciation generally for those who have to deal with distressing situations on a daily basis. Consular officers are often required to draw heavily on their personal resilience and ingenuity to deal with extraordinary situations, and to find creative solutions to help those in anguish. Their work sometimes goes over and above expectations.

Lyall Crawford never really fitted the standard image of a public servant. It was not just his amazingly long Ned Kelly–style beard. He's also a martial arts expert, and developed his Chinese-language skills to a high level over the course of two postings in China – at the embassy in Beijing and then the consulate in Shanghai. His career also took him to all the 'interesting' locations, from Kabul to Baghdad. In 2003 he was posted to the small Australian embassy in Kathmandu, under the leadership of Ambassador Keith Gardner, who had previously served as the Director of Consular Operations in Canberra.

Keith and Lyall were put to the test when an Australian climbing team encountered tragedy in May 2003 on the Tibetan side of the border with Nepal – on the slopes of Cho Oyu, the world's sixth-highest peak. The climbers were from the elite Special Operations Group of the Victorian police – they were heroes back home, where it was said that their group's acronym actually stood for 'Sons of God'. Tragically, their leader, Paul

Carr, died of altitude sickness at 7400 metres, where he and others in the climbing party had been trapped for days amid blizzard conditions.

Carr's family and supporters would simply not accept the so-called law of the Himalayas – that if you die on the mountain, you stay on the mountain. They were determined that their hero was not going to join the hundreds of frozen bodies that litter Everest and other peaks in the region. Carr had promised his family he would return, and his three surviving friends at base camp were determined to keep that promise for him. At their request, some local Sherpa people climbed back up the mountain to retrieve Paul's body. The group were able to contact Lyall in the embassy via satellite phone. Lyall was immediately focused on finding a solution, but felt he needed to explain some of the complexities, given the inaccessible location. The climbers didn't want to hear about those. They made it very clear, in their anguish, that they expected their government to step up and help.

The Kathmandu embassy had been involved in several helicopter rescues in the past, but this one was particularly difficult. The survivors were suffering to varying degrees from the conditions, and their prospects of rescue were severely complicated by their location – at about 5600 metres altitude, in Chinese-controlled Tibet. Even if the embassy could obtain permission to cross the border, the helicopters available for charter were incapable of flying at the heights required to reach the Australian group. Only the Russian-built Mi-17 helicopters, flown by the Nepalese military could conceivably manage it. So Lyall called the chief of the Nepalese Armed Forces, who said that they would be prepared to help, but only if certain conditions were met.

The first condition was that the embassy would need to cover the costs of the operation. The second was more challenging: someone would need to obtain permission from the Chinese government for a Nepalese military helicopter to enter Chinese-Tibetan airspace. If this could be achieved, then Lyall himself would need to accompany the helicopter crew as a kind of insurance, given the unusual geopolitical arrangements. Finally, no one – not even Colonel Madan K.C., the experienced senior pilot who would fly the helicopter – had any knowledge of the terrain in that part of the mountains. So they would need maps.

The embassy team in Kathmandu, under Keith Gardner's direction, kept driving the strategy, enlisting the help of colleagues in Canberra and Beijing as required. At the local level, Lyall had established a strong relationship with the deputy Chinese ambassador in Nepal. Lyall explained to him in his fluent Chinese that the surviving Australian mountain climbers would not leave without their friend, and he feared they too would die on the mountain if a rescue was not mounted. The deputy agreed to take it up with his headquarters. The Australian embassy in Beijing was also asked to raise the matter with the Chinese Ministry of Foreign Affairs. While he was waiting for their answer, Lyall went out to buy every relevant contour map of the Himalayas he could find in Kathmandu.

The reply from Beijing, when it came, was a pleasant surprise. Foreign Minister Li Zhaoxing called his acting Australian counterpart, Mark Vaile, to convey his agreement that the operation could proceed. Lyall was told to submit visa applications as soon as possible, for himself and for the Nepali air crew. This was a major breakthrough. It was simply unprecedented for Chinese authorities to lift their strict controls on Tibetan airspace to allow access by a foreign military aircraft.

In the early hours of 19 May 2003, Lyall presented himself at the airbase to join Colonel Madan K.C. and his crew as a 'guest navigator' for the perilous rescue mission. Lyall was wearing a grey business suit, dress shoes and a tie under a black insulated jacket. He had chosen to dress formally because he thought he might need to negotiate his way through more officialdom, and in his experience people 'always take you more seriously when you wear a suit and tie'. They took off from Kathmandu and dropped off a load of air fuel cans in the foothills – Lyall recalls the aviation fuel spilling a little en route and soaking through his suit trouser leg – before flying on through the unfamiliar landscape. Because of the terrain, they were forced to climb higher than 5800 metres – the very outer limits of the helicopter's operating capacity. Another 200 metres or so higher would have resulted in 'flame-out' – when the spark in the engine's combustion chamber is extinguished because there is insufficient oxygen.

Lyall describes the search in vivid terms: 'Flying over the completely white snow plateau, we couldn't find the mountaineers initially. If you imagine a white banquet tablecloth with just one shake from a pepper shaker on it, that's what the mountaineers looked like when we spotted them.'

The helicopter landed, but the team soon realised that there had been a miscommunication about the body they were to retrieve. The climbers had left Paul on the other side of a glacier when they'd relocated to the flattish rendezvous area. They expected that the helicopter could simply stop by and collect it. But it was too close to the towering cliffs, and despite Colonel Madan K.C.'s heroic efforts to fly over to the spot on his own, he could not reach it. So, to the deep dismay of the climbers, they were forced to set off back to Kathmandu without Paul's body. They felt they had failed to keep their promise to the dead man's family and friends, and were absolutely despondent. Lyall rang the helpful deputy ambassador at the Chinese embassy on return to thank him for his assistance in saving three Australian lives.

The deputy said: 'You didn't bring the body back? Didn't I give you a visa for two days? You can return tomorrow!'

So Lyall and the crew set off again at dawn the following morning. This time they were successful, and the team made it back to Kathmandu by about 9 am. Lyall made the necessary arrangements for the body and was driven back to the embassy compound where he lived.

As it happened, his arrival was observed by two Australian journalists waiting near the embassy entrance to talk to Ambassador Gardner about the operation. They could see Lyall was a staff member, and that he was arriving at his place of work well after opening hours. One of them looked at his watch and said, a little too loudly, 'It's all right for some, isn't it?' Lyall had a moment of quiet satisfaction a little later when the journalists asked the ambassador if they could meet the official who had performed these remarkable feats.

In 2021, an interviewer put it to then DFAT secretary Frances Adamson that Australian foreign service officers are 'people who are willing to get things done'. She agreed, but added: 'That's not necessarily because we are diplomats, it probably has to do with the fact that we are Australian.' I do think that this core Australian attribute – a focus on practical outcomes – is key to Australia's strong record in responding to crises, both at home and abroad. My own experience working for both Australian and other organisations, including in the United States, certainly bears this out. Australia's response to overseas disasters is helped by the 'Goldilocks size' of our government – it is small enough for those who work in the international security field to know each other well, and big enough that substantial capabilities can be brought to bear when required.

Former and experienced consular officers like to talk about the lighter, more inspirational moments, but they all carry dark memories too. There have been many difficult and dangerous situations where members of the service have shown amazing fortitude. David Chaplin's experience in those first chaotic hours at the Bali International Medical Centre comes to mind. David suddenly found himself in a situation that no one should be in, and showed phenomenal, quiet strength. There are those who helped build and maintain makeshift morgues in Bali and after the Asian tsunami, or who have otherwise supported anguished parents and siblings through the identification processes that must follow violent death – after terrorist attacks, road accidents or air crashes. One longstanding consul remembers being grateful for the tip she received before her first confronting experience with mass casualties: do not adopt the 'old trick' of trying to mask the smell of the dead with perfume or another substance like Vicks, as whatever scent you use will forever after bring death to mind.

Our officials have themselves been the targets of violence. The bombing attack on the Australian embassy in Jakarta in September 2004 was an unambiguous message of intent from the South-East Asian branch of the jihadist movement. Ambassador David Ritchie, Ric Smith's successor in Jakarta, had a very narrow escape – he was working at his desk when his office windows shattered and a large piece of steel security fencing flew past his head. The car bomb killed nine people, including the suicide bomber, and injured many more. The victims were all Indonesian – an embassy security guard, policemen, a gardener and several passers-by. In an air crash at Yogyakarta airport in 2007, two members of the Jakarta embassy team, Elizabeth 'Liz' O'Neill and Allison Sudrajat, were tragically killed along with nineteen other passengers. So, too, were AFP officers Brice Steele and Mark Scott, and Australian journalist Morgan Mellish. There have been many other cases of Australian foreign service officers receiving threats or being attacked. Some of the Australians in jail overseas are deeply suspicious of consular officers, refusing to accept that they are not somehow part of an official conspiracy aimed at keeping them behind bars. Several of our consuls have received death threats from prisoners or their families.

The Australian government gives priority to the safety and welfare of its staff and their families, but is also scrupulous about ensuring that any information shared with them about the local security situation in any given country is also shared, simultaneously, with the broader public. Similarly, any evacuation of staff or dependants from a place of potential danger is taken in strict parallel with advice to the broader Australian community that they do the same. In my time running the consular service, this approach was often described informally as the 'Lockerbie principle' – so named because of a myth that the US embassy in London had issued a warning to American officials, but not the general public, to avoid the ill-fated Pan Am flight that was destroyed by terrorists over the Scottish lowland town of Lockerbie in 1988. I don't believe there is any truth to the story, but I recall the underlying idea being a guiding principle for us in 2001, when we encouraged all Australians to leave India and Pakistan as concerns grew that the two countries were building up to a potential nuclear conflict. We knew then that it was important that our responsibilities to our 'own' people not be allowed to get ahead of our broader responsibilities.

Like police and ambulance officers, consular officials need to be on guard against the physical and mental health consequences of their exposure to natural or human-caused disasters. They might not be experiencing trauma directly, but they are experiencing others experiencing it. Experts agree that workers are at risk if they are exposed to death, grief, injury, pain or loss – as well as personal safety issues, long hours of work, frequent shifts, poor sleep and other negative experiences. It's well accepted these days, including by DFAT, that an organisation carries a significant responsibility to provide access to counselling and other professional support in circumstances where employees are at high risk of experiencing traumatic events. There has been a small team of professional counsellors employed by DFAT since the late 1990s, with Colin Rigby as its leader throughout the establishment phase.

We worked deliberately to ensure that their guidance was integrated into the consular training courses we delivered at home and overseas. Counsellors are regularly deployed during crises to attend to staff welfare and advise on the management of distressed clients. They continue to visit overseas posts on a regular basis, and can be deployed swiftly when an embassy community experiences serious stress.

It's clear to me now that in the early 2000s the department still had a way to go in appreciating the importance of counselling support. Desley Hargreaves, the Centrelink social worker, reflects that one of her initial impressions of DFAT when she first came to work with us was that there was a cultural resistance to admitting the need for help. This resonates with my own observation of how DFAT heads of mission often responded in the early phase of a consular conflict to offers of assistance, particularly staffing resources. 'Thanks, but we've got this,' was the common refrain, until the reality of what lay ahead began to sink in. I think I know the underlying issue, because I have felt it myself. There's an internal voice that says: 'This is the moment I have been preparing for, and this is the job I have been given – now I need to show that I am up to it.' Former colleagues like Lyndall Sachs and Tracey Wunder, each still with the service, tell me that attitudes within DFAT today have evolved substantially since then, and that professional counselling now has a more established role. But both say that they find this kind of support far more useful once a crisis is over. Tracey says that in order to be effective during the crisis itself, she needs to 'put up a mental wall and set my own feelings aside so that I can concentrate fully on the challenge ahead'. Lyndall agrees that taking time out to talk to someone about her own feelings mid-crisis would put that mindset at risk: 'You almost have to become an automaton to do what you need to do.'

It's sometimes claimed that the Australian public is getting 'less than it deserves' from its consular service. Some in the media jump to this kind of assertion when they witness the grief of those whose loves ones have been caught in a mass casualty event or are stranded overseas, and who just want their government to 'do something about it'. I know that consular officers take pride in supporting their fellow Australians under the great 'contract' between the Australian public and their government. They try, and mostly succeed, to deliver against reasonable community expectations. As I see it, in fact, too many members of the travelling public have failed to fulfil their own side of the contract. Prior to the Covid-19 pandemic, about one-third of Australian travellers were ignoring official warnings to take out travel insurance, imposing avoidable costs on the taxpayer and making their own lives immeasurably more difficult when things went wrong. And public expectations of the service are sometimes far from reasonable, including in 'normal' periods of travel, when people look to the consular service to cover their routine medical expenses, locate their lost luggage, arrange their work permits or book their sightseeing tours. It can also be taken for granted that the consular service will step in to help when Australians have put themselves in harm's way and things take a turn for the worse. In more recent times, consular officials across the network have had to absorb the anger of those stranded overseas by the Covid-19 pandemic when abrupt decisions were made about border restrictions by politicians at home. In many cases the anger is understandable, but very few members of the public would have stopped to think that the Covid-19 pandemic had also imposed extended separations on these DFAT staff and their families, or that our consuls were themselves facing personal hazards in continuing to work with the public in high-risk locations overseas.

Even in 'normal' times, there are some realities about life in the foreign service that don't fit with the lazy cliché of cocktail-sipping diplomats enjoying life in splendid locations abroad. First of all, it's not all Paris, London and New York. Positions also have to be filled in places like Lagos, Kabul, Baghdad, Moscow and Port Moresby. There's actually a group of DFAT officers who are drawn to these 'hardship' postings because of the nature of the work on offer, or because life in these kinds of places can be enriching in its own way. But it's not what comes to mind for many members of the public. There can be serious drawbacks, too, from a family perspective. Like the partners of many other DFAT officers, my wife, Roxanne, found herself having to 'reinvent' herself every time we arrived on a new posting. As the DFAT officer, I had ready access to a familiar, English-speaking office environment when I arrived, and my colleagues at the mission provided an instant social network. The partner at home does not have these same advantages. Families also have to think carefully about the consequences of disrupting their children's education, especially during the secondary school years. There are also many positives to the experience, and representing your country overseas really is a privilege. But it's not what many think.

It is rare for members of the consular service to receive national acknowledgement for their efforts, although I'm pleased to say that the Bali response was an exception. Many of DFAT's consular staff – in Canberra, Jakarta and Bali – were recognised for their exceptional work with awards in the Order of Australia, along with other government officials and volunteers who had stepped forward to help. We were all delighted to watch as Ross Tysoe and David Chaplin accepted their awards from Governor-General Michael Jeffery at the Government House ceremony in November 2003. These two consular officers had been the first on the scene, and had remained heavily engaged in the crisis response over the long, difficult months that followed.

It was good to see this kind of positive spotlight shone on the consular service, at least for a moment. But none of these consular officials were seeking attention from the public, and they certainly didn't want pity. They were motivated by a range of factors – compassion, satisfaction in helping others, a sense of adventure, camaraderie and a strong commitment to public service. For them, the people who mattered were the consular clients, particularly the many innocent people who find themselves in truly difficult or tragic circumstances every day.

Personally, I think it was a pity that when Paul Carr's remains were returned to his widow in Melbourne amid a blaze of media reporting, Lyall's role in the rescue didn't feature more prominently in the public narrative. There was little media coverage of the resourcefulness he showed, or of his preparedness to put his own safety at risk. I also can't help thinking about how his own family would have felt if things had gone horribly wrong.

But those things were far from Lyall's mind. He says there was a moment, when he was sitting on the Tibetan ice shelf high above the world, that he asked himself: *How lucky are you to be doing this?*

CHAPTER FOURTEEN

Moving On

BY 2004, MY FAMILY AND I felt that we were ready for another overseas posting. I'd found the chief consular position immensely fulfilling, but I had done the work for five years – longer than any of my predecessors – and did not want to burn out. This was a real risk in the consular role. I was eligible by then to apply for a senior ambassadorial position overseas, which was the natural next step in a DFAT career. But in October that year the department let me know, in its own unique way, that this would have to wait a little longer. The deputy secretary responsible for personnel called one Sunday and said, deadpan, 'I'm just ringing to check there's no obstacle to you starting as head of the prime minister's international division on 6 December?'

And so, after a brief handover and a couple of long lunches, I went on secondment to the Department of the Prime Minister and Cabinet, where my job involved supporting the head of government in all international engagements. The department ensured continuity in the consular field by again appointing Rod Smith to be my replacement – this time as head of the broader division.

My time leading the consular service from headquarters had been marked by an unusual series of crises, and in their farewell remarks, several of my DFAT colleagues put it to me that I might have been the jinx. When the Indian Ocean tsunami took place three weeks after I left the job, I had proof that it hadn't all been my fault.

Within a month of starting in my new role, I found myself standing in the rear of a C-130 Hercules military aircraft alongside Angus Houston, then the chief of the Royal Australian Air Force. (He was to be appointed as chief of the ADF five months later.) We stared wordlessly out through the windows at the western coastline of Sumatra, and the enormous brown smudge that extended along the shore, reaching several hundred metres inland. Dotted along the coast within the dirty margin lay the exposed foundations of what had, until recently, been towns and small cities. It had been a few weeks since the 'Boxing Day tsunami' had wreaked havoc across the region, and the Australian government had put everything it had into supporting its neighbours and assisting its own citizens. But it was only then, as I looked down at the scene of destruction, that I began to understand how 230,000 people could just disappear.

We'd just accompanied Prime Minister Howard on a visit to Banda Aceh, a regional centre in the north of the Indonesian island of Sumatra that had borne the brunt of the tidal wave. Howard had been invited by his still-new Indonesian counterpart, Susilo Bambang Yudhoyono, to assess the damage for himself. It had been a long day in desolate surroundings. Very few of Banda Aceh's buildings had survived, there was mud everywhere and a heavy stench hung in the air. Australian troops were on the ground alongside their Indonesian counterparts, providing engineering and other practical support. The contrast with our last stop had made it all the more surreal – I'd flown in from

Switzerland, where the PM had been attending the annual World Economic Forum at the exclusive ski resort of Davos, surrounded by Hollywood stars like Angelina Jolie and Sharon Stone, as well as U2's Bono. When we touched down in Sumatra, I felt that we were back where our work really mattered.

While I was enjoying my new job, I was struggling a little with the fact that I was not personally leading the consular response to the tsunami. I was still climbing down from the constant adrenaline rush associated with crisis leadership. Back at DFAT, the service did a superb job with Rod Smith running the operation. At headquarters, about 300 staff, half of whom voluntarily returned from their Christmas leave, worked around the clock for days, coordinating with teams on the ground to confirm the safety of Australians and identify the missing, and to keep families informed. The hotline we had established and strengthened over the preceding years took more than 85,000 calls, with over 15,000 Australians reported as unaccounted for. In the end, twenty-six Australians were killed, but the surge of anxiety at home suggested for some time that it might be much more than that – just as it had in the aftermath of September 11. The Australian missions in Sri Lanka, Indonesia, Thailand, Malaysia and India worked to identify and repatriate survivors, supporting yet another horrendous disaster victim identification process. The Australian government established temporary offices in the hard-hit Thai resort centres of Phuket and Krabi, and in the Maldives – all places where Australian tourists had been spending their Christmas breaks.

When the news of the tsunami came through, veteran diplomat Bill Paterson and his family were preparing to move to Bangkok, where Bill was to take up the position as Australia's ambassador to Thailand within a few weeks. We had attended a farewell at his home only a few weeks beforehand. Bill received new instructions on Boxing Day that his new job was starting with immediate effect. With forty others – consular staff, federal police and Centrelink counsellors – Bill arrived in Phuket on 29 December, where the team began working to evacuate injured Australians, and faced the anger of families desperate to get the bodies of their relatives released. He readily acknowledged to a journalist that he had been 'yelled at' by some family members. 'People are in a high state of emotion,' he said. 'You have to accept that. It's been a big learning experience for me.'

One of the most important legacies from the very early 2000s was the experience that our people had gained through what had been an extraordinary, sustained crisis period. The department had come to recognise the invaluable capabilities that a core cadre of consular leaders had developed, and when new crises came rolling in, key individuals were plucked from their day jobs and deployed to the scene to help guide the emergency response and pass on their knowledge and expertise to the next generation. Together, they continued to play an instrumental role in driving the consular service forward.

DFAT drew heavily on this group in responding to the Indian Ocean tsunami. Tracey Wunder, who'd been awarded the Public Service Medal for her support to the Bali victims' families, had actually been posted to the High Commission in Port Moresby by late 2004, but she was in Brisbane on a short Christmas break when the tsunami struck. She took a call summoning her immediately to Canberra, and for the following six weeks she reprised the role she had played in the wake of the Bali bombings, leading the case officers who supported the families through the victim identification process. Lyndall Sachs was once more on deck to manage the voracious media. She was actually about to set off for India from Sydney airport on a holiday when the tsunami hit, but cancelled her flights as soon as she heard the news.

The tsunami response was dark and difficult work for all concerned, including Australia's consular officials. So many other nations lost people in the disaster, particularly regional countries from Indonesia to Somalia. Rod Smith does remember one bright spot from this sustained period of grim news, when contact was finally made with a lone surfer on the island of Nias, off Sumatra's west coast. The man had been without an internet connection for days, and had actually been out on the water at the time of the tsunami. He was apparently oblivious to what had happened; the tidal wave had not been evident from his location on the open water. He was reported to have remarked that the surf had been particularly good that day.

Many of the Australian police officers, soldiers, diplomats, social workers, medical personnel and consular officials involved in the Indian Ocean tsunami operation knew each other well from the Bali response. Another of the great legacies of the 'Bali era' was a better 'whole-of-government' approach to emergency situations overseas – a collective recognition that the major crises of the modern era had broader dimensions than those of the past, and required a more integrated approach. One of the best symbols of this was the Emergency Response Team arrangement that was established in the wake of the bombings. The ERTs provided a framework to bring together representatives from each of the key agencies, ready for deployment in response to a crisis overseas. The relationships established between people representing these agencies had their own practical value, which could not be underestimated when a real crisis came along.

The Australian government's response to the tsunami built on the collective experience of the officials involved, and the lessons they'd learned from the major crises they'd grappled with in recent years. Not all countries had these 'advantages'. Sweden was the country outside Asia that lost most citizens to the tsunami – 543 Swedish holiday-makers were killed and a further 1500 injured. In the aftermath of the catastrophe many survivors and victims' families accused the Swedish government of reacting far too slowly and engaging very poorly with affected families. Foreign Minister Laila Freivalds came under great pressure for her personal handling of the situation, and was threatened with a vote of no-confidence. Twelve months after the tsunami, an independent commission slammed the government for having no crisis management mechanism in place at the foreign ministry and for allowing unacceptable delays in the provision of medical support. Sweden had never experienced anything like this before, and it showed.

In those first couple of years after the Bali bombing, some substantial steps were also taken to upgrade further the department's consular capability. The decision was taken during Rod Smith's time at the helm to form a new division at headquarters comprising two consular branches – one dealing with operations, the other with policy and public information. Rod remained head of the restructured division. DFAT won a little more money in the budget to build a substantial new crisis management centre, replacing what we had thought of in the earlier 2000s as a significant improvement on what we'd had before. The Smartraveller information service was strengthened further, and a new advertising campaign launched.

Meanwhile, Foreign Minister Downer did what he could to push back on rising traveller expectations – which, as he noted in a speech to the National Press Club in November 2005, partly resulted from his department's strong performance. 'In a way we have become a victim of our own success,' he said. 'With people now more aware of our efforts … they expect us to perform miracles. At times it seems people believe we are like the Thunderbirds … with teams of Australian heroes ready to take off in rocketships to pluck Australians to safety from any situation, any place on the planet, anytime.' As Downer emphasised, he had personally put great priority on consular work since being appointed minister, but the travelling public also had a responsibility to keep themselves informed and not subject themselves to unnecessary risk.

Terrorism continued to cast its shadow on the international stage, and Australians were still being impacted. I accompanied the prime minister on an official visit to London a few weeks after the 7 July 2005 suicide bombing attacks on the London transport system, which killed fifty-two people, including an Australian, and injured more than 700. Howard visited Australian survivors in hospital on the morning of our arrival, and we happened to be having lunch with Prime Minister Tony Blair at 10 Downing Street when Blair received the news that Islamic extremists had attempted a second series of attacks.

We had a great opportunity to watch the British head of government and key ministers move quickly to set up the 'COBRA' cross-departmental national emergency arrangements – so named because the meetings generally took place in Cabinet Office Briefing Room A. I'd heard all about their crisis arrangements through my engagement as consular head with my British counterpart, James Watt. Their procedures differed slightly from ours in their detail, but things generally looked very familiar. It was also interesting to watch Blair in action. He handled the situation with calm and polite resolve. The joint press conference between the two prime ministers that afternoon was entirely focused on the latest attacks, and the two countries' common goal of combating terrorism in all its forms.

A few months later, I had to let John Howard know that, sickeningly, there had been a second series of bombings against tourist targets in Bali. Four Australians were among the twenty victims who lost their lives on that occasion.

I welcomed the opportunity to engage at the strategic level on the global issues of the time – including global jihadism, which had dominated my work as consular head. I was witness, as a participant in conversations in the Oval Office and elsewhere, to the common resolve between John Howard and George W. Bush to counter this phenomenon. The issues that had suddenly come to demand their attention back in September 2001 were still front and centre. The United States and its allies were struggling to stabilise Afghanistan and Iraq following the fateful decisions to invade these two countries. We visited the Australian military contingent in Afghanistan's Oruzgan province that year – it's hard to forget the precautionary evasive action taken by the C-130 Hercules pilot as we landed – and flew on to meet with President Hamid Karzai in Kabul.

I had to stay on top of the higher-profile and more challenging consular cases in my new role, as they sometimes required the active involvement of the prime minister. Despite all the warnings, Australians continued to be arrested on drug-smuggling charges around the word – including in South-East Asia, where the penalties could be very severe. I was with John Howard in Singapore in 2005, when he argued strongly with Prime Minister Lee Hsien Loong to spare the life of Nguyen Tuong-van, a twenty-five-year-old Australian who had received the mandatory death sentence after being arrested in 2002 for trafficking heroin. It was to no avail – we were unsurprised, but gutted, when the young man was executed in December that year.

We were horrified to hear the news, in April 2005, that nine young Australians had been arrested at the airport in Bali on heroin-trafficking charges. The 'Bali Nine' arrests attracted widespread news coverage from the very start – in Australia, Indonesia and across the world. This was amplified by the fact that they occurred as the long-running Schapelle Corby saga was coming to a head amid frenzied reporting of the final stages of her trial. Brent Hall, Ross Tysoe's successor, would be the first in a long line of consul-generals to manage these challenging cases, each of which might lead to the death penalty being imposed by the Indonesian authorities. The group came to trial a couple of months after their arrests, and the consulate in Bali again needed reinforcement given the demands associated with the court cases and the influx of family and media.

Rowland Pocock, who had been a key member of the Canberra consular operations team in my time running the branch, was then on posting in Jakarta and was sent to Bali the day after the arrests. He remembers how frightening and aggressive the media could be – there were moments when he was in fear for the safety of the families in his care. One of the several others sent to help out was Kerin Burns, whom I had first met in Beirut, and who by that time had married and changed her surname to Ayyalaraju. Kerin visited the prisoners in Kerobokan prison and attended every court hearing for three months. They both came away from the experience struck by the tragedy of it all. Kerin admits that, before meeting them, she felt intimidated by the image projected of the Bali Nine through the media, but came to the view that they were just kids who had almost no experience of the world. In some ways it was their families who were having the roughest time. 'Their parents were good people,' Kerin says. 'I stood with them watching their kids being led in handcuffs to and from court hearings, holding cells and police vans, through media scrums, not able to help them, or reach out to hug them.'

These judicial proceedings would draw in successive Australian governments, cast a long shadow over the relationship between Canberra and Jakarta, and lead to the worst possible outcome for two of the Australians involved.

Expectations of how Australian ambassadors should engage in consular work had changed markedly during my time at the consular helm, and any lofty disdain that some might have had about consular work had fallen away. In the early 2000s, with strong support from Ashton Calvert and the rest of the DFAT leadership, we'd begun emphasising to newly appointed diplomatic heads of mission that they should move quickly, if a consular emergency occurred on their patch, to assume visible, personal leadership of the response.

I had an opportunity to put theory into practice when I was appointed as Australia's ambassador to Germany in April 2006. I'd expressed interest in the role the previous year when I realised it would soon become vacant. It had now been almost eight years since our last overseas posting, and I was keen to take up the responsibilities of Australia's envoy to Europe's largest economy. My German-language skills were still in reasonable shape after my Vienna posting years earlier, and I felt more than ready for my first ambassadorial role. Importantly, my family was up for it. Roxanne was supportive as always, fourteen-year-old Eloise was ready for adventure, and while Annabelle was already at university in Brisbane, she was looking forward to visiting us in Europe. So we were all pleased when Prime Minister Howard signed off on Foreign Minister Downer's recommendation that I be appointed to the position.

My 'day job' in Berlin ranged from global economic collaboration in the wake of the 2008 global financial crisis to engaging the Germans in our shared peacekeeping objectives in Afghanistan. I was also accredited as Ambassador to Switzerland and to the tiny principality of Liechtenstein, as Australia has no resident representation in these countries' capitals. The political, trade and investment work involved with these accreditations was wide-ranging, but it was natural for me to drop all that and show up in support of my fellow Australians when things went badly wrong.

While I was thankfully spared a major terrorist incident, natural disaster or high-profile arrest in Berlin, we had our share of consular challenges. It felt important to be experiencing consular work from the 'other side' – from the perspective of an overseas mission.

In our first year in Germany, Roxanne and I supported families and friends at the first anniversary commemoration of the tragic death of Australian Olympic cyclist and rower Amy Gillett, killed when a young German driver ploughed into the Australian women's cycling squad during a training ride in the eastern state of Thuringia. Amy's husband, Simon, later joined the Australian Cycling Foundation in establishing the Amy Gillett Foundation, to support the rehabilitation of other injured team members, provide a scholarship program for young female cyclists, and promote road safety awareness among cyclists and motorists.

Our time in Germany wasn't all dark and difficult, though, and there were reminders along the way that our fellow Australians are overwhelmingly decent, independent and respectful travellers. A peak consular moment for us was the 2006 FIFA World Cup, held in cities and towns across Germany in what was a joyous summer for the country. Up to 60,000 Australians travelled to Germany. They came to soak up the atmosphere, and many watched the football on massive screens erected in the heart of German towns and cities. At the embassy, we had elaborate plans in place for every imaginable contingency, including terrorist attacks, and we expected to have to deal with a large number of arrests for drunken behaviour at the very least. We were very pleased to be wrong. The Australian fans caused very little trouble, and actually became very popular in the towns they 'occupied'.

Roxanne and I were delighted to attend each of the Socceroos' World Cup matches. It was the very least we could do. I did wonder, when the Australian team was bundled out of the competition in Kaiserslautern, after Italy won a questionable penalty right in front of the goal mouth, whether there would be any bad blood that night. Within minutes of the final whistle, Roxanne and I and our official party had been dropped off at the edge of the centre of Kaiserslautern's old town and were scrumming our way through a dense crowd of Australian and Italian fans. We were accompanying the visiting Australian sports minister, Rod Kemp, and his wife, Danielle, to a restaurant, and Roxanne, worried that she would lose the petite Danielle in the crowd, was holding tightly onto her hand. A big, slightly drunk Aussie lad noticed the look of grim concentration on Roxanne's face as she wove through the intensely packed crowd with the minister's wife. He frowned for a moment, and then called out cheerily: 'Smile – we done good!' He was right. We had done good – every single one of us.

As it turned out, one of our more significant consular preoccupations during my time in Berlin was an event that took place thousands of kilometres from Germany. It had become a matter of established principle by 2006 that Australia's entire diplomatic system should consider itself at the disposal of a major consular emergency response. It was understood that personnel in Canberra or at other missions not directly in the firing line should immediately swing in behind the crisis response if needed. The large-scale evacuation of Australians from Lebanon, which began in 2006, was a case in point. It required staffing support and coordination from many other points in the network – including, as it turned out, from Berlin. It was also a major moment in Australian consular history.

Attacks on Israeli territory and the abduction of Israeli soldiers by the Lebanese-based Hezbollah movement in July that year met with swift retaliation in the form of Israeli missile and air attacks, and the situation quickly escalated. Israel's formidable firepower rained down on southern Lebanon and Beirut. The Australian government was quickly besieged by calls for help from citizens desperate to flee the conflict following the destruction of the country's international airport. There were around 25,000 to 30,000 Australian citizens in Lebanon at any given time. Consular officials were joined by colleagues from the ADF and the Australian police for a mammoth evacuation operation. The first step for most was a rough voyage to Cyprus, about 260 kilometres across the water, or to Mersin on the southern Turkish coastline. Australian officials in Cyprus arranged reception, accommodation and onward travel to Australia on specially chartered flights.

The backbone of the consular response was formed by the 'repeat offenders' of the consular world. Our ambassador in Lebanon in 2006 was none other than Lyndall Sachs, who had worked so closely with the consular crew to manage the Australian media through the September 11, Bali bombing and tsunami responses. Lyndall was little more than three months into her first ambassadorial posting when the Lebanon crisis began to unfold. She and her colleagues at the small embassy struggled to sleep at night as bombs exploded around town. There was a moment when Lyndall and the team were working to get a large group of Australians onto a bus heading for the relative safety of Syria. She struggled to keep her patience in the middle of all this when someone from Canberra called her mobile phone to remind her that all the passengers should sign waiver releases. At one point, the phone conversation was punctuated by a 2000-kilogram bomb going off not far away.

Rod Smith recalls that one of the most challenging aspects of the Lebanon evacuation was locating ships. Australia was not in the same position as many European governments, which could call on naval assets already positioned in the Mediterranean. Australian officials had to find shipping agents they could rely on, and with their help find shipping vessels that were seaworthy, safe and fit for purpose. As Rod says, 'We couldn't risk a ferry full of refugees going down at sea.' The competition for vessels was intense and there was one moment when the Australians were 'gazumped' by another government that had made the shipping agent a better offer.

Bill Jackson, who had led the operations team in Canberra through the Bali ordeal, was despatched to Cyprus to lead the consular effort there. Many of the evacuees who were flooding into Cyprus from Lebanon had been under fire, and some exhibited signs of emotional dislocation. Others were keen to explain to the officials arranging their onward flights from Cyprus that they only flew business class. Organising this crowd of people, attending to their accommodation and other needs, and prioritising them for onward flights was an enormous logistical exercise. There was a moment Bill felt so crushed by the challenge that he locked himself in a toilet cubicle and wept. In his own words, he 'sucked it up' after a few minutes and returned to work. He mentioned this experience later to the DFAT counsellor responsible for supporting consular and other staff, who had actually been in Cyprus at the time. She asked him why he had not spoken to her then – that was, after all, why she'd been there! Bill's response was: 'Because I'm an Australian male of a certain age, that's why.' Bill was relieved when another former colleague from a consular branch, Jeff Roach, appeared one day in the door of his office, having flown in from Paris, where he was then posted. Jeff was soon applying himself to the task of allocating people to flights. Desley Hargreaves and her Centrelink social workers were also soon in Cyprus, dealing with evacuees in need and alleviating the burden on the consular team. The comfort these people had with each other made a challenging situation more manageable.

Things were also hectic at the Canberra end. The media was constantly baying for more information, family members and representatives of the Australian Lebanese community were constantly on the phones, and their local members of parliament were also keen to get involved. The logistics involved in coordinating a large number of Australian officials deployed across a wide region were complex, to say the least. The Australian ambassador in Tel Aviv, Tim George, was well plugged in and able to provide very useful information on what the Israeli military was likely to do next, or when there would be lulls in the bombardment. These represented brief opportunities for ships full of evacuees to leave port safely. Rod recalls that an Arabic-speaking DFAT officer was immensely resourceful in fielding calls from people in the conflict zone. Over time he found that she was even phoning local taxi firms in Lebanon to coordinate the transport of Australians from their homes to the ferry assembly points.

DFAT officers were redeployed from across the network to support the evacuation effort. A consular officer named Peter Nagy was sent from the Australian embassy in Budapest to help coordinate the seaborne evacuation of Australian citizens from Beirut to the Turkish port of Mersin. He crossed the Mediterranean Sea twice as part of this operation, helping bring hundreds to safety. He wrote later in an internal staff bulletin that to describe the voyage as an awful experience was an understatement – it was hard enough to keep his balance, but he did what he could to hand out sick bags, reassure others and appear confident. 'There is a feeling of absolute despair and helplessness which I hope few people experience in the course of their consular work. A feeling that makes you want to lock yourself in the bathroom and just cry. But I couldn't do that – there were people who looked up to us as points of stability and hope, voices of authority. Besides, by then the bathrooms were in an unmentionable state.'

It wasn't long before our mission in Berlin was asked to swing in to support the evacuation. My deputy, Daniel Sloper, was deployed to Beirut to support Lyndall in running the logistics for the ever-growing operation there. My staff and I worked with the German government, which had very strong links in Tel Aviv and was coordinating its own mass evacuation. Then, a couple of weeks into the operation, we received the news that Qantas would be using Frankfurt, in western Germany, as an evacuation hub. Several hundred Australian evacuees would be flown to Frankfurt from Cyprus, where they would need to be accommodated and otherwise supported for several days, pending the availability of aircraft to take them on to Australia. The consular team from my embassy in Berlin relocated to Frankfurt, where they hired out one of the airport hotels, and I travelled down there myself to greet the evacuees when they arrived. There was an exhausted cheer when I used the intercom on the Qantas Boeing 747 to welcome them all to Germany.

I was back in Frankfurt when they all flew out to Australia on another chartered flight five days later. By that stage my staff and I were every bit as keen to see them on their way as they were to get home. There were a few of us from the embassy at the airport terminal to see them onto the plane. I was on the phone to one of my young colleagues, Alison Carrington, who was at the other end of the building shortly before take-off, when I saw a group of three young Australians heading in the wrong direction – away from the departure gate. I ended the call with Alison and asked them where they were going. They said that they had forgotten to let their families know when to collect them from the airport, and were looking for a phone. I handed over my mobile and told them to be quick. It was well after midnight in Australia. They made their calls, thanked me and handed back my phone, and I moved on. I then noticed that we needed an extra couple of wheelchairs for some elderly evacuees at that end of the building, so I hit the green redial button on my phone to ring Alison – the last number I had called. I said to the female voice that answered, 'Look, we need three wheelchairs at this end of the terminal – can you arrange pronto, please?' It took me more than a few seconds to work out that I was talking to someone's startled mum in the middle of the night in Sydney. She seemed, from her confused responses, to be trying to work out how best she could help. You've got to love an Australian mum.

The Lebanon evacuation eventually concluded, and over the following years the embassy in Berlin continued to respond professionally to the deaths, hospitalisations, welfare cases and occasional arrests that make up the daily consular agenda. We provided support to Australians who were flown in with serious injuries from Afghanistan and Iraq to the Landstuhl Regional Medical Center, an overseas military hospital operated by the US Army in the south of the country. This was the nearest treatment centre for those serving with the international coalition forces in the Middle East. During my time as ambassador, an Australian civilian contractor died at Landstuhl in August 2006, and an Australian soldier was hospitalised there for an extended period after sustaining serious injuries from a roadside bomb that killed one of his Australian mates. My defence adviser, an army colonel, visited regularly to check on his welfare.

I was regularly reminded that Australians abroad don't always 'live down' to the poor standards of behaviour that are sometimes imagined. I decided that it was an important part of my duties to call on the police chief in Munich in the wake of the Oktoberfest festival – to express my appreciation for the work of his force and to apologise for any difficulties my compatriots might have caused. The police chief welcomed me and thanked me warmly for the bottle of good Australian red that I gave him. He was at pains to assure me that the Australians were not his biggest problem during Oktoberfest. 'Yes, Mr Ambassador,' he said, 'your people drink too much, but they are happy drunks who spend their money in our town, and they really don't cause us too much trouble.'

I visited Munich each October for the rest of my posting, just in case.

CHAPTER FIFTEEN

Homecoming

We watched from our home in Berlin as Kevin Rudd and the Australian Labor Party were swept to victory in the November 2007 federal election. Like many other DFAT colleagues of my generation, I was already acquainted with the new prime minister. He'd been a mid-level DFAT officer himself when I joined the department in 1988, but had returned home to Queensland at the end of that year to lay the foundations for his political career. His election win was a significant political watershed for Australia after John Howard's eleven years in power. But there would largely be continuity between the Liberal and Labor governments on global security issues, and no fundamental change when it came to the consular field. Over the following six years, under both prime ministers Kevin Rudd and Julia Gillard, the government continued to prioritise support for Australians overseas, while struggling with the challenge of rising traveller expectations. Meanwhile, the difficult cases and crises kept on coming, requiring the country's new political leaders to engage intensively with the consular service as it responded to each new challenge.

The global financial crisis began to unfold soon after Rudd was elected, and the Australian prime minister was keen to engage Germany, then the world's third-largest economy, on the international response. I was in almost constant contact with Chancellor Angela Merkel's economic advisers at the direct request of the prime minister's office, and arranged several telephone conversations between the two leaders on how best to use the framework of the G20 – the international forum that brings together the world's largest economies, including Australia – to avert a global depression. But I did not catch up with Kevin Rudd in person until he visited Berlin in July 2009, when my term as ambassador was drawing to an end. It was a state visit with all the formalities, including a ceremonial welcome at the military airport. At one point on the drive into town from the airport, Rudd asked me what I wanted to do next.

I knew that the position I considered to be the best in the Australian diplomatic service would soon fall vacant: Australian High Commissioner to Papua New Guinea. I told Rudd that I wanted the role, and took him through my reasons. I was keen to get back to the Indo-Pacific region, where Australian foreign policy matters most. As I've mentioned, I had spent my childhood in PNG, where my parents were among the generation of Australians who helped prepare the country for independence, but that was not why I wanted the job. The country is Australia's closest neighbour – its southern coastline lies less than four kilometres from the nearest Queensland islands in the Torres Strait. PNG struggles with a range of serious development challenges, and Australia is closely engaged in efforts to improve health, education and governance outcomes across the country. The Australian High Commissioner there has oversight of extensive bilateral political links, a substantial defence cooperation relationship and an aid program worth more than half a billion dollars. Australian diplomats who build relationships and trust can play an influential role in the country. I wanted to be at the leading edge of Australian foreign policy, and that was in PNG.

What neither Rudd nor I knew was that a consular tragedy was about to unfold in PNG that would in the future require my personal involvement. On 11 August 2009, an Airlines PNG Twin Otter aircraft crashed into the side of a mountain bordering the Kokoda Valley in southern Papua New Guinea. There were thirteen people on board, and nine of them were Australian – a group of eight visitors and a tour guide, on their way to walk the famous Kokoda Track, following in the footsteps of the Australian soldiers who'd fought back the Japanese in 1942. The walk can take up to ten days, and traverses some of the most majestic country on the planet. At that time, the number of people walking the track each year had risen to about 5000. They walked to pay tribute to the fallen, as a rite of passage or as a test of fitness. The numbers subsided after the air crash, but steadied for several years afterwards at an annual rate of around 3000 each year.

Air accident investigators later established that the plane deviated from its flight path because cloud cover obscured visibility, causing the flight crew to misjudge their proximity to the ground. The aircraft was reported missing, and an air and ground search began across the mountainous jungle region south of the Kokoda airstrip. The families could do nothing but wait – just as our family had waited after the plane carrying Roger disappeared in Vanuatu back in 1991. The Australian deputy head of mission in PNG, John Feakes, played a personal role in coordinating the search, working the mountainous terrain with PNG colleagues and liaising with the ADF, which deployed helicopters and transport aircraft to support the operation. When the aircraft was eventually found high on a remote mountainside with no survivors, John walked in and helped safeguard the victims' remains. From then on it was a matter of identifying the bodies, advising the relatives and getting the deceased home.

I remember reading reports about the Kokoda air crash in Berlin and thinking sympathetically about what it must be like for my colleagues on the spot. Stephen Smith, who had replaced Alexander Downer as foreign minister when Labor came to power, had already developed considerable experience with the consular function since taking up the role, and was directly involved in managing the response. He intervened where necessary to ensure that sufficient military resources were deployed, and participated in daily phone hook-ups with the consular division in Canberra and the High Commission in Port Moresby. After word came through that there had been no survivors, Smith held the media off until consular staff confirmed that all the next of kin had received proper notification of their loved ones' deaths. If considered strictly on the basis of consular operational objectives, the response was executed flawlessly, and was a credit to all those involved – Australians and Papua New Guineans alike. But it was another devastating human tragedy.

There are moments in the consular field when you are reminded that Australia can be a very small place. In my own time running the service from headquarters there were several moments when the names of people I knew in my childhood appeared in the daily summary of consular cases. It's hard to convey the connection you sometimes feel with the community you serve. At one point during the Kokoda air crash response, Stephen Smith asked if anyone from Western Australia had been on board the aircraft. It was a fair question – he was the foreign minister, but he also represented the electorate of Perth. The answer came back in the negative – the Australians on board were all from the eastern states. So he was shocked to discover through the media a few days later that one of the victims was the son of an old Perth schoolfriend. The young man had moved away from Perth a few years before the crash, and his Western Australian links hadn't been immediately obvious. Smith rang his friend to offer his personal condolences, and apologised for not making the connection any earlier. The bereaved father responded that his and the other families had received the best possible assistance from the department, and that Stephen had nothing to apologise for.

Towards the end of our time in Germany, I learned that my application for Port Moresby had been successful. We said goodbye to staff, colleagues and friends in Berlin, and then spent three months back in Canberra, where a Papua New Guinean tutor helped me brush up on my Tok Pisin – the national language of PNG, which I had learned as a child. It came back quickly enough, but she did tell me a couple of times that my phraseology was a bit, well, childish – and that there were a few words I should forget. Roxanne and I were both really looking forward to the posting, and most of my friends understood why. But PNG has a distorted and negative reputation with those who have never been there, and a couple of acquaintances asked me, only half-jokingly, what I'd done wrong. They were people from outside the foreign service who didn't fully understand the priorities and motivations that factor into a diplomatic career.

In January 2010 I took up the role of Australian High Commissioner in Port Moresby. It was like a homecoming, with childhood friends emerging from my distant past to greet me during the first few months. People seemed to welcome my personal connection with the place – I was often referred to in the PNG press as a *mangi lo ples*, which roughly translates to 'a local kid'. It was all new to Roxanne, but like most Australians who spend time in PNG, she quickly came to love the place and the people. She seized the opportunity to play an important leadership role of her own, promoting the causes of the disabled and those with cancer, helping establish the Safe Motherhood Alliance, and supporting the special care nursery at the Port Moresby General Hospital. Both our girls were at university in Brisbane by then, but they were looking forward to exploring the country on their breaks. And Brisbane was less than three hours' flight away.

The work in PNG was very wide-ranging. In our first couple of years we launched some important development initiatives, including a program to restore a regular supply of medicines to health centres across the country. We supported a peace-building process in the troubled island region of Bougainville, and assisted the PNG government with technical advice as it worked to modernise its mining and gas industries, both significant contributors to national revenue. But our consular responsibilities to the 20,000 Australians who live in PNG were never far from mind.

I had a particular accountability, as an employer, for the safety of a sizeable community of Australian government officials and their dependants in Port Moresby – a city beset by law and order challenges. There were a hundred Australian officials at the High Commission itself, but if you included the police officers and advisers working on loan with PNG government agencies, the official establishment was about double that. Many were accompanied by their families – the largest residential compound was full of Australian children.

I met with every newly arrived Australian staff member, some of whom had been scared witless by the security briefings they had received on arrival. I tried to help them put the situation in perspective. Expatriates in Port Moresby rarely encounter real trouble, but car-jackings do occur around town. The modus operandi is consistent: a gang traps a vehicle when it is stationary and forces the driver at gunpoint to abandon it. Those who cooperate normally walked away unscathed. I reinforced with new arrivals all the messages about avoiding unfamiliar areas, keeping the doors and windows locked, and taking local advice. I also told them that I could guarantee that the vast majority of locals would go out of their way to help if they saw a foreigner in difficulty. We recommended that until they understood the environment better, they should either drive with others in convoy or ask one of our security vehicles to tail them. I used this service myself when I was driving at night with other passengers in the car, but otherwise felt perfectly comfortable in my old home town. For her part, Roxanne drove all over Port Moresby by herself during the day.

Bad things did happen. We took a call one night to hear that two young women whom we both knew very well had been carjacked at a notorious bend in the road about a kilometre from our residence. One was a High Commission employee, the other a Papua New Guinean professional. They had handled the situation well, jumping from the vehicle and running in their bare feet down the road to the safety of the Crown Hotel. Roxanne and I were very fond of them both, and my blood was boiling as I drove down the hill to the Crown. I sat with them for a few minutes – they were shaken but okay – then the High Commission security officer who was on duty at the time informed us that the carjackers had run the vehicle into a wall only a few hundred metres from the scene of the crime. I was told that one of the carjackers had been detained, and I felt a strong urge to drive around and tear strips off him, but instead I did the sensible thing and drove our two young friends home.

The first anniversary of the Kokoda air crash came around a few months after Roxanne and I arrived in the country. In the lead-up, we did whatever we could to make things bearable for the family members who would be returning to the country to mark the occasion. Several of them were intent on walking the track and commemorating the anniversary at the crash site. We were anxious to ensure that the local residents near the site responded with kindness to the grieving Australian relatives when they arrived on their memorial pilgrimage. We'd heard that there might be some resentment simmering – the accident itself and the investigation that followed had been traumatic intrusions into their lives in the remote mountains. John Feakes flew to Kokoda again and walked into the village in advance to talk to them.

All went well in the end, and the families returned to Port Moresby after their trek, heartened by the warm welcome they had received. We conducted a quiet ceremony with the visiting families around a newly established memorial on the grounds of the High Commission. The families had wanted to plant a memorial stone near the crash site, but we'd persuaded them that it would deteriorate very quickly in the mountains, where it would be impossible to maintain and vulnerable to vandalism. I have continued to visit the High Commission in Port Moresby regularly in more recent times, and I often walk over to the spot after my meetings to spend a few quiet moments.

After the families had left the country, we worked with Dame Carol Kidu, the country's minister for community affairs, to establish what practical assistance we could offer the tiny village near the crash site through our discretionary aid allocation. We were keen to show our appreciation for their kind response to the Australian families. I suppose we were thinking about toilet blocks, community halls or road improvements – all things we regularly supported around the country. Some PNG communities could be demanding when they sensed an opportunity to leverage engagement with the Australian aid program. But all the villagers asked for was ducks. They were keen to supplement their existing farming practices with duck breeding, and politely asked for one of each gender. When we asked if that was really all they wanted, they replied tentatively that a football and a netball for the kids would be nice. So a few weeks later, Dame Carol and I had the experience of flying into one of the more remote parts of the country in a small helicopter otherwise full of ducks and sporting equipment. We spent a happy hour or so with the villagers, who were very pleased with their gifts.

Meanwhile, Foreign Minister Stephen Smith and the rest of the consular service were dealing with one crisis after another across the world. I recently asked Smith about how he found his interactions with the service during his time as foreign minister. He said he came to appreciate, in his first weeks in the role, the sheer volume of cases managed by the department. He knew that he was only drawn in when a situation became very difficult or assumed a high profile, or when complaints were made – to him or the media – about the way the consular service was handling a case. Only a very small proportion of cases ever went anywhere near him or his office, but when they did, he remembered well the high level of coordination required between his office and DFAT's consular arm when the system was confronted with 'red alert' situations. While the government's first focus was always on the victims and their families, he was conscious that consular officials were often responding to difficult situations in the public spotlight, and that harsh judgement would follow if they failed to meet community expectations.

Smith also remembers very clearly how John McCarthy provided us all with a master class in consular crisis management in 2008. At that point John was the Australian High Commissioner in India. Since joining the department in the late 1960s, he had also served variously as Australia's ambassador to Japan, Indonesia, the United States, Thailand, Mexico and Vietnam. He'd been posted earlier to more junior positions in Damascus, Baghdad and Vientiane. It was hard to think of anyone more experienced.

On the evening of 26 November that year, ten members of Lashkar-e-Taiba, the Islamic terrorist organisation that David Hicks had fought with back in 1999, began a four-day killing spree in Mumbai. They targeted the exclusive Taj Mahal Palace and Oberoi Trident hotels, as well as a crowded railway station, a cafe and a hospital. When it was all over, there were thirty-nine foreigners among the victims. Two Australians were killed and a further two injured, while several more had the terrifying experience of being trapped in the two hotels for days. Most of the 179 dead were Indians who had been innocently waiting at the railway station.

High Commissioner McCarthy happened to be on the spot in Mumbai, visiting the city on official business. In fact, he had checked out of the Taj Mahal Palace the night before the attacks and moved to a hotel on the northern side of the city. John told me that he saw the initial local reports that evening in his hotel room. 'Christ, what's this?' he thought, and picked up the phone to ring the Australian consul-general in Mumbai. This was followed by calls to Canberra and New Delhi to set the consular wheels in motion. The local authorities in Mumbai were encouraging the city's inhabitants to stay behind closed doors, but John had work to do.

Information came in that an Australian man had been killed and his wife badly injured in the shooting, and John made his way to the hospital where the wounded woman was receiving care. She had been drifting in and out of consciousness, and awoke to find the Australian High Commissioner sitting in a chair at the foot of her bed. He extended his deepest sympathies on the death of her husband, and assured her that the Australian government would get her, and her husband's body, home to their family.

John then got hold of the deputy manager at the Taj, where most of the foreigners were at risk, and obtained the registration details of all of their Australian guests. This was important information for the consular emergency staff in Canberra and India, who were working to resolve the whereabouts inquiries that were pouring in on the public lines. Australia was at a significant advantage because a resourceful, experienced head of mission happened to be on the spot; most ambassadors of like-minded nations flew into Mumbai the day after the attacks commenced. The expectations of Australian heads of mission in these situations had clearly also come to apply to other nations.

The jihadist movement was also still making its presence felt in Indonesia. The Marriott Hotel in Jakarta was bombed again in July 2009, along with the nearby Ritz-Carlton. This time there were three Australian casualties among the nine killed. Stephen Smith had just landed at Perth airport from an overseas visit when the news reached him. He rang home from the car to say that he was on his way, but that he might need to be off overseas again very quickly – and, sure enough, he was on his way to Jakarta the following day to oversee the response and encourage Indonesia to support a joint investigation with the AFP.

Smith had another of those 'small Australia' experiences soon afterwards. At a Canberra memorial service for one of those who had been killed, the mother of the victim accepted Stephen Smith's condolences graciously and asked after his son by name. Mystified, Smith asked how she came to know his son. She explained that she had been a nurse at the neonatal clinic in the Canberra hospital where he was born, premature, in the 1990s. She and the other staff knew that Smith was working for Paul Keating, prime minister at the time, and had watched with quiet interest as Smith visited his boy every night after finishing late at Parliament House. She and her family had continued to watch from afar as his career had progressed over the years. They felt that they had a personal, albeit remote, connection with him. Sometimes in Australian consular work, it really does feel as if you are supporting members of your own extended family.

We didn't have a monopoly on air crashes in PNG. In June 2010 an aircraft carrying the entire board of the Perth-based Sundance Resources mining company went missing over thick jungle on a flight from Cameroon to the Republic of the Congo. Once again, it took days to find the wreckage and to establish that there were no survivors. Ian McConville, Australia's Lagos-based High Commissioner at the time, has described the task of coordinating the search, and then retrieving the bodies of the seven Australians, as the most challenging assignment of his career. The devastating experience led Australian companies to establish new rules that restricted the number of corporate directors and executives permitted to fly together on the same aircraft.

In June 2010, Kevin Rudd was deposed as prime minister by his own party and replaced by his deputy, Julia Gillard. The new prime minister appointed Rudd as foreign minister to replace Stephen Smith, who moved to the defence portfolio. This arrangement would last until March 2012, when party tensions led Gillard to reshuffle her cabinet again, appointing former New South Wales premier Bob Carr to the foreign portfolio.

Foreign Minister Rudd and the consular service were soon facing a new challenge in the Middle East, where the Arab Spring was underway – a series of demonstrations, protests and uprisings against repressive regimes across the region, starting in Tunisia in late 2010 and spreading over following months to many other countries, including Egypt and Libya. By January 2011, thousands were protesting on a daily basis in Cairo, where they demanded that President Hosni Mubarak step down. The president resigned in early February and transferred his powers to the military, ushering in further confrontations. Meanwhile, protests were breaking out against Muammar Gaddafi's regime in Libya, sparking an uprising that would soon turn into a civil war.

During these uprisings, many Australians ignored early official consular advice that they should leave by available means, and then found themselves stranded when the commercial flights began to dry up. It did not take long for calls for government action to emerge. In response to growing criticism that the government was not doing enough, Rudd announced that additional consular staff had been sent to Egypt and highlighted the operational challenges associated with the conflict. The government ended up sponsoring charter flights to evacuate Australians from Cairo, and also funded evacuation voyages from Libya. Some of those on the Qantas charter flight out of Cairo asked whether they would be awarded frequent-flyer points!

Speaking publicly about these issues soon afterwards, then DFAT secretary Dennis Richardson made the point that rising, and sometimes unreasonable, public demands of the consular service were not limited to Australia, or even to Western countries. He recounted that he'd been in Beijing for talks with Chinese officials soon after the Libyan uprising; their description of their citizens' demanding behaviour had been what you might have expected from officials from the United Kingdom or the like. Expectation management had become a global problem.

Another event in 2011 provided an opportunity for the renewal of a longstanding professional partnership. In March that year, Tracey Wunder and Bill Jackson, both veterans of the Bali bombing era, were deployed to Japan after a tsunami swept away coastal communities and flooded the reactors at the Fukushima nuclear power facility, releasing radioactive contamination into the atmosphere and sea. There were about 100 Australians living in the affected region, including teachers, footballers playing in the Japanese league, and others who had married locals and made their lives there. Tracey was based in Tokyo, coordinating and providing guidance to the embassy officers who had been conscripted to support the consular effort. Bill, who had recently completed a three-year posting in Japan, joined the embassy consular team in the Fukushima area to assess the situation and help oversee the evacuation of Australians. Our team limited their exposure to radiation as much as they could while working to distribute rations, water and anti-radiation drugs, and to facilitate the departure of those who chose to leave.

The Fukushima response provided a great example of the selfless approach that DFAT's locally engaged staff often show during crises affecting Australians overseas. When Bill arrived in the devastated area, he was greeted by Masayasu Yoshimoto, a longstanding local employee of the embassy in Tokyo who had been Bill's driver during his own recent posting to Japan. Yoshimoto had volunteered to drive into the disaster zone shortly after the tsunami to establish the forward consular base. He'd been working in the area for an extended period, so Bill told him that he'd done enough and should consider returning to Tokyo. His reply was brief and unequivocal: 'If you stay, Mr Jackson, I stay.' Yoshimoto remained in the disaster zone for the duration of the consular mission, sourcing fuel and food for the team, and working out the logistics as they travelled long distances. At one point he also volunteered to drive a round trip of 750 kilometres through exclusion zones to deliver anti-radiation drugs to Australians in affected areas. He was later recognised with a medal in the Order of Australia.

We were not free of new consular preoccupations in PNG at this time. Sadly, a further air crash took the lives of fellow Australians during our posting, and there were one or two occasions when an Australian fell victim to a violent assault. Where appropriate, I travelled to the scene or reached out to the victims myself. I also took a direct interest in our contingency planning to protect the substantial Australian community in PNG in the event of civil unrest or natural disaster.

We had to dust these plans off again in late 2011. In December that year, a confused constitutional battle for PNG's prime ministership threatened to descend into conflict between armed factions loyal to the two contenders. Michael Somare, who had led the country to independence in 1975 and was often referred to as the 'father of the nation', was supported by the courts; Peter O'Neill, the representative of a younger generation, had the backing of parliament. Two opposing police contingents came to blows, and at one point shots were fired amid a physical struggle outside the governor-general's residence. The commander of the PNG defence force came under real pressure from one of the factions to intervene. It was important for me to register my government's concern about these developments, but I also needed to avoid accusations of interference in what, in the end, was a domestic political dispute. I knew both the protagonists well, and emphasised to them in a succession of phone calls and personal meetings that their differences should be resolved politically, as PNG's stability and reputation were at stake. I spoke to senior military officers, encouraging them to stay out of it, and we brokered meetings between the two rival police factions, which helped keep the temperature down.

Canberra was, naturally, very focused on what was happening, mindful of the security implications for the large Australian community in PNG if the situation worsened. I was in constant touch by phone and video conference with Prime Minister Gillard, Foreign Minister Rudd and other members of the National Security Committee. I have to say, though, that the thousands of Australians living in PNG were unperturbed by what was happening. They had seen it all before. And I felt, deep down, that Papua New Guineans would not let things go too far. But I couldn't be completely sure of that, and we had to be prepared. If things turned nasty, the task of protecting or evacuating the broader expatriate community – not only Australians – would inevitably fall to us.

Prime Minister Gillard took a supportive interest in our work, making a point of showing her appreciation for the mission's efforts. There was a moment early in her prime ministership when her easy, informal approach took me by surprise. We were having breakfast on the balcony when my mobile phone rang. A female voice said: 'Hi, Ian, it's Julia here.' I very nearly replied, 'Um, sorry – Julia who?' Fortunately, I recovered my wits quickly enough to say, after a small pause, 'Good morning, Prime Minister,' and to then proceed with a briefing update for her.

(I have been pleased to have the opportunity to work again with Julia Gillard in much more recent times, as Australian representative for the World Bank's Global Partnership for Education, which she chaired until mid-2021. She continues to show the same respect and appreciation in her everyday dealings.)

The saga continued for months, with many twists and turns along the way. It was ultimately resolved at the ballot box: Peter O'Neill's party won the most seats in the mid-2012 national elections, and he quickly pulled together a substantial coalition majority. I was not at all surprised when his erstwhile adversary, Michael Somare, joined O'Neill in coalition. PNG politicians are nothing if not pragmatic.

Our latter period in PNG provided me with the opportunity to get to know the woman who would be Australia's next foreign minister. As the opposition's lead on foreign affairs, Julie Bishop visited PNG frequently, investing considerable time and effort in establishing relationships with the country's leaders. She understood well the importance of the relationship with our nearest neighbour, and had felt a strong affinity with the country since having a penfriend in the PNG highlands as a schoolgirl. Our encounters laid the foundations for a positive professional relationship, which would strengthen further after she took on Australia's lead foreign policy role.

My posting to PNG ended in 2013, and Roxanne and I returned to Brisbane. I took long-service leave and contemplated my next steps. The PNG role, I knew, had spoiled me: there are few other positions available to a career officer that combine high levels of autonomy, influence and resources. There was also the pull of family – a nomadic life becomes less attractive when your children have grown up and are no longer with you. And the prospect of traipsing from one head of mission posting to another until we reached retirement age held little appeal for either of us. So when the private sector came knocking later that year, I decided to take the opportunity to apply my skills and knowledge in the international corporate world.

I tendered my resignation and Roxanne and I flew down to Canberra to attend a farewell dinner, finalise the paperwork and settle our personal affairs. When we walked out of the DFAT headquarters building together, it was a major milestone for both of us. But the next phase of our lives would provide plenty of opportunity for us to stay connected with my former colleagues as they grappled with the never-ending challenges of the consular world.

CHAPTER SIXTEEN

Dark Times

THE CRISIS I HAD ALWAYS feared as head of the consular branch – the downing of a major commercial aircraft overseas with a large number of Australians on board – came to pass about a year after I left the Australian foreign service. Malaysian Airlines Flight 17 from Amsterdam to Kuala Lumpur was shot out of the sky on 17 July 2014 by Russian-backed separatists as it flew over eastern Ukraine, killing all 298 people on board, including thirty-eight Australians. The flight was meant to connect with onward flights to various Australian cities. Also on board were several foreign passengers on their way to an international AIDS conference in Melbourne. It was an even bigger disaster for the Netherlands, which lost 193 of its citizens. Malaysia was also reeling – forty-three of its people had been on board, and the atrocity came on the heels of the unexplained disappearance of another Malaysian Airlines flight, MH370, on its way from Kuala Lumpur to Beijing in March 2014.

The conflict on the ground had been underway since February that year, when Russia responded to the overthrow of Ukraine's pro-Russian president by annexing the Crimean Peninsula and mounting attacks against Donbas in the country's east – both internationally recognised as part of Ukraine. International civil aviation authorities had warned of risks to commercial aircraft flying over some parts of Ukraine over previous weeks and months, but these did not cover the MH17 crash region. The Ukranian authorities had issued restrictions on aircraft flying below certain altitudes, but had not closed the air space. As many as thirty-seven airlines had continued flying over the country in the weeks before the crash.

Julie Bishop took personal command of the Australian response in the aftermath of the MH17 atrocity. She had been appointed as Australia's first female foreign minister ten months earlier, after the September 2013 Australian elections removed the Labor government and restored the Liberal-National coalition under Prime Minister Tony Abbott.

I had several opportunities around this time to talk to Julie. My new corporate career had taken me to Washington DC for a period, where I was advising major US companies on their dealings in the Indo-Pacific; I was also maintaining my direct involvement in the region through pro bono roles with a range of Australian think tanks and development organisations. Part of my motivation to leave DFAT had been to spend more time with Roxanne in Australia, and it felt for a while that I may have taken a wrong turn. The new foreign minister was a frequent visitor to the United States, Australia's most important alliance partner, and we would catch up regularly, in Washington or New York, to discuss regional and other foreign policy issues. But I didn't really ask her what the MH17 experience had been like from her perspective until several years later, after she had left politics.

Julie had been in Brisbane for a conference with visiting PNG ministers when she heard the news that the flight had gone down. She was quickly on the phone to her Dutch counterpart, Foreign

Minister Frans Timmermans. These two would form an important partnership over the following weeks and months. They agreed to push for a strong response by the United Nations Security Council to what was both a clear violation of international law and a threat to international security. Julie flew first to Sydney, where the Russian ambassador to Australia happened to be on a visit. She summoned him for a tense meeting, and also spoke about the matter to Prime Minister Abbott. Then she flew to Washington via Japan. She spent the Tokyo transit speaking to the families of the victims, and boarded the onward flight deeply saddened. In Washington, Julie met with the US intelligence agencies, who were able to give her some insights into the kind of weapon that had been used, including its undoubted Russian provenance. She then caught the train to New York, where she caught up with Frans Timmermans in person. Australian diplomats had drafted a resolution by the time the two foreign ministers arrived. It called on the separatists at the crash site to ensure the bodies of the victims were treated with respect, underlined the need for an independent investigation and demanded military activities in the area cease to enable access to the site. It further demanded that those responsible for this incident be held to account.

Julie and her Dutch counterpart shared the work of trying to convince each Security Council member to support the resolution. Among others, Julie was allocated the Russian UN ambassador, Vitaly Churkin. She resorted to every argument she could think of to get him over the line – no small task, given the close links between the Russian state and the rebels who had shot down the plane. She had Australian newspapers on display in the room, complete with photographs of the dead, and appealed to him as a father. She could see that he was deeply moved. The Russians asked for some minor text changes, and a day or so later Julie eyeballed Churkin as the president of the

Security Council called for a vote in support of the proposed resolution. He slowly raised his hand.

Resolution 2166 was passed unanimously on 21 July – a vital point of pressure to allow access for investigators to the crash site, and to allow the MH17 victims to be returned to their loved ones. The Russians were to prove less cooperative a few days afterwards, when a further resolution came before the council to establish a special tribunal to prosecute those responsible.

Next, Foreign Minister Bishop moved to Kyiv, where the Australian task involved creating a functional government presence in the Ukrainian capital from scratch – effectively an embassy capable of supporting a massive consular and diplomatic operation. A hotel in central Kyiv became the base for a forty-five-person Australian team led by former defence chief Angus Houston. He and I had been together in Sumatra in the aftermath of the 2004 tsunami, and he was also a regular visitor to PNG during my time there. He is just the kind of man you want by your side in a crisis. Kerin Ayyalaraju was again among the DFAT contingent, this time with media management responsibilities. She recalls Julie Bishop's extraordinary physical resilience with wonder – the foreign minister would be up in the middle of the night to call in to a National Security Committee meeting in Canberra, rise again at dawn to go for her daily run and then work a very long and intense day. She would top it all off in the evening by insisting that the staff join her for drinks at the bar. I've spent a few days on the road with Julie. It's very hard to keep up.

The key imperative for Australia, the Netherlands and others was to secure Ukrainian agreement for hundreds of Australian police investigators and accompanying defence personnel to join a Dutch-led international security force in securing the crash site, which adjoined separatist territory. To deploy this kind of force on Ukrainian soil required a formal agreement between the two countries. Senior DFAT legal personnel negotiated an agreement, which Julie signed with her Ukrainian counterpart on 25 July. This was a great step forward, but the Ukrainian parliament also needed to indicate its backing for the agreement before it came into effect. And with exquisitely bad timing, the Ukrainian parliament rose that same day, after a week of argument and physical confrontations in the chamber led to the resignation of the prime minister. The next session was not scheduled for another three weeks.

When asked for his advice, the Ukrainian president said that the only option he could see was for Australia to lobby the main parliamentary factions to reconvene parliament for this one important item of business. This seemed ludicrous – it's hard to imagine Ukrainian officials convincing the Australian parliament to resume when it had risen for an extended break. But the Australians accepted the advice and commenced another intense advocacy exercise. Somehow they managed to win enough support for a parliamentary quorum to reconvene, but Julie's heart was in her mouth as she watched from the gallery as the results appeared on an electronic screen. It was a positive outcome in the end, a success that Julie attributes in no small part to the Ukrainian perception of Australia as an active member of the Western alliance – the bulwark, as they saw it, against Russian aggression and expansionism.

Over time, the bodies of victims were secured and the identification processes began. The remains were placed in coffins and flown to Eindhoven, in the Netherlands, where the coronial inquest was to take place. The dead were received with great dignity in the ceremony organised by the Dutch government.

Julie has since described supporting the Australian families of the MH17 disaster as the most emotional experience of her life. She certainly won great loyalty from DFAT staff for her close identification with the work of the consular service, and for the way she led from the front in the aftermath of the MH17 disaster. She was to earn the admiration of many more in the broader Australian population when she confronted Russia's President Vladimir Putin over his nation's failure to cooperate with the crash probe. It was Prime Minister Tony Abbott who had publicly threatened to 'shirtfront' Putin, but Julie did it more diplomatically. Recalling the encounter several years later in an interview with ABC Perth, following Russia's invasion of Ukraine, she described Putin as 'menacing'. He was 'very steely, very calm,' she said. 'He stared at me, his eyes didn't leave my face. He didn't blink. Not once. But he disagreed with the points I'd made calmly, politely, almost respectfully.'

The consular officers who graduated from the Bali bombing era continued to provide the core of the service for many years after I left. Bill Jackson had finally retired in mid-2012 after what his colleagues described as his 'farewell world tour' – he filled in at a number of overseas posts on a short-term basis after his Fukushima experience in 2011. But Tracey Wunder was still at it when I last spoke to her in 2021. Between postings, she spent time in Canberra doing her old consular management job and training new consular officers there. In addition to the Japanese tsunami operation, she was deployed repeatedly on some challenging missions. In 2019 she was a member of an all-female team of DFAT officers who pulled off a very delicate operation to bring home the orphans of Australian jihadists who had been killed overseas. By 2021 she was on a posting as the regional consular officer for Africa, based in Pretoria, and was doing everything she could to help stranded Australians get home as Covid-19 spread through the region.

Rowland Pocock, who had been there at the very beginning as a member of the fledgling Consular Emergency Centre, retired in 2014 but was called back less than two years later to help as a contractor. He has been there ever since. I rang him in 2021 to ask about a couple of details I'd forgotten, and had to laugh when he said that he would have to make it quick because he needed to head into DFAT shortly to commence his shift at the Consular Emergency Centre. Tracey reckons he'll still be at it when he's pushing a Zimmer frame.

Kerin Ayyalaraju is also still in harness. The MH17 disaster was not the only consular emergency response in the first year after my departure from DFAT, and it wasn't the only one Kerin was involved with. She was one of many sent to the Philippines in November 2013 when Typhoon Haiyan left more than four million people homeless across Asia. There were about 300 Australians living in the most heavily affected region – mostly older Australians who had married Filipino nationals and settled there. The response was another significant moment in Australian consular history.

Kerin was told that she would be working at the embassy in Manila, but on arrival she was asked to fly straight on to Tacloban, at the crisis epicentre, to help trace missing Australians. When she arrived, she joined forces with a Philippine police officer and a retired Australian volunteer. They borrowed a utility vehicle and began to work through a list of priority names. The rain was constant, and Kerin shared a tent prone to flooding each night with four others. She was receiving inquiries direct from family members on her phone, and drew on the local knowledge of the other team members and any local intelligence they could collect to track down missing Australians. She recalls the sense of triumph each time they found an Australian who turned out to be safe and well. 'There was one man who we'd been looking for … we walked into a courtyard to find him standing in the sun, in all his glory, being hosed down by his wife. Consular welfare confirmed!'

Kerin is now the Australian Ambassador in Copenhagen, where she is accredited to Denmark, Iceland and Norway.

The issues that we had grappled with in those early years were still present in the second decade of the century. The jihadist movement was far from a thing of the past. The service had to step forward to help manage public anxiety again in November 2015, when coordinated terror attacks in Paris killed people at a football stadium, cafe district and rock concert. The same terrorist cell pulled off a further series of attacks in Brussels the following year. In the end, none of the casualties was Australian, but as we had learned many years previously, there was generally little correlation between the number of Australian casualties and the number of concerned callers to DFAT's emergency lines. Regrettably, two Australians were killed in the London Bridge atrocity of 2017: Sara Zelenak, a twenty-one-year-old from Queensland, and Kirsty Boden, a twenty-eight-year-old nurse from regional South Australia, who was killed as she rushed to give first aid to a victim.

Something we had not 'fixed' in my time was the perennial gap between expectations of the consular service and what it was actually set up to do. A 2013 Lowy Institute report on the 'consular conundrum' provided a useful snapshot of the situation. It noted the following requests and queries on the consular emergency lines: 'Could DFAT feed my dog while I'm away?'; 'Will the sand in Egypt upset my asthma?'; 'How much spending money should my cousin bring with him on his visit to Australia?'; 'I haven't heard from my friend for three years; I'm worried about him and I also want his motor cycle out of my garage.'

As foreign minister, Julie Bishop did what she could to temper public expectations. In 2015 she launched a review of consular services, which aimed, in large part, to promote greater self-reliance in Australian travellers. It signalled an intention to cut back on what she described as a 'gold-plated' service. This involved renewed efforts to convince Australians to take out travel insurance, a tougher stance towards reckless and obstinate travellers, and signals that consular assistance would be reduced to the 'absolute minimum level' if Australians acted negligently or abused the system. She mentioned, for example, circumstances where travellers persisted with their travel plans despite DFAT warnings. Consular service, she made it clear, was a privilege, not a right. It was all worth trying, but the unreasonable expectations lingered.

The consular review did lead to a number of other much-needed reforms. Policies were developed to limit consular assistance to permanent residents and dual nationals in their country of other nationality, and the foreign minister cancelled hundreds of passports of reportable sex offenders after Australia became the first country to introduce laws to deny these people passports. The Act made it an offence for reportable offenders to attempt to leave Australia without the permission of a competent authority. Meanwhile, the organisation's response capabilities were upgraded through the establishment of a unified Australian government Global Watch Office and a comprehensive upgrade of the department's crisis centre.

A long, searing consular issue that had begun back in 2005, when I was working with the prime minister, reached a dreadful point of culmination ten years later. The so-called 'ringleaders' of the Bali Nine, Myuran Sukumaran and Andrew Chan, had been sentenced to death in 2006 by the district court in Bali. Since then, the two men and their supporters had tried and failed, several times, to escape the ultimate sanction. The death sentence had been upheld on appeal by the provincial Supreme Court, and again by the Indonesian Supreme Court in Jakarta. President Joko Widodo, known as 'Jokowi', had come to power in 2013 on an anti-drugs platform, and was clearly disinclined to grant clemency. This came during a period of strain in the bilateral relationship between Australia and Indonesia: a Wikileaks report had asserted that Australian intelligence agencies, under the Rudd government, had been spying on the wife of former president Susilo Bambang Yudhoyono. And now, in late 2014, the fate of the two Australians emerged as a major issue of contention between the two countries.

The heroin trade has many victims, and even in Australia there are still those who say they support the death penalty in cases of drug trafficking. But Australia's longstanding, bipartisan and universal opposition to capital punishment reflects a broader community view. Some Australians were moved to describe the pending executions as a barbarous affront to civilised values and a betrayal of an important bilateral relationship. Many others were persuaded by the self-redemption narrative that these cases offered. Both men had found solace in Christianity, and the governor of the prison described them as being very positive influences on other inmates. Chan married while in jail, led church services and was a mentor to others. Sukumaran gave lessons in English and graphic design, and was completing a fine arts degree by correspondence at Curtin University. He had been recognised as a gifted portrait artist by Ben Quilty, himself a winner of the prestigious Archibald Prize for portraiture. As Julie Bishop reflects, they had become model prisoners, and in many ways represented everything that a prison sentence was meant to achieve.

The Australian government, spearheaded by Bishop and the ambassador to Indonesia, Paul Grigson, left no stone unturned in its efforts to convince President Jokowi to grant the men clemency. Julie had countless conversations with her Indonesian counterpart, Retno Marsudi, and Grigson led a comprehensive advocacy strategy on the ground in Jakarta. The Australian prime minister and governor-general made direct representations to their Indonesian counterparts, and the European Union and the United States were both convinced to support the cause. There were moments even at the very end when Julie held out hope for success, but it was not to be.

By March 2015, the two men had been moved to the Nusa Kambangan prison island, near Cilacap in central Java, where they were to be executed along with several prisoners from other countries. The tone of public exchanges between Australia and Indonesia deteriorated rapidly as the execution date neared. Australians became offended by the stories that emerged about the rough treatment of the men's families. By all accounts, the official advice about the specific timing of the executions was delivered very abruptly and without compassion, and there was little the embassy team could do to soften the blow. Family members were reportedly shunted from one hotel to another to make room for the many senior Indonesian officials who descended on Cilacap in the lead-up to the executions. The families and their representatives had to deal with confrontational pro-execution protests and heavy-handed shows of strength by the military and police. As Julie Bishop pointed out publicly at the time, the Indonesians seemed to be singling out the Australians for aggressive treatment.

In among all this anger, tragedy and sadness was an act that leaves me feeling optimistic about the future of the Australian foreign service.

A young policy officer from the Jakarta embassy, Monty Pounder, was in Cilacap as a member of the Australian team deployed to support the families through the awful ordeal of the men's execution, and to manage the voracious Australian, Indonesian and international media. The contingent was led by the highly experienced Majell Hind, a successor of Ross Tysoe as consul-general in Bali, who had established strong relationships with the families. Monty was selected as a member of the team because he spoke Indonesian fluently, had experience in dealing with Indonesian officialdom and was a natural fixer.

After the executions had been carried out, Monty took on the task of ensuring that Myuran Sukumaran's paintings were properly secured and transported back to Jakarta, where they could then be handed over to his family. Sukumaran had thrown himself into his painting with renewed energy since being transported to Nusa Kambangan from Bali, and produced some quite extraordinary works through this period. Monty's father had been an art dealer in Sydney, and Monty knew that oil paintings take a long time to dry, and even longer to cure. He was determined that they would not be damaged while in his care, and made some calls home to get some practical advice. There was not enough space for about ten of the largest paintings on the two buses that would soon be taking them all back to Jakarta, so he stacked them in a hotel room and typed up a 'contract' in Bahasa Indonesia with the hotel's management – under which they agreed, for a stated sum, not to allow access to the room to anyone other than an Australian embassy staff member. Monty couldn't be sure they would be secure from those who might try to profit from the situation. He jammed a card in the air-conditioning slot and joined the silent fifteen-hour bus ride back to Jakarta with the families of the executed men.

Monty was back in Cilacap within a week. He acknowledges that he could have asked for someone else to go, but says: 'If someone smeared one of those works I wouldn't have been able to forgive myself.' He was relieved to find the pictures were just as he had left them. He and an embassy driver carefully tacked the backs of each canvas to wooden planks, and then joined the resulting structures together in a series of 'boxes'. He spent that night in the room, surrounded by the images. Unsurprisingly, he didn't get a lot of sleep. The following day he bubble-wrapped the pictures, packed them into the vehicles and set off for Jakarta again.

An exhibition of Myuran Sukumaran's work toured Australian towns and cities for the following several years. It has been described by Ben Quilty as the strongest imaginable standing protest against the death penalty.

It might not seem like 'core consular business', but to me there is something moving about the determination Monty showed as he worked to salvage something positive from what must have seemed an otherwise irredeemable situation. Australians can take pride in how he, like many DFAT officers before him, stepped forward to bring some humanity to bear in the bleakest of circumstances.

CHAPTER SEVENTEEN

Hostage Diplomacy

I HAVE LITTLE DOUBT THAT the vast majority of Australian citizens who are arrested around the world each year actually have a case to answer. But sometimes our fellow citizens are held captive overseas in circumstances that are obviously wrong.

Kidnappings by a terrorist cell or a criminal gang are nightmares for the victims and dreadful experiences for their families. These incidents also place governments in an invidious position. There are no reliable rules for dealing with a group that is operating well outside international law or convention. One false move might lead to death for the captive. The Australian government is further constrained in these situations because it won't countenance any involvement in the payment of ransoms. Nor will it consider granting any political concessions to extremists. It rightly takes the view that criminality should not be rewarded – that to do so would only encourage the practice. An armed rescue attempt can only be contemplated if the location of the hostage is known, and this option is always extremely risky. And Australia can't just deploy its own special forces at will when one of its citizens is taken hostage in another country.

The 1994 David Wilson case in Cambodia had underlined all these limitations.

It's rare that hostages taken by extremists survive the ordeal, but there have been some exceptions. I was still working as head of Prime Minister Howard's international division in May 2005 when Douglas Wood, an Australian engineer working on construction projects in Iraq, was kidnapped by an extremist group. They released a video showing Wood pleading for his life and calling for US and Australian troops to be withdrawn from Iraq. Howard asked Nick Warner, a deputy secretary at DFAT and a predecessor of mine in the PNG role, to deploy to Baghdad to lead the response team. I'd worked closely with Nick before, and have again since. We have become good friends over the years. I remember speaking to him shortly after he'd been told about the assignment, and then getting on the phone to Defence headquarters to relay the PM's 'request' that an RAAF aircraft fly him immediately to Iraq. Nick drew together a strong Australian team in Baghdad, and I kept the prime minister informed about their progress over the following weeks as they worked to trace Wood's whereabouts. In Washington DC, President Bush instructed the US security and intelligence agencies to treat the case as if Wood were an American citizen. Australian Muslim leader Sheik Taj El-Din Hilaly involved himself in support of the government's efforts, broadcasting public appeals and travelling to Iraq to seek out intermediaries.

Nick's team was beginning to establish lines of communication with the kidnappers when an Iraqi military unit undertaking a counter-insurgency sweep in Baghdad's outskirts received a tip-off and raided the house where Wood was being held. Back in Canberra, a national security meeting of the Australian cabinet was taking place when the news came through that Wood had been rescued alive. I happened to be in the cabinet room at the time. Howard was handed a note and then read its contents aloud, beaming, to the meeting participants. After his return to Australia, Douglas Wood revealed publicly that Iraqi captives had been murdered right next to him during his time in captivity. He went on to support a number of Iraqi charities, and in 2009 lobbied the Australian government to provide humanitarian visas for the Iraqi military personnel who had been involved in his rescue.

Queenslander Nigel Brennan also survived a kidnapping by Islamic insurgents, but as far as he and his family were concerned, this was no thanks to the Australian government. Brennan, a photojournalist, was kidnapped in Somalia in August 2008 by fundamentalist insurgents, along with his Canadian colleague Amanda Lindhout and their Somali translator and drivers. The Somalis were freed in January 2009, but the two foreigners were held in isolation for fifteen months. Lindhout was brutally and repeatedly assaulted by their captors. Back in Australia, DFAT consular officers and members of a special AFP negotiating team initially established a positive relationship with Brennan's family, but this soured over time, and echoes emerged of the tensions we had seen back in the 1990s with the Wilson family over ransom policy. Brennan and Lindhout were ultimately released in November 2009 when a private deal was struck to pay a ransom. After his release, Brennan told the media that his freedom was the result of his family's hard work and commitment, and nothing else. He and some of his supporters described DFAT's overall efforts as ineffectual and accused the AFP of incompetence. In response to these criticisms, Foreign Minister Stephen Smith defended the government's approach, underlining that government involvement in the payment of ransoms would only encourage kidnappers and put Australians more at risk into the future.

Stephen Smith asked John McCarthy, by then retired, to conduct a review of DFAT's handling of the Brennan case. McCarthy made a number of suggestions to promote better coordination, and recommended that if the next of kin wished to proceed with a private contractor with expertise in ransom negotiations, the government should 'provide them with the names of a couple of companies known to the Government that might be able to help'. A Senate inquiry into the government's response to the kidnapping of Australian citizens overseas, launched in 2011 in response to the Brennan case, backed this and a number of McCarthy's other suggestions. The government accepted these recommendations and procedures were tightened as a result.

Negotiating with extremists and criminals is one thing, but it's something else entirely when another national government resorts to taking hostages.

This isn't a reference to cases like that of Schapelle Corby, where the arrest and imprisonment of an Australian by another government attracts public attention because the media 'storyline' is compelling, or because many Australians identify strongly with the individuals or the cause they represent. In these situations, Australian officials may come under public pressure to 'do something about it', but there is no firm basis for defying international convention and pressing the other government to release the prisoner.

However, over the years, our citizens have been imprisoned by governments for reasons that are seen as purely political – and sometimes for no apparent reason other than to gain advantage in their relationship with the Australian government. When the charges are clearly false there is naturally a widespread expectation at home that our government will go beyond the normal consular boundaries to press hard for the apparent victims' release. The case of Kerry and Kay Danes, which I dealt with back in 2001, had some of these hallmarks, and it was neither the first nor the last. More recent, very serious cases that clearly fall into this category include those of Peter Greste in Egypt, Dr Yang Hengjun in China and Kylie Moore-Gilbert in Iran.

The number of such cases seems to have grown substantially over time, and the Australian government is clearly not the only one to think so. In 2021, an international coalition of fifty-seven nations signed a joint statement calling for an end to the practice of international arbitrary detention. Australia was a strong supporter of this Canadian-led initiative, describing politically motivated imprisonment as a fundamental breach of human rights. This joint diplomatic action was widely understood to have been sparked by a series of incidents in which foreign nationals were seized in Iran, China, Russia, North Korea and Myanmar.

The first country to be raised in discussions about 'hostage diplomacy' is usually China. Beijing's efforts to convince the rest of the international community that China is a benign and responsible global power have been consistently undercut by a pattern of hostile targeting of foreigners and dual nationals for alleged espionage, national security transgressions or financial crime. In the past decade, China has made international headlines by detaining, in circumstances that others find doubtful, the citizens of countries including Canada, Japan, the United States and Australia. At times, this behaviour has been depicted as part of a bargaining strategy; at others it has appeared to be attempted coercion. Australia has had several experiences of this kind with China. In recent years, the Chinese authorities have been accused of arbitrarily imprisoning many Australian citizens or dealing out 'justice' to them that is unacceptably harsh in order to send a deliberate message to Canberra: that it needs to adopt a more compliant approach in its dealings with Australia's largest trading partner.

It is hard to avoid the conclusion that there is a direct link between Beijing's approach to Australian citizens and the state of the Australia–China relationship. The pattern goes back to at least 2009, when the Chinese-speaking Kevin Rudd was still the Australian prime minister, and Stephen Smith his foreign minister. First an Australian Defence statement ruffled feathers by expressing concern about the modernisation of the Chinese military, and then Canberra imposed limits on a proposed investment in Anglo-Australian miner Rio Tinto by Chinalco, a major Chinese state-owned enterprise. China accused Australia and the company of colluding to keep the iron ore price high. In July 2009, the authorities arrested Stern Hu, an Australian citizen of Chinese heritage who headed Rio Tinto's iron ore business in China, on charges of bribery and espionage, along with two of his Chinese colleagues. Rudd and Smith both warned publicly that China's handling of the case would determine how it was seen by the international community. When Hu was sentenced to ten years' imprisonment in a secret trial, Prime Minister Rudd stated bluntly that China had missed an opportunity to prove its case to the world. Stern Hu was to serve eight years before he was released.

There were several other Australians arrested in the years that followed. Australian cardiac surgeon Du Zuying, Sydney banker Matthew Ng and Perth-born Carl Mather were among several arrested for fraud amid disputes with local business associates. Some might question whether all this was really directed by the Chinese leadership, but people who know more than I do about China say that it didn't really need to be. Those involved at the local level just needed to read the signals from the top and act accordingly.

The relationship between the two countries began to recover around the time that Rudd was replaced as prime minister by

Julia Gillard. China had taken a substantial interest in gas fields off the Australian north-west coast in late 2009, and high-level visits were subsequently resumed in both directions. Things began to improve in the consular field in turn, with China and Australia finalising a prisoner transfer agreement in 2011, which allowed Australians imprisoned in China to be sent home to finish their sentences and vice versa. Both Carl Mather and Australian–Chinese businesswoman Charlotte Chou, who had been in jail since 2008, had their sentences reduced substantially shortly after Prime Minister Gillard visited Beijing in 2013. By the end of the following year, Chou and Du Zuying had been released, and Matthew Ng had been transferred to Australia under the prisoner transfer agreement to serve out the remaining eighteen months of his sentence. These releases coincided with the finalisation by the Abbott government of a free trade agreement with China, and a state visit to Australia by Chinese president Xi Jinping in November 2014.

I visited Beijing myself in 2014, when China hosted the APEC leaders' meeting. The company I was representing on that visit was a sponsor of the APEC 'CEO Summit', where national leaders mixed with senior private-sector representatives. China was riding high as it played host to world leaders, including US president Barack Obama, Russia's Vladimir Putin and Australia's Tony Abbott. Between the speeches, I spoke to diplomatic observers from a range of countries about where China was headed, and the message was consistent: this was a ruthless autocratic regime and it was intent on making its presence felt on the world stage. It was clear that Xi Jinping was moving deliberately to consolidate his personal power by encouraging an aggressively nationalist stance at home.

Abbott's successor, Malcolm Turnbull, was the last Australian leader to date to visit Beijing in 2016. The relationship began to deteriorate a few months later, when the Australian government joined others in calling on Beijing to respect an international ruling against its territorial claims in the South China Sea. In 2017, Australia joined the governments of Japan, India and the United States in revitalising their quadrilateral security dialogue, which China sees as a military alliance aimed at preventing China's resurgence.

Meanwhile, the Turnbull government became increasingly concerned about Chinese spying activities and the intimidation of Chinese students on our university campuses. Australia launched a review of its espionage and foreign interference laws, and then, in August 2018, banned Chinese tech giant Huawei from participating in the construction of its 5G telecommunications network.

Taking their cue from above, the Chinese media referred to Australia variously as a 'paper cat' and a 'British offshore prison'. Inevitably, things took a turn for the worse in the consular field early the following year, by which time Scott Morrison had replaced Turnbull in a further leadership upset. Chinese-Australian novelist Yang Hengjun was detained in Guangzhou in early 2019 and held without charge for more than seven months. Marise Payne, who had replaced Julie Bishop as Australian foreign minister in 2018, was forthright in her public response, describing Yang in a media release as having been 'criminally detained'. She has consistently labelled this case as 'arbitrary detention'. The third anniversary of Yang's imprisonment passed in early 2022, and by then his friends were growing increasingly anxious that his deteriorating health would see him die in prison.

The bilateral relationship has seen some very challenging times since then. In July 2020 the Morrison government announced a significant increase in defence spending in the context of China's more active presence in the Indo–Pacific region. By then, we had seen Beijing respond angrily to Australia's call for an independent investigation into the origins of the Covid-19 pandemic. Beijing moved to impose serious trade restrictions on some products, and Chinese officials strengthened their aggressive rhetoric.

Cheng Lei, who grew up in Australia after moving here with her family at the age of ten, was detained in August 2020. Cheng had become a well-known and successful television news anchor in China. Like Yang Hengjun, she was held in an undisclosed location and without comment for an initial period, and it was not until February 2021 that she was formally arrested and charged with 'supplying state secrets overseas'.

Australian Ambassador Graham Fletcher was denied access to the closed-door proceedings of the national security court in March 2022. The court deferred its decision, prolonging the uncertainty for Cheng Lei and her family. By then it had been more than eighteen months since she had seen her children. Foreign Minister Payne issued a statement criticising the lack of transparency and stating that 'Australia stands by Ms Cheng and her family at this difficult time'.

Many of the Australians to fall foul of the Chinese authorities were of Chinese ethnicity. Members of this group are more likely than other Australians to be immersed in the risky Chinese private sector. They are doubly vulnerable at times of tension in the Australia–China relationship. They are potential objects of suspicion because of their Australian links, and China doesn't really recognise them as Australians. I think the Australian media and some members of the broader public are sometimes guilty of a similar mindset.

There has been much debate about how the Australian government should best deal with arbitrary detention – whether it takes place in China or elsewhere. The families of some Australian detainees have asserted that DFAT has discouraged them from 'going public' with their cases because it wants to limit public pressure and minimise any damage to its international relationships. They argue that 'quiet diplomacy' is not always the best approach, and that public attention can lead to improvements in prisoners' conditions and treatment. This criticism has come up in consular cases across several countries. The department generally advises against 'megaphone diplomacy', asserting that mounting a public advocacy campaign is a decision for the families alone to make.

On the face of it, journalist Peter Greste's experience of detention in Egypt seems to repudiate the 'quiet diplomacy' argument. The situation in Egypt was extremely tense in the latter half of 2013: the Islamic government that had emerged in the aftermath of the Arab Spring was overthrown in a military coup in June that year. Violent clashes followed, and hundreds of protesters were killed by the security forces. Thousands of supporters of the former government were rounded up and imprisoned, and the military regime imposed a prolonged series of night-time curfews. Egypt was locked down.

A highly experienced foreign correspondent working at the time for the Al Jazeera news agency, Greste was arrested by the Egyptian authorities in late 2013, along with two colleagues – one Canadian and the other Egyptian. They were accused of falsifying news, damaging national security and having a negative impact on the country's international image.

I've had the pleasure of getting to know Peter in recent years, and have talked to him about his experiences over a series of coffees, lunches and dinners in Brisbane. I've also briefly met his delightful parents, Juris and Lois. As the couple told Richard Fidler in an ABC *Conversations* interview after their son's release, they 'dropped absolutely everything' in their lives as soon as they heard of Peter's arrest, and set about organising a public campaign to highlight the injustice of the case. With their sons, Mike and

Andrew, they took it in turns to travel to Cairo. Juris told me that they quickly decided that a family member should always be available to visit Peter, every time it was permitted.

Peter's case was a protracted and very serious preoccupation for Foreign Minister Julie Bishop and the consular service. The campaign on behalf of the imprisoned men became truly global, with governments and international organisations backed by strong public and media support. Core to the campaign was the theme of press freedom. The Australian government took a leading role, making repeated representations on Peter's behalf. Bishop involved herself directly in the dialogue with the Egyptian government, and made it public that she was 'appalled' when the journalists were convicted and seven-year sentences were imposed on them in June 2014. The campaign to correct this injustice continued unabated over the months that followed. Peter speaks with appreciation of the efforts of the Australian ambassador to Egypt, Ralph King. He could not be fully aware of the extent of the efforts that were underway on his behalf, but as he says, 'every now and again news leaks in, and it made all the difference'. Ultimately, Peter was deported without explanation on 1 February 2015. He then dedicated himself to securing the release of his two colleagues, who were pardoned in September that year.

Peter's experience leaves him with the firm view that public advocacy can be very helpful in seeking to win the release of someone who has been unjustly imprisoned, but that campaign strategists need to think about the targets of their messaging, and what will support them to move in the desired direction. He says that different message tracks are required for different targets – one for your own government; another for the authorities who actually hold the keys. In both cases, the approach needs to have a facilitative quality, rather than just being about 'applying pressure'. At the Australian end, his supporters' aim was to show that the cause had solid public support among the government's own political constituency, encouraging it to set aside cautious arguments about precedent and stretch itself to achieve a result. Consistent with this 'supportive' approach, Peter's team worked to ensure that their messaging in Australia avoided any sense that they were conspiring with the political opposition to hector the government.

Julie Bishop's recollections of the public dynamics associated with the case are entirely consistent with Peter's. She saw the family's campaign as supportive of her own efforts, and those of the consular service, rather than targeting the Australian government.

At the Egyptian end, Greste's family and friends were conscious of the need to help the authorities preserve some element of 'face'. They highlighted in positive terms the guarantees for the freedom of the press in the Egyptian constitution, and characterised the journalists' detention as an anomaly that needed fixing. All that was required was action to ensure full alignment between the nation's official stance and its practices. They were also careful to ensure that the debate was always about protecting press freedom, rather than allowing it to become about what the trio had or hadn't done. Peter and his supporters are confident that the Egyptian authorities were able to distinguish between the family's careful messaging and the 'public noise' of social media, human rights organisations and the international media. This noise had its own value, though, keeping other governments focused on the case and giving them a reason to raise the matter with the Egyptians.

Of course, Peter Greste had some things going for him that other victims of arbitrary detention do not. For a start, Egypt is not China. The charges against him and his colleagues were risible, and the international media was on hand to call out the situation for what it was – an attack on the freedom of the press. By dint of his background, experience and connections, Peter's family also had access to a group of advisers with highly relevant experience. Peter underlines the value of having a team with relevant expertise who can guide the public approach in a thoughtful, almost dispassionate way.

Egypt may have been susceptible to international public opinion in this case, but some countries play a tougher game. In recent times, the Islamic Republic of Iran has used arbitrary detention, imprisoning many foreigners and dual citizens for long periods on highly questionable grounds. Tehran doesn't recognise dual citizenship at all: if one of a person's nationalities is Iranian, it refuses to allow consular access by foreign governments. Dual nationals are treated with great suspicion and are particularly vulnerable to the regime's often paranoid behaviour. An Iranian-Canadian conservationist died in custody in early 2018 shortly after being arrested for alleged espionage. The authorities said it was suicide and rebuffed the Canadian government's demands for further information.

There can be little doubt about Iran's willingness to use prisoners with foreign connections as pawns in their international dealings. An American history student of Chinese heritage who was arrested for 'espionage' in 2016 was released in a prisoner swap in 2019 for an Iranian scientist imprisoned in the United States for attempting to smuggle restricted biological material to Iran. And as recently as March 2022, immediately after the British government paid an 'historic debt' of more than $700 million connected with arms sales to the previous Iranian regime, Tehran finally released Nazanin Zaghari-Ratcliffe, a British charity aid worker, who'd been arrested six years previously for 'attempting to topple the regime'. Also released was dual Iranian–British national Anousheh Ashouri, who had spent three years behind bars on charges of espionage. The Iranian foreign minister claimed the timing of the British payment and prisoner's release was 'just a coincidence'.

Australia, too, has had some experience of Iran's transactional approach to foreign prisoners.

Kylie Moore-Gilbert attended school in Bathurst, New South Wales, and went on to study Asian and Middle Eastern studies at Cambridge. She is Australian but also holds British citizenship. Her doctorate from the University of Melbourne involved sociopolitical analysis of contemporary Bahrain. Kylie travelled to Iran in September 2018 to attend an academic conference, and was arrested at Tehran's international airport at the end of her visit. She was accused of espionage – a charge that she and the Australian government have consistently dismissed as baseless.

Kylie's incarceration only became known to the public about a year after her arrest, when the detention of two Australian travel bloggers for three months by the Tehran regime drew media attention and led to reporting on her case. Even then the coverage was muted and her family remained silent. Watching from a distance, I was struck by the absence of a public campaign, and assumed that a tactical judgement had been made that this was in the best interests of securing Kylie's freedom. I gathered from the media coverage that the Australian embassy had been able to obtain some access to Kylie in prison, and that she had been able to make occasional phone calls. The case assumed a greater profile as time wore on, and some of her friends and supporters did speak out, holding a public vigil on the second anniversary of her imprisonment and releasing extracts from her letters that had been smuggled out from prison.

It appeared that Foreign Minister Payne was giving the case priority, and my longstanding friend and colleague Lyndall Sachs was Australia's ambassador in Iran at the time. I gathered from DFAT statements and the media that she was handling the case personally. I felt that Kylie was in good hands in that sense, at least.

Kylie's release was announced on 25 November 2020 by the Iranian media, who revealed that 'an Iranian businessman and two Iranian citizens who were detained abroad on baseless charges were exchanged for a dual national spy named Kylie Moore-Gilbert'. State television footage showed the arrival of the three Iranians from Bangkok and Kylie's departure. Marise Payne limited her public commentary to welcoming Kylie's release. But it became clear from media reporting over the following few days that another old friend, Nick Warner, who had worked to obtain Douglas Wood's release from Baghdad all those years ago and was by this time head of the Office of National Intelligence, had also led the team that secured the 'deal' to release Kylie. As she has since confirmed in her own compelling account of her experiences, *The Uncaged Sky*, it was Nick who flew to Tehran on a RAAF aircraft to finalise the arrangements and escort her back to Australia. He also introduced me to Kylie a few months after she returned home.

Kylie had been subjected to unacceptable treatment by her captors, and the conditions were dreadful. She was shunted back and forth between different locations, and as time went on the prison where she was being held became riddled with Covid-19. When asked about how she managed to get through it, she says: 'You can't just check out of the experience; there is no other option but to hang in there – and you find those reserves of strength that you never knew you had.'

She has told me that in the absence of any evident progress in negotiations, she felt she needed to devise her own plans and tactics. She went on hunger strikes to secure attention, and sought to maximise the very few opportunities that arose for her to communicate with the outside world. At one point, she staged an 'emotional meltdown' during an embassy visit to create an opportunity, amid the confusion, to let the Australians know that the Iranians were attempting to recruit her as a spy.

Kylie says she is grateful to the Australian government for securing her release. She made a point of thanking the prime minister in person soon after her return to Australia. In my own discussions with her, she has spoken particularly warmly of the individual Australian officials who helped her along the way – certainly Nick Warner and Lyndall Sachs, but also Lyndall's predecessor, Ian Biggs, who was the ambassador in Tehran when she was first incarcerated. But she firmly believes the government was wrong to discourage her family from mounting a public campaign. She told Sky News in early March 2021 that the government's 'line' was that 'trying to find a solution diplomatically behind the scenes with Iran was the best approach for getting me out, and that the media would complicate things and could make Iran angry and piss them off and make things worse for me'.

As the person inside the prison cell, Kylie took a different view. She says there was 'no way' the Iranians would have imposed a ten-year sentence if her case had been made public earlier. She has observed that once the case was made public, much greater attention was paid to her health and conditions. She argues that the more public attention is given a case, the better off a prisoner will be. 'Sunshine,' she says, 'is the best disinfectant'. Prime Minister Morrison, when asked about this perspective shortly after Kylie's release, made a broad reference to national security considerations and said that she 'couldn't be aware of all the things the government has been involved in to secure her release over a long period of time'.

Kylie has not changed her mind. She maintains that she was in a strong position to provide input into the Australian negotiating strategy. The skills and knowledge that helped her through the ordeal, combined with her knowledge of the Iranians' interrogation tactics, meant that she had significant value to add. But she was disappointed that the official Australian approach didn't take her views into account. She feels strongly that any justification for the government's opposition to a public campaign was substantially reduced after her case became public, and believes DFAT could have been much more transparent with her family about what was happening in the negotiations. She makes the point that confidence evaporates in the absence of news, and the risk therefore grows that prisoners or their supporters will strike out publicly in uncoordinated and potentially unhelpful ways. She acknowledges that the approach needs to be adjusted depending on the particulars of the case, or the country concerned, but her plea is for the government to show more trust by bringing victims and their families more 'into the tent'. She can't help concluding that the government's strong emphasis on 'quiet diplomacy' reflects a deep-seated preference for staying in sole control of proceedings, and a hardwired aversion to working in genuine partnership with detainees and their supporters.

I find Kylie's view persuasive, but I am not really in a position to judge what might have been. I have no real insight to how my former colleagues in DFAT saw the situation as they managed the case to what was, in the end, a successful outcome. But the cases of Peter Greste and Kylie Moore-Gilbert lead me to the conclusion that thoughtful and collaborative public efforts by a prisoner's family and supporters can assist official attempts to secure a favourable outcome, and that the consular service should be more alive to this opportunity.

Since they were released, Peter and Kylie have both shown an enduring commitment to highlighting the situation of those who remain victims of arbitrary detention. One Australian in this situation is Sean Turnell, an economic adviser to Aung San Suu Kyi, long-term symbol of her country's democratic movement. In February 2021, when Myanmar's military staged their latest coup,

Turnell was arrested for breaching secrecy laws along with Aung San Suu Kyi herself, who by then held the senior national position of State Counsellor. The regime's handling of the case, including its reluctance to communicate clearly with the Australian embassy about it, fell far short of acceptable international standards. There are many others who are imprisoned on objectionable grounds in Myanmar. Many of them are local journalists. Peter Greste, interviewed by the ABC in November 2021 following the release of an American journalist from Myanmar, expressed his joy at this development but made the point: 'There are literally dozens and dozens of other journalists in Myanmar who don't have the support of a foreign government to advocate for them, or to negotiate their release, and who are languishing in prison simply for doing their jobs.' Not everyone is supported by a consular service that will at least try its best to provide support in such circumstances.

CHAPTER EIGHTEEN

It Never Ends

IT'S ABUNDANTLY CLEAR, LOOKING BACK, that the 'end of history' proclaimed by some after the collapse of the Soviet Union was just the close of one fleeting chapter in the ongoing narrative of world affairs. The war in Yugoslavia and global terrorism quickly surfaced as new challenges to international security in the years that followed. More recent events have made it clearer still, that the story is not over. The first few years of the current decade have seen the emergence of a pandemic and the ignominious end to the West's intervention in Afghanistan, which had first been launched in the wake of the September 11 attacks. Resentment about the blow inflicted on Russian prestige at the end of the Cold War has contributed to a new, dangerous European conflict. Each of these developments has had direct implications for the safety of Australians overseas, and thus for the Australian consular service.

We had little inkling of any of this in the period leading up to 2020, which now looks like it may have been the high-water mark of globalisation. The number of Australians travelling and living abroad climbed steeply in these years, as budget travel became even more accessible, and opportunities to live and work internationally mushroomed. Australians made more than eleven million trips in 2019 – more than three times the number made two decades earlier. The consular service dealt with about five death cases, five hospitalisations and three arrests every day that year. Each of these numbers was about triple what they had been twenty years before. The number of complex, time-consuming and sensitive cases also increased dramatically through the age of terrorism, as some nations took to detaining foreign nationals to achieve their political ends. The profile of Australian travellers continued to evolve, too. By 2019, far more Australians were embarking on their first overseas trip, and at a younger age, than ever before. Older Australians were also travelling in much larger numbers, and the trend towards more exotic destinations and adventure activities had strengthened. The world had truly become a much smaller place.

I remained one of those Australian frequent flyers. Roxanne and I returned home to Brisbane in 2016, after I joined the leadership of an Australian company with operations in West Africa, Indonesia, PNG and the Americas. I was on the road to these and other destinations on a regular basis to engage with governments and other partners on behalf of the business. I enjoyed working for an Australian organisation after my time based in the United States. I came to appreciate even more, the typically Australian characteristics that I'd experienced in my DFAT career – a welcome directness of communication and a tendency to not take ourselves too seriously. My corporate work, and my pro bono roles with organisations, such as the Lowy Institute, The University of Queensland, the Australia-Indonesia Centre and the Kokoda Track Foundation, kept me in close contact with former colleagues in the Australian government.

Despite the growth in demand for its consular services, DFAT's funding almost flatlined in the two decades after the

September 11 terror attacks. By contrast, budgetary allocations for defence, along with the intelligence and security agencies, grew by factors of between three and five. Successive DFAT leaders did what they could to shield the consular service from the department's straitened circumstances, given the immediacy of this field of work and political sensitivity to the expectations of the travelling public. But this often involved diverting resources from policymaking and international influence-building – core capacities which should be considered as national assets, but that unfortunately lack a serious constituency. A lingering and completely misplaced public perception of cocktail-sipping diplomats, regrettably sometimes shared by Australian ministers and finance officials, may have something to do with the reluctance to boost the department's finances.

It took a global pandemic to convince the Australian government to belatedly increase DFAT's funding.

The pattern of Australian outbound travel changed dramatically when the coronavirus spread across the globe in the first half of 2020. The Australian government closed our borders, and overseas travel quickly became limited to those with essential work reasons or who were responding to a family tragedy. (Sometimes not even these circumstances passed the test.) But the pandemic also revealed to the Australian public just how many Australian expatriates were out there in the world – working long-term everywhere, from London to San Francisco to Mumbai, often with international families, but still calling Australia home. More than 600,000 of these Australians had returned home by mid-2021, a little more than twelve months after the government began advising them to do so. But the number of Australians seeking DFAT assistance brought to mind Norman Lindsay's self-generating 'magic pudding'. Until border restrictions began to ease later in the year, it seemed that no matter how many

Australians returned to the country, through either commercial or government-sponsored repatriation flights, there were still tens of thousands left.

This, then, became an overwhelming focus of the consular service. The challenge was to attend to the ongoing consular business of arrests, hospitalisations and deaths overseas, while also running a global repatriation operation. Consular officials worked to stay in touch with registered Australians, prioritising the most vulnerable cases for flights and providing welfare assistance to those in financial stress or ill health. Many thousands of the Australians who returned home did so on special repatriation flights organised by DFAT. Duty officers at the Consular Emergency Centre took scores of thousands of calls, and their counterparts at overseas missions took many more. They also dealt with sustained and misdirected attacks, directly and through social media, from aspiring returnees and their supporters as airlines bumped passengers to comply with the ever-changing limits on Australian arrivals back home. Many consular clients felt justifiable frustration and anxiety as they tried to engage with a consular network under extreme pressure.

While the rest of us were in relative security behind our hard borders in Australia, most DFAT officers and their families remained at their posts, experiencing never-ending periods of isolation and home schooling in countries where the virus was running rampant. It rarely occurred to their critics that in some of our overseas missions, consular teams were depleted because staff members had themselves been infected by the coronavirus. By April 2021, when the government's vaccination program finally got underway, 132 diplomats were reported to have contracted Covid-19, and the figure for Australia's locally engaged staff overseas can be assumed to have been much higher again. At that point, very few Australians at home knew anyone who had contracted the virus. Friends and former colleagues of mine packed up their families to go out into the world in the midst of all this, glad at least that they were prioritised under the government's vaccination program after it began to be rolled out. The work of the department – global security, trade and investment, health and other development support to our neighbours, and consular work – couldn't simply be put on hold.

The Covid era saw the Australian authorities placed in situations where they felt they had to choose between the interests of Australians overseas and the broader population at home. Limitations on Australia's quarantine arrangements meant that decisions had to be made to restrict the number of Australians who could return in any given week. Many airlines simply discontinued their services to Australia because they were being forced to carry passenger loads that were too small to be viable. At one point in 2021, the cost of an airfare from London to Sydney peaked at $38,000. Those who were still out there, despite their best efforts, felt abandoned by their government, and said so.

Public debate about these issues took on an 'us or them' tone, with some asking why these people hadn't come home earlier. This attitude tended to overlook the reality of people's lives.

They had work commitments and their children's education to take into account. Family illness and tragedies at home meant that those who had settled elsewhere needed to come back when they hadn't originally intended to. And the critics were also missing how fundamentally Australia has changed in recent times. Nearly a third of all Australians were born overseas, and about half of us have at least one parent born in another country. For the many Australians whose families straddled international boundaries, the situation was very challenging indeed.

There was one moment during the pandemic which underlined that many Australians still didn't appreciate how much their country has changed. In an unprecedented step, the Australian government effectively made it illegal in May 2021 for some of its citizens to fly home. The Delta variant of the coronavirus was spreading fast in India at the time, and the government first moved to suspend direct flights from India. Then, when some Australian citizens managed to find their way back via other countries, Health Minister Greg Hunt issued a biosecurity determination instituting 'a temporary pause on travellers from India entering Australian territory if the passenger has been in India within fourteen days of the person's time of departure'. The accompanying ministerial press release made it clear that failure to comply with the determination would incur a financial penalty or five years' imprisonment, or both. The government defended itself against the outcry this move provoked, emphasising the temporary nature of the determination.

For these Australians, this was a denial of their inalienable right of abode in their own country. Almost all were of Indian heritage, and naturally took offence when some public comments, including from at least one senior government figure, seemed to suggest that they were not 'real' Australians. Many had been born in Australia or had surrendered their Indian citizenship to become Australians. Indian-Australians have become our country's second-largest group of migrants, and they have a voice. Many people in the broader Australian community saw the situation from their perspective, and there was such a backlash against these measures – both in the media and in the form of online petitions – that the government lifted the ban within weeks.

I had understood, from an early stage in my DFAT career, how we have a responsibility to all Australians overseas, even if they don't conform to traditional notions of what an Australian looks like. The fellow citizens I had encountered in the Balkans in the 1990s, the Australians who were evacuated from Lebanon in

2005, and the Australians of Chinese origin detained by Beijing were representative of our increasingly multicultural society. Our 'immigration nation' makes little sense unless we treat all Australians equally, irrespective of their origins.

For me, the Covid era coincided with a move out of formal employment and into a more independent life. When Roxanne and I returned to Brisbane, an old friend calculated that we had made eighteen household moves, including seven across international borders, only to end up one kilometre from where we'd started our married life. We established a strategic advisory business that supports companies as they negotiate challenges in the Indo–Pacific, and I took on roles with a range of international development organisations. This work took me to Canberra when interstate travel restrictions allowed and provided opportunities to catch up along the way with the latest leaders of the Australian consular service.

Kate Logan was appointed in mid-2021 to run the Consular and Crisis Management division, as it was by then known. Kate already had serious consular experience to draw on – she'd spent a substantial period running the crisis branch before being promoted to lead the broader division, and her last overseas post had been as ambassador to Greece, where there were about 250,000 Australian passport holders at any given time. I've spoken a few times with Kate and some of her senior colleagues about their experiences.

The department had come to recognise, through the first year of the pandemic, that it needed to bolster its capacity to reach out proactively to check on the welfare of Australians abroad. So-called 'tiger teams' were established within the division to identify, track and initiate contact with vulnerable Australians overseas – this was several steps beyond what we had envisaged twenty years previously, when we first established a global consular emergency line at headquarters. The team also worked to overhaul its ability to manage data about the whereabouts of Australians at risk. These improvement efforts were bolstered from May 2021, when the federal budget finally allocated an additional $200 million to support the global consular operation and strengthen the department's overseas network with additional positions. It was not before time.

Until mid-2021 Australian media attention was almost entirely focused on the pandemic, and public interest in the global security situation waned for a while. International conflict and terrorism seemed remote from behind Australia's hard borders. Indeed, al-Qaeda, which captured global attention with such violence in 2001, almost seemed to have petered out twenty years later. Osama bin Laden was dead and the organisation's remaining affiliates were relatively quiet. Even Islamic State, the movement that stepped into al-Qaeda's shoes in the early 2010s, inflicting unspeakable horror on the people of Iraq and Syria, had suffered some serious setbacks. But its decline at the centre was accompanied by steady growth in its 'provinces' and affiliates across the world. ISIS activity was moving steadily from the Middle East to sub-Saharan Africa, where an increasing number of its victims were being killed.

Meanwhile, the international military presence that had moved into Afghanistan in the wake of the September 11 attacks was withdrawn in 2021 as the Taliban strengthened their control against the country once again. Australian troops returned home and our embassy in Kabul was shut down because of security concerns. A key question hanging over the future of Afghanistan was whether the birthplace of al-Qaeda would once again become a safe haven for terrorists intent on waging jihad against the Western world.

On 15 August 2021, the Taliban retook Kabul following the shockingly fast collapse of the internationally backed government. Taliban co-founder Mullah Abdul Ghani Baradar made it clear in media interviews that even he was surprised by the speed of the takeover. It felt to many, including the Australian soldiers and officials who had committed much of their working lives to the Afghanistan project, that a mission of hope had been destroyed in a single day. It was a particularly devastating setback for the women of Afghanistan, who had dared to believe in a future where they, too, could access education and employment opportunities.

In the days and weeks that followed, as the twentieth anniversary of the September 11 attacks loomed, international coalition partners launched a desperate effort to evacuate their citizens and those Afghanis who had worked with them. I followed events closely as my consular successors, working with military and other counterparts, pulled off one of the most challenging and dangerous evacuations in our nation's history. Working with many others, the Australian government managed to bring more than 4000 people to safety after Kabul fell, in the back of RAAF C-130 Hercules and C-17 Globemaster aircraft. Included in this number were hundreds destined for other countries. There were still too many left behind, and questions continued to be raised about why the United States and its allies had not seen it coming and acted sooner. But the bitter feeling of unfinished business should not detract from the achievement of the Australian officials involved.

At the Canberra end the whole operation was severely complicated because the Australian Capital Territory was locked down by a Covid outbreak at the time, necessitating the rapid establishment of a 'virtual' crisis centre to bring the agencies together to execute the mission. Lynn Bell, who had only just taken over the crisis management branch in July 2021 following Kate's promotion, was required to isolate for fourteen days because of a Covid outbreak at her son's school. Her work on the repatriation effort was done from a desk in her bedroom at home. Newly appointed DFAT Secretary Kathryn Campbell slept in the office through the crisis response period because of the timing and tempo of the work.

In response to public pressure, state and territory leaders halved the quarantine quotas for international arrivals amidst the repatriation effort from Afghanistan, making things even harder for Kate, Lynn and their colleagues as they worked to get evacuees onto flights within tight quotas for incoming international arrivals. Lynn describes this process as a 'massive jigsaw puzzle'. She reflects on the sheer scale of the operation and the level of collaboration with other government agencies. At the Commonwealth level, this included the departments of Defence, Health, Prime Minister and Cabinet, Infrastructure and Home Affairs, as well as Emergency Management Australia. But as Lynn also notes, the term 'whole of government' was not really adequate to describe the operation. It had really been a 'whole of Federation' effort, with each of the states and territory governments collaborating as best they could to accept evacuee arrivals. As I listened to her, I was reminded of the Bali evacuation of 2002, which had required a similar, truly integrated national response.

As 2021 turned into 2022 the inter-agency team continued to work behind the scenes to facilitate onward travel to Australia by citizens and visa holders who'd managed to escape Afghanistan into Pakistan. This operation had not been fully wound down when the consular team began to turn their attention to another escalating crisis – this time in Europe.

The conflict in eastern Ukraine, first brought to Australians' shocked attention by the downing of MH17, had settled into a static struggle unnoticed by many outside the region. Then, from late 2021, a major build-up of Russian forces on Ukraine's borders coincided with sharpened rhetoric from Russian President Vladimir Putin, who accused the Zelensky government in Kyiv of conspiring with the West to threaten Russia. He even publicly questioned Ukraine's right to exist. In late February 2022 Moscow formally recognised the 'independence' of the eastern Donbas region and launched a full-scale military offensive against Ukraine. The western world responded with unprecedented sanctions against Russia and by providing arms supplies to Ukraine, and the Ukrainians themselves mounted a heroic resistance against the invaders. Missiles and shells rained down on towns and cities across the country, and millions of Ukrainian women and children sought refuge in neighbouring countries. Like others, I was transfixed. The images of devastation, the spirited attitude of the defenders and the reports of war crimes transported me back to Bosnia and the mid-1990s.

The consular service was determined to get ahead of this one. Contingency planning personnel began visiting Ukraine early in the year to plan the crisis response with the small embassy in Kyiv. The Australian government urged its citizens to leave Ukraine from early February, as concerns grew over the Russian military build-up. There are more Australians in Ukraine at any given time than many might expect. Almost 50,000 Australians claim Ukrainian ancestry, about 4000 Australians visited Ukraine each year prior to the pandemic, and an estimated 1400 were resident in the country at the beginning of 2022. Not all of them chose to follow the Australian warnings to leave. Public messaging was complicated by the Ukrainian authorities themselves, who initially played down the prospects of an invasion and expressed irritation towards countries they thought were showing undue alarm.

Following the outbreak of hostilities, the Australian embassy moved first to Lviv in western Ukraine, and then to Poland. Four regional consular response teams were established to support Australians fleeing the country – two in Poland, and one each in Romania and Moldova. These teams included staff flown in from Australia; senior regional consular officers from Berlin, London and other capitals; and local staff with the required language skills and homegrown knowledge. They reported to Andrew Goledzinowski, another senior DFAT officer with decades of international experience. Andrew based himself in eastern Poland near the Ukrainian border, where he could liaise closely with local officials and like-minded partners. With the assistance of their colleagues in Canberra, these officials stayed in phone, text and WhatsApp contact with Australians seeking to escape Ukraine. The 'tiger teams' established as part of the Covid response were again put to good use, actively tracking and reaching out to registered Australians. They facilitated border crossings by assisting families with travel documentation and arranged to be present at checkpoints when their fellow Australians made it through.

Every consular crisis throws up unusual challenges, and the Ukraine operation was no different. The country is a popular destination for surrogacy – it has a legal framework which recognises married heterosexual couples as the legal parents of a child born through surrogacy, and it permits arrangements with foreign intended parents. Between 2000 and 2500 babies are born to surrogate mothers in the country each year. The outbreak of war was a catastrophe for many intended parents, surrogates and infants. More than ten Australian couples were among the many foreign parents who found themselves in the distressing situation of being cut off from their babies. Meanwhile, the surrogates and the babies themselves were left to contend with uncertainty and do their best to shelter from the war.

Alba was one of these babies. She was born in Ukraine, eleven weeks premature, on 22 February – two days before Russia commenced its invasion. She was suffering from bleeding on the brain and lungs, and was moved into the neonatal intensive care unit of a hospital in Odesa. Her parents, Jessica van Nooten and Kevin Middleton of Melbourne, scrambled immediately. All flights into Ukraine were cancelled while they were en route, so they made their way instead to neighbouring Poland and then Moldova, where they stayed in close contact with the consular teams. The couple were not going to be put off by official warnings against entering Ukraine – they have shared publicly that they'd previously undergone multiple failed rounds of IVF and endured a miscarriage. They were determined to extract Alba from Ukraine and get her to high-quality medical care. Their research indicated that the best option was Great Ormond Street Hospital for Children in London.

The couple finally crossed the border into Ukraine and were united with their baby in Odesa more than two weeks after her birth. Once Alba was sufficiently stabilised they made their way back to Moldova. The Australian consular crew were there in the background, staying in touch and helping them with the documentation they needed to cross the border, and then working with the Department of Home Affairs on Alba's application for Australian citizenship by descent. This is required for all Australian children born overseas and needs to happen before a passport can be issued by DFAT. This all happened very quickly, and the little family were soon on their way to London in an air ambulance covered by an online funding campaign.

This was, above all else, a story of parental love and determination, but I know how much satisfaction being part of this kind of operation can bring for the consular officials involved. It's one of the great things about this field of work that never changes.

Otherwise, the consular service has come a long way from the 'cottage industry' operation I'd inherited two decades previously. Rowland Pocock, who is still turning up for his shift at the CEC, marvels at how much the department's crisis arrangements have scaled up since those early years. The current arrangement, under which the department has an entire headquarters division of about

200 people focused solely on consular and crisis management issues, is a long way from the small branch of thirty or so people I once ran. The CEC, which Rowland and his colleagues once managed through the night alone, now has two or three people on duty at any given time. DFAT's twenty-four-hour arrangements also include the standing Global Watch Office established under Julie Bishop's ministerial direction in 2015, where at least two officers monitor the world through the night for important political and economic developments. These arrangements are underpinned by technology that we couldn't have imagined in our time.

There has also been a complete revolution in public online interaction with the consular network and its travel advisory service since we launched the original, modest Smartraveller website with Alexander Downer at the Sydney Opera House in the wake of the Bali bombings. The growth of the internet and the ubiquity of the smartphone enables more independent travellers to chart their own way through difficult situations rather than turn to the consular service, but the rising influence of social media has become both an opportunity and a challenge. As Marinella Padula has noted in an Australian and New Zealand School of Government report, it makes it easier for DFAT to issue warnings and monitor live developments but is just as easy for people to use those forums to disseminate rumours and misinformation. Social media campaigns can rapidly mobilise support for a person or cause but can also raise unrealistic hopes or misrepresent the work of the foreign service. We saw some of this during the Covid era.

Some members of the public have very high expectations of the Australian consular service, and politicians remain very sensitive to public demands. Successive governments have tried to address unrealistic expectations, but it remains an unresolved issue. I am sometimes left wondering how much of this we brought on ourselves. Every time the service pulled off a high-profile emergency response, the bar of expectation was raised a little higher. I remember that moment in September 2001, when the foreign minister of the day made an invidious decision to abandon precedent and follow the British government in paying for victims' families to travel to New York. We were troubled at the time about how this would be seen by people whose loved ones died in less extraordinary but still tragic circumstances overseas, and yet who would not receive this kind of support. It now looks almost insignificant compared to subsequent government actions and decisions.

It doesn't help to shake our heads and say that DFAT's emphasis on consular support has got completely out of hand – that Australians just need to regain their personal independence and stop relying so heavily on their government. The 'contract' between Australians overseas and their government at home has indeed changed over time, but I still believe that the majority of Australians are independent, resourceful travellers. In any case, the genie cannot be put back in the bottle. Future Australian governments should by all means re-engage the public in a discussion about where individual responsibility begins and ends. But they also need to ensure that we have a well-resourced consular service that keeps pace with social and technological change, and which retains a capacity to both anticipate and respond to crisis in an ever-changing international environment. The Australian consular service that is emerging from the last few turbulent years is probably at the global leading edge, but it could lose this status quickly if the commitment to continuous improvement is allowed to flag.

None of this should be – or needs to be – at the expense of resourcing DFAT's capability to advance our national interests and exert influence in a more complex and contested world. Our diplomats need to be able to both shape foreign policy and provide consular services. It is well within Australia's means to maintain a highly functioning foreign ministry, able to deliver good policy advice, exert strong diplomatic influence and provide high-quality services to the travelling public.

Over the last quarter-century, our consuls have contended with rapidly growing traveller numbers, a radical global movement intent on hurting Australians among others, rising expectations carried on the back of the communications revolution, rogue governments playing politics with our citizens' lives, a global pandemic that left many of those abroad desperate to return, and a new European war. Of all these factors, I think that it was the global terrorist movement, emerging as it did after the fall of the Berlin Wall, that played the most significant role in reshaping DFAT's consular service. Its impact on the Australian government extended well beyond stimulating consular reform – the travelling experience was changed fundamentally by new security arrangements, and Australia's security and intelligence agencies were also forced to overhaul their operating models.

The deadly impact of extremism will always be with the Australians who lost loved ones in Bali and in other attacks over the years. Nothing can fill the gaps that have been left behind, and things still happen to remind them of those times. A key figure in the 2002 Bali attacks, Aris Sumarsono, was jailed in early 2022 after spending more than seventeen years on the run, while Abu Bakar Ba'asyir was released from prison in early 2021 after a ten-year stretch. Many of the victims' families are still monitoring these developments carefully. In recent times experts have also highlighted a worrying rise in right-wing terrorist capabilities in the United States, Europe and other developed societies. The murderous assault by an Australian on mosques in Christchurch, New Zealand, in March 2019 confirmed that white supremacism is a serious threat to public safety, and that Muslims can be the targets of terrorism, too.

It would be foolish of us to lose focus on the risks associated with terrorism in the increasingly complex world. The drumbeat may once again be muffled, but the international terrorist movement has shown great resilience over time.

The Australian consular officers of the early twenty-first century can feel some pride in how they showed up. Each of us, in our time, supported our fellow Australians as best we could. During and between crises, we handled challenging individual cases with flexibility and careful thought – always with the aim of ensuring that our actions aligned with what the Australian community would expect. We built systems and established new ways of thinking that would make it easier for our successors. Mistakes were made along the way, and sometimes our clients were left disappointed or angry, but we tried to learn from each experience, conducting formal reviews after every significant operation to identify areas for improvement. No one can predict what the next crisis will look like, so the goal was to build on the experience we'd gained and put in place flexible and resilient systems that can adapt quickly to whatever comes next.

The quiet consuls behind the media headlines aren't looking for pats on the back. They are generally well-intentioned people who want to get it right – even if they don't always succeed. They are motivated by a range of factors, including human compassion and a sense of adventure. They also feel a strong pride in working for their country. Some would call it patriotism, but it is not mere flag-waving nationalism. It is based much more firmly on a sense of personal connection with their fellow Australians – a community they identify strongly with because they are members of it, too. They would instinctively understand what Roger Strickland was thinking about all those years ago, when we were graduate trainees: It really is a great feeling, knowing they are doing this for Australia.

Acknowledgements

My primary intention in writing this book has been to draw attention to the important work that is done, every day of the year, by the men and women of the Australian consular service. There are countless members of the service who deserve recognition for outstanding work, including at times of crisis, but who are not mentioned in this account. I hope they will understand that those who *do* feature in my narrative stand as representatives for them, and for every consular generation.

I'm grateful to the current and former DFAT officers who agreed to speak with me as I developed the manuscript. In some of these 'interviews', we reminded each other about experiences we'd shared many years before; in other cases I heard blow-by-blow accounts for the first time of events in which I did not participate. It was not just a matter of sharing old war stories, although there was an element of this. I was struck by how open they all were about their experiences – about what had gone wrong as well as right. These discussions often proved cathartic for both participants.

Several who are still in active service found the time to talk

amid their demanding working lives. My warm thanks go to
Kerin Ayyalaraju, Lynn Bell, Philip Green, Kate Logan, Rowland
Pocock, Monty Pounder, Tracy Reid, Jeff Roach, Lyndall Sachs,
Greg Wilcock and Tracey Wunder. I also consulted several
former Australian officials who have worked hard, in difficult
circumstances, to support their fellow Australians over the years:
Lyall Crawford, Keith Gardner, Desley Hargreaves, Bill Jackson,
John McCarthy, Rod Smith, Ross Tysoe, Nick Warner and Frank
Yourn.

I relied on my own memory and the public record in describing
the contributions of many other former colleagues. It would be
redundant to repeat all their names – the references in the book
speak for themselves. Some people whose achievements I have
recounted, like Ric Smith, David Chaplin and John Feakes, will
just have to forgive me for describing their actions in my own
words and telling them about it later. I know how self-effacing
they all are, and they would just have tried to tone down the
references to themselves. I also want to pay tribute again here
to the important role played by the late Chris De Cure in the
emergency phase of the Bali response, and the dedication shown
by the late Victoria Owen across any number of consular issues,
including as ambassador to Egypt at the time of Mamdouh Habib's
detention there. Both Chris and Victoria passed away too soon.

I have been honoured to get to know some of the 'clients'
of the consular service. Melissa Lysaght, who lost her husband,
Scott, in the 2002 Bali bombings, became a friend, and Scott's
parents, Daniel and Pauline, showed me unexpected generosity
through their letters and other interactions. There were many
others like them. I also spent time with some who were sharply
critical of DFAT's approach after losing loved ones overseas, like
Peter Wilson and Brian Deegan, and I regret that we fell short
of their expectations. Former prisoners Kylie Moore-Gilbert and

ACKNOWLEDGEMENTS

Peter Greste are both impressive Australians who offered me thoughtful perspectives on the work of the consular service. They have both told their own compelling stories. Peter and his family collaborated to write *Freeing Peter* (Penguin, 2016) and Peter has also authored his own memoir, *The First Casualty* (Penguin, 2017). Kylie's courage is on full display in *The Uncaged Sky* (Ultimo, 2022). Both displayed enormous resilience while behind bars, and since then have shown an enduring commitment to those who remain incarcerated overseas. So has Kay Danes; I have not spoken to her, or to her husband, Kerry, since 2001, but in telling their story I have drawn in part on Kay's published accounts of their ordeal, *Deliver Us from Evil: Bad Things Do Happen to Good People* (Crown Content, 2002) and *Nightmare in Laos: The True Story of a Woman Imprisoned in a Communist Gulag* (Maverick House, 2006).

Several of the Australians who emerged from Taliban-controlled Afghanistan in the wake of the 2001 US-led offensive have also written their own books, or participated actively in those written by others. In seeking to bring their personal stories together, I drew partly on Mamdouh Habib's *My Story: The Tale of a Terrorist Who Wasn't* (written with Julia Collingwood; Scribe 2008) and David Hicks' *Guantanamo: My Journey* (Heinemann, 2010), as well as Sally Neighbour's extraordinary account of Rabiah Hutchinson's personal journey, *The Mother of Mohammed: An Australian Woman's Extraordinary Journey into Jihad* (Melbourne University Publishing, 2010). Sally Neighbour's investigative work in this area has been carried by a range of media outlets, including ABC TV's *Four Corners* and *The Weekend Australian*. In the case of Joseph Terrence 'Jihad Jack' Thomas, I looked to the media interviews he provided, including to Mark Dunn of the *Herald Sun* on 11 May 2013. I otherwise relied on the public record in describing official handling of these sensitive cases, including Senate Estimates hearings and the 2011 public report of the Inspector-General of Intelligence and Security into the Australian government's handling of the Habib case.

There has otherwise been surprisingly little public research or analysis of DFAT's consular work. Alex Oliver was an exception to this rule when she was with the Lowy Institute, contributing useful perspectives on trends in the field – particularly the problem of expectation management. I have referred to her work several times.

I would also like to acknowledge the supportive role of Australian government leaders over the years. I served six foreign ministers and five prime ministers – from both sides of politics – as an independent public servant. I've also maintained strong working relationships with the holders of both these offices since departing the service. Alexander Downer was foreign minister throughout my time running the consular service, and John Howard was prime minister. They both showed strong support for our work at critical times. Kevin Rudd, Julia Gillard and Stephen Smith all backed the service strongly during my time as a head of mission overseas, and I enjoyed a very positive relationship with each of them too – as I have subsequently with foreign ministers Julie Bishop and Marise Payne.

Of the political office holders, I chose only to interview Stephen Smith and Julie Bishop – because I felt I needed their recollections and 'voices' to cover properly some periods and events of which I had little knowledge myself. I am indebted to them both for their time and their openness, and to Julie for her kind foreword. I also appreciate the support of Murray Hansen, Julie's former chief of staff and current business partner.

Some great Australians have served as secretaries of DFAT in recent decades, and each has shown strong support for the consular service in their time. The late Ashton Calvert, Michael L'Estrange, Dennis Richardson, Peter Varghese and Frances

Adamson all exhibited strong leadership and showed me personal friendship. I wish Jan Adams, the incumbent (at the time of writing), the very best as she works to ensure (among other things) that the consular service is well equipped for tomorrow's challenges.

This is my own, independent account. Frances Adamson, who was secretary of DFAT when I began the project, confirmed that she was willing to offer me access to the department's classified records – subject, of course, to the proper clearance processes that must apply to anything written on this basis. But I found that my own recollections, checked against the memories of others and the public record, were enough for the purpose I had in mind. So I did not end up taking this formal route after all. I doubt that the department would have sought to influence the narrative anyway, but I feel that this approach might help avoid any perception that the book is some kind of officially endorsed public-relations project. DFAT did, however, facilitate my access to serving officers of the department for interview purposes, and I also provided the department with an advance copy of the text – both as a courtesy and to confirm that I had not breached my obligations under the Acts dealing with official secrets and privacy. I am obliged to DFAT officers Tracy Reid and Katherine Grant for their support with this.

I am truly grateful to UQP for showing confidence in me as a first-time author. I first met publishing director Madonna Duffy when I was posted in Berlin more than ten years ago, and when we saw each other intermittently over the years she would often say, 'I think you've got a book in there, Ian.' She has been my principal professional guide through the process. It has also been an enormous pleasure to work with editors Jacqueline Blanchard and Julian Welch, without whom the manuscript would have been a lot poorer. I have been greatly encouraged by the enthusiasm and professionalism shown by marketing gurus Sally Wilson and Louise Cornegé. I'm also grateful to Peter Greste, Rod Smith and Jonathan Pryke of the Lowy Institute for providing feedback on the draft.

Roger Strickland's parents, Mary and Lester, have never been far from my mind, and nor has Roger's widow, Chrissy Strickland, my sister-in-law. My daughters, Annabelle and Eloise, who grew to adulthood in the years covered in this book, have shown keen interest in the project since its inception. In many ways, the story of the consular service is a kind of background track for their own childhood. It hasn't stopped them from taking the mickey out of me along the way.

My wife, Roxanne Martens, has been alongside me at all the key moments in my professional life, including the challenging consular years, as thoughtful adviser and friend, sharing both the highs and the lows. Meanwhile, she has worked in her own field to the benefit of others – both overseas and in Australia – while always keeping her focus on family. She has been my first reader as I have developed my drafts, offering incisive commentary and suggestions. As always in our life together, she has also provided me with my best lines.